13-95

Agriculture in Chains

Bangladesh: A Case Study in Contradictions and Constraints

Stefan de Vylder

Zed Press, 57 Caledonian Road, London N1 9DN.

Vikas Publishing House Pvt Ltd, New Delhi/Bombay/Bangalore/
Calcutta/Kanpur

This book was first published in 1982 by:

Zed Press
  57 Caledonian Road, London N1 9DN

Vikas Publishing House Pvt Ltd,
  5 Ansari Road, New Delhi 110002
  Savoy Chambers, 5 Wallace Street, Bombay 400001
  10 First Main Road, Gandhi Nagar, Bangalore 560009
  8/1-B, Chowringhee Lane, Calcutta 700016
  80 Canning Road, Kanpur 208004

Typeset by Donald Typesetting
Proofread by Penelope Fryxell
Cover design by Jacque Solomons
Cover photo by Eva Asplund
Printed by Redwood Burn, Trowbridge,
Wiltshire.

British Library Cataloguing in Publication Data

Dr Vylder, Stefan
    Agriculture in chains
    1. Agriculture — Economic aspects —
       Bangladesh
    I. Title
    338.1'09549'204   HD1410.6.B/
    ISBN 0-86232-041-0 ✓

U.S. Distributor
Lawrence Hill and Co., 520 Riverside Avenue,
Westport, Conn. 06880, U.S.A.

Contents

6, 15, 18, 138

List of Tables

Figure

Acknowledgements

The large number of scholars, from Bangladesh and elsewhere, who are quoted approvingly, and often at length, in this book will indicate to whom the study owes most of its intellectual debt. But while it has been relatively easy to acknowledge my debt to written sources, it is more difficult to thank all my friends and colleagues who have both encouraged me and criticized my thoughts and writings during seminars and informal discussions. I cannot mention them individually, but I wish to thank them all. A particular word of thanks should, however, be given to the researchers at the Bangladesh Institute for Development Studies (BIDS), whose friendly co-operation was indispensable, and to Daniel Asplund, without whose support and thorough knowledge of Bangladesh this book would never have been written.

The customary reservation that the author alone is responsible for all errors, omissions and misinterpretations must be stressed, especially since some of those whom I have cited have expressed very different opinions on several of the points that are raised in this book.

I would finally like to express my sincere gratitude to SIDA (the Swedish International Development Authority), my employer when I first started to work on rural development problems in Bangladesh, and to SAREC (the Swedish Agency for Research Co-operation), whose financial support enabled me to complete this book.

Stefan de Vylder
Stockholm

Bangladesh: Basic Data

Rice Crops and Cropping Seasons

There are four major rice crops in Bangladesh:

i) *Aus*: This is the early monsoon crop harvested in July and August which is either broadcast or transplanted. *Aus* rice occupies roughly 33% of the paddy acreage while contributing 25% of total production.

ii) *Broadcast Aman*: These are the deep-water varieties that are highly photo-sensitive, sown from February to April on land usually flooded from between 1 and 3 metres deep, harvested from October to December. Cultivated on some 18% of the acreage and contributing 14% of total paddy production.

iii) *Transplanted Aman*: This is sometimes called *shail* to distinguish it from the deep-water Aman. It is transplanted on puddled land from July to September and harvested from November to early January. Occupies 41% of the acreage and contributes 46% of total production.

iv) *Boro*: This rice crop is transplanted from December to February and harvested from late March to the end of June. Cultivated on 9% of the acreage and producing 14% of the total paddy in the country.

The two main crop seasons are:

i) *Kharif*: the summer and monsoon season. Main *kharif* crops are *Aus* and *Aman* paddy, tropical vegetables, jute, chillies and mung.

ii) *Rabi*: the dry winter season from October to April-May. Main *rabi* crops are *boro* paddy, wheat and other temperate cereals, rape, mustard, pulses and temperate vegetables.

Administrative Divisions in Bangladesh

Administrative Units		Local Councils	Size of
Name	Number		Population
Division	4	–	20 million
District	19	Zilla Board	4 million
Sub-division	62	–	1.3 million
Thana	464	Thana Parishad (council)	200,000
Union	4,355	Union Parishad (council)	15-20,000
(Ward)	13,000	–	5-7,000

Common Abbreviations of Officials and Institutions

CO	Circle Officer – highest Thana official.
SDO	Sub-divisional officer.
DC	Deputy Commissioner, highest District official.
Union Chairman	Chairman of Union Council, elected separately by Union electorate.
TPO	Thana Project Officer. IRDP officer posted in TCCA as executive officer under elected co-op managing committee.
IRDP	Integrated Rural Development Programme, semi-autonomous government institution in charge of agricultural co-operative programme (commonly also used to denote the programme as such).
KSS	Krishi Samabay Shamiti – agricultural primary co-operative society.
TCCA	Thana Central Co-operative Association, the second, upper tier of the IRDP co-operative structure.

Currency

1 taka (Tk) = 100 poisha.
1 U.S.$ = around 20 taka (as of February 1982).

Measures

1 maund = 40 seers = around 37 kilos.
1 bigha = $\frac{1}{3}$ acre = 0.13 hectares.

Country Data

Area
144,000 km^2, out of which 6.5% are rivers.
Density: 590 inhabitants per km^2, as of 1978.
              960 inhabitants per km^2 of cultivable land.

Geography
Largely a deltaic plain formed by the outlet of the Ganges (Padma) and
Brahmaputra (Jamuna) Rivers into the Bay of Bengal. These two rivers also
efficiently divide the country into an Eastern and a Western part. Except for
the hilly areas in the Northern and Southeastern parts of the country, average
altitude is less than 10 metres above sea-level. Bangladesh is surrounded by
Indian territory except for the border with Burma in the Southeast and the
sea-coast in the South.

Climate
Tropical monsoon climate with heavy rains in May-September. Annual rainfall
from 1.4 to 5 metres. Temperature between 22 and 38°C.

Population
Around 85 million (1978) out of which 98% are Bengalis and 1 to 2% tribal
people.
Birthrate: 45-47/1,000.
Deathrate: 17-20/1,000.
Rate of growth: 2.8% per annum (1965-70).

Religion
Muslims (mainly Sunnis): 85%.
Hindus: 10-15%.
Other: 2-3%.

Government
Bangladesh has since independence in 1971 been a People's Republic, based
on the four stated principles of democracy, nationalism, socialism and Islam
(the latter introduced in 1977). The Constitution and Parliament were
suspended after the military coup against the Awami League Government
under Sheikh Mujibur Rahman in 1975. In 1978 the military ruler, General
Ziaur Rahman, was elected president. Parliamentary elections were held in
February 1979 ending the formal military rule. With his assassination in 1981,
subsequent presidential elections were held.

Education
Literacy: less than 20% of the population.
Enrolment in primary schools: 55-60% of eligible age group.
Drop-out rates: extremely high.

Health
Population per doctor: 11,000 (1975).
Population per hospital bed: 5,300 (1974).
Percentage of population consuming less than 90% of minimum calorie intake: 62% (1975).
Infant mortality: 130 per 1,000 live births.
Life expectancy: 42 years.

Distribution of Income
Top 20% of population take 40% of National Income.
Bottom 20% of population take 7% of National Income.

Distribution of Agricultural Land (1977)
10% largest landowners own 45%.
10% smallest landowners own 1%.
Rural households owning no land or less than 0.5 acres of agricultural land: 48% (1977).

Per Capita Income
G.D.P. per capita (1977): U.S.$ 91.

Structure of G.D.P. (1977-78 estimate)

Sector	Percentage
Agriculture	57.0%
Manufacturing	8.5
Construction	4.5
Power and Gas	0.5
Housing	4.5
Trade, Transport and Other Services	25.0
Total	100.0

Foreign Trade (1976-77) (in U.S.$ millions and %)

Exports			*Imports*		
Item	Value	% age	Item	Value	% age
Raw Jute	114	27%	Food Grains	147	17%
Jute Goods	172	41	Other Consumer Goods	34	4
Tea	36	8.5	Intermediate Goods	236	27
Leather	42	10	Capital Goods	227	26
Fish and Shrimps	22	5	Miscellaneous	221	26
Other	35	8.5			
Total	421	100.0	Total	865	100.0

Introduction

The International Context

During the last few decades, dozens of countries in Asia, Africa and Latin America have been converted into net importers of foodgrains. The Third World's trade deficit in cereals has increased from just a couple of metric tons in the early 1950s to around 30 million tons in the mid-1960s, 52 million tons in 1973–74 and 66 million tons in 1977–78. In recent years food production has increased remarkably in several major areas, most notably in Asia, but all forecasts nevertheless indicate that the developing countries' trade gap in foodgrains will continue to rise in the foreseeable future. According to World Bank estimates, the Third World countries will, if present trends in agricultural production continue, need to raise their imports of foodgrains to a level of 90–100 million tons per year at the end of this century just to maintain the present – and highly insufficient – nutrition standards.

This alarming trend of high and rising food deficits in the poor countries may appear paradoxical. The large-scale introduction since the 1960s of the improved seed–fertilizer technology popularly known as the Green Revolution would lead us to expect an increase in self-sufficiency in food. Today, the improved seeds, or High-Yielding Varieties (H.Y.V.s) of wheat and rice are estimated to account for over 30 and 20% respectively of the total acreage of these crops in the Third World: average yields per acre have increased spectacularly in many countries. Yet the rapid diffusion of the H.Y.V. technology has not been associated with higher self-sufficiency – let alone grain exports from the Third World – but rather with a drastic increase in imports of cereals from the industrialized countries.

Another paradox is the co-existence of large food surpluses and widespread hunger and malnutrition in many countries. This phenomenon is not new, of course, but it has been accentuated by the introduction of the H.Y.V. package of modern inputs and concomitant production increases and socio-economic changes. The last decade's impressive rise in food production in India is a good illustration of this situation: in India, agricultural modernization and favourable monsoons gave rise to an unexpected surplus which by the end of the 1970s reached the fantastic figure of almost 20 million tons of grain. Still poverty and malnutrition continued and while tens – or

1

even hundreds — of millions of Indians were unable to meet minimum daily calorie requirements even during the record years, the farmers were complaining loudly about the low prices of grain, and began to cut down investment and production. A new food crisis may not be far away in India.

Food: A Problem of Poverty

What the Indian case illustrates is the obvious but sometimes forgotten fact that the food problem is essentially a problem of poverty. Much of the theory and practice of the Green Revolution strategy is implicitly based on the assumption that the food problem should almost exclusively be attacked from the supply side, i.e. by the introduction of new seeds, agricultural inputs and methods of production which permit higher yields per acre. Once we recognize that insufficient effective demand may be the ultimate barrier to increased production of food, it must also be recognized that the distribution of the consequent gains in output and income is a key issue. The poor are hungry because they are poor, and as long as they remain poor, it will simply not be profitable to grow the food that they need.

A production-oriented strategy which, further, often results in the dispossession and proletarianization of small farmers and tenants and massive increases in landlessness, unemployment and poverty, can therefore never be a solution to the food problem, let alone to broader development problems — however large the production increases of the privileged farmers. The result is more likely to be a shift in production activities from less efficient to more efficient producers — efficiency is here understood in private, not social, terms — while the overall production increase may be quite small and, in the long run, even negative. But this is almost inevitable with a strategy which concentrates exclusively on production while neglecting the role of effective demand and income distribution. Another common effect is a tendency towards deterioration in the domestic terms-of-trade for agricultural products and a concomitant increase in the transfer of resources from rural to urban areas and activities. The situation thus resembles the case of 'immiserizing growth', well-known in international trade theory: confronted with a low elasticity of demand, a country — or, in this case, the agricultural sector within a country — which lowers production costs in the export sector may lose in deteriorating terms-of-trade what it gains in increased output, the result being that a growth of output actually reduces real income in the country/sector as a whole.

Some Third World countries have turned to export strategies to solve the contradiction between enhanced production possibilities and insufficient domestic purchasing power for basic food staples. Thus we find an expansion of exports of cash crops, fruit and vegetables, meat, etc. to the industrialized world (and some oil-exporting countries) where the best markets are to be found. This is paralleled by a drastic increase in imports of foodgrains from the developed countries, above all from the United States, which today accounts for over 50% of world exports of cereals. Food aid, and subsidized food imports, are instruments that have been used extensively to facilitate this reallocation of agricultural production away from basic necessities. The almost constantly over-valued foreign exchange rates in the Third World, in combination with selective export incentives of various kinds, reinforces the process.

The present study deals with Bangladesh. From what has been said above, it should however be clear that many of the tendencies and mechanisms that we will find in Bangladesh are operating in many parts of the world, although Bangladesh certainly has its own, particular features. A far-reaching process of technical and socio-economic change — spearheaded by transnational agribusiness corporations — is today taking place in the global agricultural sector, a process which has only recently begun to affect rural Bangladesh but which in the future is likely to affect the lives of millions of Bengalis far more than the dramatic political events that have shaken East Pakistan/ Bangladesh during the last decade.

This Study: Its Scope

The study begins with an attempt to summarize the extent and causes of rural poverty in Bangladesh. The very first chapter, entitled 'Development Problems', is thus a brief, descriptive overview of a number of 'poverty indicators' and an equally brief identification of the three main, and mutually inter-related, causes of poverty: landlessness, inequality, and under-employment. These are the 'big' development problems whose combined effect is to perpetuate, and even increase, the appalling misery of millions of rural households and which any development strategy worthy of its name must be able to tackle.

The 'population explosion', which many people have been accustomed to identify as the number one development problem in densely populated Bangladesh, will not be dealt with at all. Not that I deny that it is a problem — it is; and it will become a big problem. But I think — and this has become a commonplace nowadays — that high fertility is a symptom rather than a cause of underdevelopment. In Bangladesh, numerous studies have demonstrated that it is, from the individual family's point of view, a rational response to poverty and insecurity to decide to have many children. The obvious corollary to this insight is that any strategy which aims to reduce the present rate of population growth — which, if it continues unabated, will double today's population of approximately 90 million people in 25 years — must first of all attack the basic causes of poverty instead of fighting, in the name of 'population control', the poor themselves.

In Chapter 2, Bangladesh's development potentials are tentatively assessed. The point of departure is the trivial but nevertheless revealing recognition of the fact that there exist in Bangladesh vast human and natural resources which, if properly mobilized, could easily bridge the entire 'food gap' by narrowing the wide gulf that separates the agricultural potential of the country and its actual levels of production and employment. The agricultural sector as a whole, and its different components right down to the individual farm, can be looked upon as economic units working very much below their capacity, as expressed in, among other things, low yields of the main crop, rice, and in the small degree of diversification.

After this introductory overview of major development problems and potentials, we turn to an analysis of a number of distortions, of a combined economic, political and social character, which impede both a better utilization of the rural community's resources and a more equal distribution of the agricultural produce. The main body of the study is a discussion of these distortions, or biases, which are summarized under the following eight headings: the urban bias, the foreign bias, the bureaucratic bias, the capital bias, the production bias, the landlord bias, the rice bias, and the private bias. It must, however, be emphasized that this way of compartmentalizing the problems and constraints into a number of different 'biases' is made for the sake of exposition, not as the formula for a forward plan. These distortions are not to be taken as 'correctible' deviations from the best of all possible worlds as found in text-books on neo-classical economics. Rather they are development obstacles which reduce the rate of capacity utilization of both human beings and material forces of production but they cannot be attacked one by one, in a piecemeal, fragmented manner. On the contrary: they are the manifestations of the interaction of a particular setting of simultaneous social relations and power configurations; most, if not all, of them could be summarized under one single heading — class bias. The fact that the biases are presented separately, one by one, should thus not be misinterpreted: it is by no means to suggest the possibility of eliminating one or two of the most harmful, rather it is necessary to confront the central dynamics of the society as a whole.

Methodological Considerations

Many different statistics from a wide range of sources will be presented in this study. I have tried to use the best figures available, but it must be acknowledged at the start that the overall quality of agricultural statistics in Bangladesh is quite poor, often very poor. In some cases I have indicated that the figures used are highly approximate and, possibly, misleading but, in order to avoid a number of tedious repetitions, I have normally refrained from making any explicit reservations. I am, however, conscious of the fact that several statements that are substantiated by figures of dubious accuracy might have to be revised were better data available; but it is unlikely that these statistical inadequacies invalidate the main conclusions.

Another reservation has to do with the up-to-dateness of the material. Although the study is intended to cover the post-Independence period up to around January 1980, when the second of my two stays in Bangladesh was concluded, it has sometimes been impossible to get good data from 1978 and 1979. Instead of using preliminary estimates based on small samples and/or doubtful forecasts, I have normally chosen to rely on older, but more reliable, data.

Certain changes in the government's agricultural policies announced in the recently published *Five-Year Plan* have intentionally been neglected. The new *Five-Year Plan* envisages, among other things, a higher share than in the past of development expenditures allocated to agriculture, and a modification and strengthening of the rural co-operative structure. These developments, although marginal and unable to tackle the fundamental problems, should be welcomed. Judging from past experience in Bangladesh, however, it is easy enough to give nominal recognition to agriculture's pressing claims for priority and the need to create viable peasants' organizations, without translating this into action. To evaluate the future by listening to the words of today may be just another case of wishful thinking.

1. Development Problems

The Dimensions of Poverty

After several consecutive years of relative political stability,* and massive inflows of foreign economic assistance, the immediate outlook for the Bangladesh economy today looks better than ever before since Independence. The disruptive effects of the war of liberation and of the natural and man-made disasters during the first years of Bangladesh's existence have largely been overcome, and despite a severe drought in 1979 — when huge food imports compensated for the loss in domestic production — the country's stocks of foodgrain have remained acceptably high. Inflation has been reduced, and the problems of smuggling and the black market that only a few years ago threatened the entire food distribution system with virtual collapse have been controlled quite successfully.

However, the economically disastrous period 1971–74 left the per capita consumption of both food and industrial goods in 1979 still appreciably below its pre-1971 level. And since no major reforms or improvements in the protection or productivity of the soil have been undertaken, the vulnerability of the economy to adverse natural or other conditions is as great as before. The margins of safety in Bangladesh are small or non-existent, and new floods, droughts and cyclones will inevitably take a heavy toll in deaths and human suffering, as they have done in the past.

But, even in the absence of natural calamities, many people in Bangladesh will continue to starve. For the majority of the population, poverty is permanent. And the last few years' economic recovery cannot conceal the fact that the long-term situation has deteriorated. For several decades agricultural production has stagnated while population and food imports have spiralled upwards. On average, the rate of population growth has exceeded the rate of growth of food production by more than 1% per year. The number of people living below the subsistence level has increased both in relative and absolute terms. Thus, according to one study, while only 5% of the rural population

* This was written, of course, before the murder of President Zia in mid 1981. *Publisher's Note.*

in Bangladesh could be characterized as 'extremely poor' (defined, in this context, as unable to obtain 80% of the recommended daily average calorie intake) in 1963–64, this proportion rose to 25% in 1968–69 and to a staggering 41% by 1975.[1]

In a recent World Bank report,[2] the findings are summarized in the following way:

> *Trends in Rural Areas*
> Except for the top 5% of the population, all expenditure classes experienced a decline in average per capita expenditure during 1963–76. Expenditure of the bottom 40% declined more than the average, dropping in 1976–77 to about two-thirds of that in 1963–64.
> *Trends in Urban Areas*
> All income groups in urban areas experienced a sharp decline in per capita real expenditure during 1963–76. Average per capita expenditure in 1976–77 was one-third lower than in 1963–64. . . . Between 1963–64 and 1976–77, the incidence and the extent of poverty have continued to increase. During 1963–76, the rural population increased by 36%, while the number of those in poverty increased by 76%. During the same period, the number of 'hard core' poor increased from almost none to a massive 45 million, about 60% of the rural population. Similar trends are observed in urban areas. . . . The number of poor increased by 152%, from less than three million in 1963–64 to nearly 7 million in 1976–77. The proportion of 'hard core' poor increased from almost none in 1963–64 to over 40% of the urban population (3.3 million) in 1976–77.

In another study, 79.4% of all rural households were found to be below the poverty line — some four-fifths of the rural population were thus unable to meet their minimum food requirements.[3] The exactness of the figures may be questioned, but the tendency is clear: the vast majority of the population, i.e. the urban and rural poor, have suffered a steady decline in their living standards. This trend, which is confirmed by a number of independent studies[4] on production and incomes, income distribution, real wages for rural and urban workers, food consumption and nutrition levels, etc., is summarized in dramatic terms by one of Bangladesh's best-known economists, Dr. Md. Yunus: 'Domestically, for a long time we made ourselves believe that we are in a kind of subsistence equilibrium; a sort of being at the bottom of a pit which cannot be any worse. Presently, a rude awakening is gripping us all. The impossible is happening. We are sinking deeper, and fast.'[5]

The rural poor, who have suffered most, would probably tend to agree with Dr. Yunus's description. Thus, in a survey of attitudes among male villagers in rural Chittagong, 86% of the respondents thought that the country was in a worse condition than in the past, and 80% considered their own situation to be 'less happy' than that of their forefathers.[6] And there is little doubt that Yunus and these villagers are right, even more so if we extend the perspective to more ancient times. During the Moghul era, which lasted from the late 16th Century to the incorporation of Bengal into the British colonial empire some 200 years later, the entire region enjoyed, according to travellers' reports and contemporary writings, a prosperity which has definitely not been matched since then.

Inequality

The dimensions of poverty in today's Bangladesh are reflected in a variety of ways. Average income is low — around US $ 100 per capita annually — and unevenly distributed. The top 20% of households received, in 1973-74, over 40% of total income, whereas the lowest 20% received only 7.3%.[7] Two-thirds of all households have incomes of less than 500 *taka* per month. In rural Bangladesh, the one-fifth of the population which lives above the poverty line is estimated to receive one-half of all rural income.[8]

In 1962-64, a national nutrition survey revealed that at least 45% of all rural families had calorie intakes below the acceptable level. Since then, declining food availability per capita and a marked shift towards inferior dietary patterns due, above all, to a considerable drop in the production of fish and pulses, have resulted in a further deterioration in the overall food and nutrition situation. Thus, the per capita consumption of *all* major foods and nutrients declined significantly in rural Bangladesh between 1962-64 and 1975-76, when the second national nutrition survey was undertaken. The average daily energy intake has been estimated to be around 150 calories less in 1975-76 than in 1962-64. According to U.N. statistics, in the early 1970s Bangladesh had the lowest average energy intake per capita of the 12 Asian countries investigated.[9] Some two-thirds of the population are estimated to suffer from protein deficiency. The 1975-76 nutrition survey also disclosed that one-quarter of all children were severely and another half moderately undernourished. 50,000 children are estimated to go blind each year due to lack of Vitamin A.[10] The rate of infant mortality is 140 per 1,000 live births, and about one-quarter of all children die before the age of five.

Other indicators of the material standard of living reveal a similar picture. Housing and sanitary conditions are poor in both urban and rural areas. The majority of houses have only one room and no running water, and hardly any have electricity. The consumption of manufactured consumer goods is among the lowest in the world. 80% of the population is illiterate. The absolute number of both physicians and dentists was lower in 1975-76 than in 1961 — or even 1951.[11] For most people in Bangladesh there are simply no public health services.

Whatever criteria we choose, the same picture of appalling misery and inequality stands out. While the privileged few — including, certainly, the foreign community clustered around a handful of fashionable avenues in Dacca — enjoy a comfortable life and absorb a sizeable part of the country's meagre surplus, life for the average Bangladeshi has been getting harder and harder.

Landlessness

Intimately connected with the overall problem of rural poverty are the twin problems of landlessness and unemployment. With land by far the most valuable asset in rural Bangladesh, its unequal distribution determines most inequalities in other fields as well.

There is an almost total lack of large, commercial estates of the Latin American — or Pakistani — type in Bangladesh, and this has led to the false impression that the land tenure structure is comparatively egalitarian. According to the 1978 Land Occupancy Survey, estates larger than 15 acres occupy only slightly more than 15% of all agricultural land — a figure which, even if we adjust for a likely underestimation of the true size of the big farms, is very low compared to almost any country in the world. However, this phenomenon is more a reflection of the general shortage of land than of any egalitarian land ownership structure. Indeed a vast proportion of all farms are tiny by any standard. Table 1.1 is based on the 1978 survey which, the authors acknowledge, considerably underestimates the true degree of land concentration. Even so it reveals both the absolute scarcity of land and the glaring inequality of its distribution.

Table 1.1:
Distribution of Agricultural Land, 1978

Acres Owned	% of Rural Households	% of Land Area
Landless	28.8	—
0.01–2.00	47.8	21.7
2.01–4.00	12.8	22.4
4.01–10.00	8.2	30.7
10.01 or more	2.5	25.2
Total	*100.0*	*100.0*

Source: Based on F. Jannuzi and J. Peach, 'Bangladesh: A Profile of the Countryside', U.S.A.I.D. (Dacca, 1979).

We thus see that over half of all agricultural land is owned by a small minority of surplus farmers (i.e. those owning more than four acres of land per household). We also note that the share of households owning less than two acres of land is almost 80%, i.e. approximately the same as the percentage of households living below the poverty line in the studies referred to earlier. Around 50% of all rural households can be regarded as functionally landless, owning less than 0.5 acres each. If we make the dividing line one acre, then over 60% can be classified as landless peasants.

The implications of this situation for the choice of development strategy are far-reaching, and will be discussed on several occasions later in this study. But here we can point out that policies which benefit smallholders with as little as one acre of land still exclude over 60% of the rural population. Since the 'hard core' of rural poor, the landless or near landless, constitute a majority of the entire population in Bangladesh, no development strategy can reasonably ignore them.

There are also political implications arising out of the high extent of landlessness in Bangladesh: the data clearly reveal that the majority of rural Bangladeshis have nothing to gain from maintaining the present agrarian structure. Nonetheless landlessness continues and increases unabated. There are also indications of a trend towards the concentration of land ownership in the hands of a relatively small number of people. Although good data on sales and purchases of land are lacking, and the land registers are hopelessly inadequate, the few studies that do exist disclose — not unexpectedly — that the sellers tend to be poor, and the buyers medium-sized or big farmers.[12] It is also widely believed by observers in Bangladesh that land purchases by urban, absentee landowners have become more and more frequent during the last decade.[13] There is nothing new in this trend towards landlessness. While only 14% of all rural households were classified as completely landless in 1951, and 17% in the agricultural census of 1960, the percentage had risen to 28.8% in 1978. In absolute terms the increase has, of course, been even more spectacular. Another dimension of the problem is that the number of landless has been increasing around two and a half times faster than the agricultural population as a whole during the last twenty years.

For the individual farmer who loses his land, the process is likely to be irreversible; few people in Bangladesh have heard of cases of a poor peasant who has lost his land and later been able to buy it back. Although the causes behind the process of increasing landlessness remain to be investigated more thoroughly, it is clear that the present rate of population growth, combined with subdivision of land according to the prevailing Muslim laws of inheritance, rapidly reduces the average size of the farms, thus placing more and more small farmers in the category of 'near landless'. And this situation is precarious, especially since virtually all smallholders are in debt during at least part of the year. The margins are small, and a variety of circumstances — harvest failures, daughters' marriages, accidents, illness, etc. — can easily force the unfortunate peasant first to mortgage, then to sell, his land. According to one survey, about half of the people who are landless today have lost their land during the last two decades.[14] Each drought or flood creates many new landless; when a natural calamity occurs, there is a powerful 'ratchet effect' operating against the small landowners which makes it almost impossible for those who have been ruined to recover their land.

It is not merely the fact that there has been a decrease in the average size of landholdings. What this means is an accelerating fragmentation of farms. Around 95% of all farms are estimated to be fragmented, and well over half of them are split up into six or more different plots. The average size of a fragment has been reduced to a mere 0.15 acres. Such a high degree of fragmentation has considerable effects on land use and productivity: fragmentation causes loss of productive time as the farmers have to travel, drive work animals, carry tools, etc. between their scattered plots; it becomes difficult to use even minor irrigation devices efficiently; scarce land is wasted because every fragment has to be surrounded by permanent ridges demarcating the property.[15]

Unemployment

The farmers who lose their land lose their only source of security and are forced to join the ranks of rural poor, competing either for work as wage labourers or for land to cultivate on a sharecropping basis. Their prospects are bleak: a greater and greater proportion of the rural population are being pushed into the already overcrowded labour market, thereby bidding down real wages even further.

Looking back a few decades, the overwhelming majority of the rural population did control some land of their own after the abolition of the Zamindar system around 1950.[16] Unemployment at that time was mainly a seasonal problem, caused by climatic and other natural factors which made crop production during part of the year difficult or impossible. Today the situation is different, and most people are fully or partly dependent upon sharecropping or wage labour for their subsistence. Both the number of employment opportunities and the wage level have therefore become of decisive importance for the majority of people in rural Bangladesh.

The agricultural labour force can be estimated at slightly over 20 million people. In 1975–76, total agricultural employment was calculated at around 12.8 million man-years,[17] indicating a rate of unemployment of about 35%, a figure by and large consistent with findings in other studies.[18] This does not mean, of course, that over one-third of the rural population is permanently unemployed — what it means is that some people are un- or underemployed most of the year, and that most of the people are un- or underemployed part of the year, the average of working-days wasted being around 35%. (There is a further discussion of this in Chapter Two).

The demand for agricultural labour is highly seasonal, with a peak in April–May when daily labour requirements in crop production, accounting for some 70% of total agricultural employment, are almost twice as high as during the slack seasons. Traditionally, there has been a shortage of labour in rural areas during the peak season, when daily wages have been pushed up above the subsistence level. These short periods of high wages have been very important, enabling workers to save some rice and/or cash for the rest of the year, when they are likely to be underemployed. Today, however, the structure of the labour market and payment system is in a state of transition, and the supply of labour has begun to outstrip demand throughout the year. Migrant labourers are becoming an increasingly important source of labour during harvesting and transplanting, and with the influx of outside workers and the spread of wage labour relations on the village labour markets, the old kinship and patron-client relationships are gradually crumbling away. This process, which is still in its initial phase but is necessarily being accelerated by the rapid growth of landless or near landless peasants, has tended to erode the high wages during the peak season and reduce the workers' share of the agricultural produce, thereby contributing to the impoverishment of the rural poor.[19] According to estimates based on official statistics, real wages of agricultural workers in Bangladesh were 30 to 40% lower in 1972–75 than in 1949.[20]

In the cities, the employment situation is almost equally difficult. The urban population has increased by over 7% per year over the last decade, while the rate of growth of employment opportunities has been more modest. 'Past rural-urban migration has,' as Edward Clay has pointed out, 'merely shifted part of the unemployment and poverty problems to the towns.'[21] With over 80% of the total population working within the agricultural sector, it is obvious that urban activities, even if they expand rapidly in relative terms, can play only a marginal role in solving the employment problems of the rural poor in the foreseeable future.

In this chapter, I have concentrated on a brief overview of the three inter-related, and mutually reinforcing, problems of poverty: inequality, landlessness and the low utilization of labour. The present situation is alarming, and even more so the fact that the underlying trends clearly indicate that the situation in all three respects has been getting worse during the last decades. There is no reason to adopt a deterministic, Malthusian vision of the future, however; the main constraints to development are not physical but man-made, and Bangladesh has a potential to feed and give employment to a much larger population than the present one.

References

1. A.R. Khan, 'Poverty and Inequality in Rural Bangladesh' in I.L.O., *Poverty and Landlessness in Rural Asia* (Geneva, 1977), p. 147.
2. I.B.R.D., *Bangladesh: Current Economic Position and Short-Term Outlook* (Washington, D.C., 21 March 1980), Annex 2.
3. M. Salimullah and A.B.M. Shamsul, 'A Note on the Conditions of Rural Poor in Bangladesh', *Bangladesh Development Studies*, No. 2, 1976.
4. See, for example, S.R. Bose, 'Trend of Real Income of the Rural Poor', *The Pakistan Development Review*, Autumn 1968, A.R. Khan *The Economy of Bangladesh* (London, Macmillan, 1972); K. Griffin and

A.R. Khan, 'Poverty in the Third World: Ugly Facts and Fancy Models', *World Development*, No. 3, 1978; M. Alamgir, 'Some Analysis of Distribution of Income, Consumption, Saving and Poverty in Bangladesh', *Bangladesh Development Studies*, No. 4, 1974 and 'Some Reflections on Below Poverty Level Equilibrium Trap: The Bangladesh Experience' (Stockholm, Institute of International Economics 1977); E.J. Clay, 'Institutional Change and Agricultural Wages in Bangladesh', *Bangladesh Development Studies*, No. 4, 1976.

5. Yunus, Md. 'Planning in Bangladesh: Format, Technique and Priority and Other Essays', Rural Studies Project, Department of Economics, Chittagong University, June 1976, p. 12.

6. M.B. Duza, *Cultural Consequences of Population Change in Bangladesh*, quoted in W.B. Arthur and G. McNicoll, 'An Analytical Survey of Population and Development in Bangladesh', *Population and Development Review*, Vol. 4, No. 1, September 1978, p. 74.

7. Based on *Statistical Pocket Book of Bangladesh 1977*, Table 13.

8. Salimullah and Shamsul, op. cit.

9. Asian Development Bank, *Asian Agricultural Survey 1976* (Manila, 1977), p. 45.

10. F.A.O./U.N.D.P./Government of Bangladesh (Agricultural Mission 1977), 'Nutrition', Working Paper No. III (Dacca, 1977).

11. *Statistical Pocket Book of Bangladesh 1978*, Table 10.8.

12. See M. Alamgir, *Bangladesh: A Case Study of Below Poverty Level Equilibrium Trap*, Bangladesh Institute for Development Studies, 1978; and Mahabub Hossain, 'Foodgrain Production in Bangladesh: Performance, Potential and Constraints' B.I.D.S., mimeo (Dacca, March 1980); see also F.T. Jannuzi and J.T. Peach, 'Bangladesh: A Profile of the Countryside' (Land Occupancy Survey) U.S.A.I.D., mimeo (Dacca, 1978). They conclude (pp. 11-12): 'The data of our field research indicate that the ownership of land in rural Bangladesh is highly concentrated. The data also indicate that the degree of concentration of ownership is increasing.'

13. In an interview conducted by myself in March 1978, the then Secretary of the Ministry of Land Reform confirmed the existence of this trend. When asked if the government had any plans to impose restrictions on the purchase of land by urban dwellers, the Secretary answered, as if it were a big joke: 'Absentee landownership? Legislation? Well, you see, we are all landowners here [i.e. at the Ministry]; each and every one of us, even the most modest official, owns some land here and there. Do you really expect us to take any action against absentee landlords?'

14. E. Jansen, 'Choice of Irrigation Technology in Bangladesh: Implications for Dependency Relationships between Rich and Poor Farmers', *The Journal of Social Studies*, Vol. 1, No. 5, 1979.

15. For a discussion of these and other negative effects of the high degree of land fragmentation see, for example, Md. Sattar Mandal, 'An Economic Analysis of Resource Use with respect to Farm Size and Tenure in an Area of Bangladesh', unpublished dissertation, Wye College, University of London, August 1979, p. 85 ff.

16. The zamindars were large landholders who collected taxes for the

British and acted as economic and political middlemen in general between the British colonial administration and the rural population. After 1947, many zamindars of Hindu origin left for India, and their lands were distributed among the mainly Muslim farmers who remained in Pakistan.

17. E.J. Clay and S. Khan, 'Agricultural Employment and Underemployment in Bangladesh: The Next Decade', Working Paper, mimeo (Dacca, 1977).

18. See, for example, I. Ahmed, 'Employment in Bangladesh — Problems and Prospects', mimeo (Dacca, 1973); M. Muqtada, 'The Seed-Fertilizer Technology and Surplus Labour in Bangladesh Agriculture', *Bangladesh Development Studies*, No. 4, 1975; M. Alam, M. Alamgir and N. Chowdhury, 'Rural and Urban Unemployment and Underemployment in Bangladesh: Concepts, Magnitude and Policies', B.I.D.S. mimeo (Dacca, 1976); R. Islam, 'Approaches to the Problem of Rural Unemployment' Working Paper, Village Study Group, University of Dacca/B.I.D.S. mimeo (Dacca, 1977); A.R. Khan, 'Capital Intensity and the Efficiency of Factor Use: A Comparative Study of the Observed Capital-Labour Ratios of Pakistan Industries', *Pakistan Development Review*, Summer 1970; see also the references found in these works.

19. E.J. Clay, 'Employment Effects of the H.Y.V. Strategy in Bangladesh: A Rejoinder', mimeo (Dacca, March 1978), p. 4.

20. For a discussion, see E.J. Clay, 1976, op. cit.

21. E.J. Clay, 1978, op. cit., p. 4.

2. Development Potential

Bangladesh's limited and poorly diversified natural endowment places severe strains on her capacity to expand the range of economic activities. Apart from natural gas, there are few economically important non-agricultural resources within the country's borders. The key to economic development in Bangladesh is, therefore, to raise agricultural production and employment by a better utilization of her three main assets: human labour, land and water. Of these assets, only land can be considered scarce.

Land and Soil Capacities

If Singapore and a handful of other city states are excluded, Bangladesh is by far the most densely populated country in the world. However since most of the area consists of soils well suited for agricultural production, the ratio of population to agricultural land is not extremely high by international standards. Indeed Bangladesh has about as much cropland per inhabitant as Great Britain and West Germany, and twice as much as South Korea or Taiwan (see Table 2.1). Moreover, the quality of Bangladesh's rich alluvial soils is second to none, and the climate permits the cultivation of up to three crops per year in many parts of the country.

Taking multi-cropping into account, the total cropped area of Bangladesh is effectively about one-third higher than the cultivated area, or around 30 million acres (see Table 2.2).

As can be seen in Table 2.2 there is little scope for increasing production by further expanding the cultivation frontier. Virtually all arable land is already under cultivation and, as urban demands and requirements for housing and infrastructure grow, the total acreage available for agricultural use is likely to decrease rather than increase in the future. A higher level of food production can thus be achieved only through a more intensive utilization of existing cultivated land.

Despite an abundance of labour power, yields per acre remain very low in Bangladesh. Average yields of rice are estimated to be approximately the same as in India, but only about one-quarter those of Australia, one-third those of Japan, and one-half those of Taiwan or China — figures which are

Table 2.1:
Cropland in Relation to Population for Selected Countries, early 1970s
(estimates)

	Acres of Cropland per Person
Bangladesh	0.32
China	0.32
Taiwan	0.15
South Korea	0.17
Japan	0.37
India	0.74
West Germany	0.32
United Kingdom	0.32
Haiti	0.16
U.S.S.R.	2.40
Argentina	2.60
United States	21.50
Australia	42.50

Source: Based on World Bank, *Land Reform, Sector Policy Paper*, May
1975, p. 50 (hectares have been converted to acres above).

Table 2.2:
Land Utilization in Bangladesh (estimates)

	Millions of Acres	*%*
Forest	5.4	
Not available for cultivation	6.7	
Cultivable waste	0.7	
Total	*12.8*	
Current fallow	1.8	
Net cropped area	20.7	
Total	*22.5*	
Cropping intensity		139%
Total cropped area (Intensity x total)	*31.2*	

Source: Based on *Statistical Pocket Book of Bangladesh 1979*, pp. 196–7.

both an insult to the fertile soils of Bangladesh and a challenge and source of
optimism for the future. Discussing the contrast between people's poverty
and the richness of the soils, the French agronomist René Dumont observes:

Technically speaking, the agricultural potentialities of Bangladesh, by square mile of arable land, are much higher than those of India, China and Japan. The quality of soils and the average amount of rainfall are much higher than in India. The climate does not know any real winter, like most of China and Japan. Floods are the bigger constraint, but if all potentialities from flood-free areas in summer, and irrigation in winter (with much higher reserves, by desilting rivers and tanks) would be used, the agricultural production of Bangladesh could be at least doubled, inside actual cropping patterns, even with overwhelming rice domination, only with well-known techniques. By multiple cropping, diversification of crops, full development of fisheries, productive trees on hills, vegetable gardening, fodder and animal production intensification, etc., the actual production could at least be trebled. Technically speaking, it is not true to say that the future of Bangladesh is without any hope, and not only in agriculture.[1]

Other estimates tend to corroborate Dumont's rather intuitive impressions. A World Bank report in 1971[2] concluded that the current rice production of about 13 million tons per year could be quadrupled by the end of the century with the help of already known technologies in combination with a gradual development of irrigation and drainage facilities. The limitation of all such technocratic exercises is that they explicitly abstract from political and socio-economic constraints; still the estimates by the World Bank do serve to highlight the contrast between present and potential levels of production. Table 2.3 summarizes the major findings of the report and indicates the technical means necessary to reach the potential targets. The importance of water conservation and control emerges clearly.

Table 2.3:
Potential Rice Production (million tons)

	Inputs Only	*Inputs + Irrigation*	*Inputs + Full Irrigation and Drainage*
1983	16	26	35
1993	19	32	42
2003	22	38	51

These figures refer to rice production only, but it is worth noting that whilst Bangladesh is a rice economy par excellence, there are vast, although largely untapped, possibilities for diversifying the present rice monoculture thereby raising both the nutritional content and the economic value of the agricultural output. For the present, however, I will restrict my comments to some of the factors that explain the low level of rice yields. In this chapter I will mainly consider the natural and technical barriers to be overcome, while the far more important political and socio-economic constraints will be dealt with in subsequent chapters.

Water Resources

There is one crucial natural factor limiting both the extension and effectiveness of the improved seed-fertilizer technology popularly known as the Green Revolution. Cropping intensity and possible increases in yields per acre are related to the use — and misuse — of available water resources. Although Bangladesh receives more rainfall per year than can ever be effectively used, there are extreme seasonal variations typical of monsoon climates. During part of the year, roughly May to October, the high level of rainfall leads to a rise in the water flows of the big rivers which combines with the flat terrain to cause excessive flooding.[3] It is estimated that over 60% of the total cultivated area is flooded annually up to depths of three feet and above,[4] and that approximately 15% of the land area is flooded to an extent of about six feet or more, making crop production virtually impossible during the monsoon season. The rest of the year, however, is almost dry, river levels are low, and the amount of rainfall is so small in most parts of the country that effective cultivation is impossible without irrigation. In addition to this, there is the added constant danger of natural disasters such as cyclones or the tidal waves that inundate part of the country with salt water. Indeed major disasters, which reduce total agricultural production by over 10% compared with normal years, are expected to affect the country once every three to five years.

The topographic and hydrological conditions in Bangladesh thus combine to produce a highly precarious environment. Since crops are often destroyed by abnormal floods, a large part of the rice acreage must be planted with relatively low-yielding, but flood-tolerant, rice. Under these conditions the application of improved seeds and expensive fertilizers and pesticides is a hazardous experiment which the majority of farmers do not dare to undertake as long as they are poor, indebted, and in constant danger of losing their land through crop failure. With the help of appropriate embankment systems and other flood protection measures, the high risks during the wet season could be drastically reduced, although a truly efficient system of flood control would require the co-operation of neighbouring countries that share the great rivers with Bangladesh.

Protection of cultivated land against serious flooding cannot be separated from the necessity for efficient irrigation. In addition to increasing rice production, this would produce an increase in the extremely poor yields of crops other than rice, many of which would thrive in the soils of Bangladesh. It would also allow an extension of their existing limited utilization. However, at present only around 3.5 million acres, or a little more than 15% of the total cultivated area, are actually irrigated, although the potential in this respect is considerable. Adequate underground water resources for irrigation exist in all regions in Bangladesh except two, and estimates indicate that 16 million acres, or more than 75% of the present cultivated area, could be irrigated with the help of underground water resources.[5] Several additional millions of acres could also be irrigated from surface water if excess water from the great rivers could be diverted through channels. Technically speaking, even in the absence of reservoirs and other sophisticated means to store the water from the monsoon season, most of Bangladesh could be irrigated with the appropriate use of the available surface and underground water supplies.

The question of irrigation policies will be returned to several times in this study. For the present, it is adequate to emphasize that the increase in total irrigated area to date has been far from impressive when we consider the size of the financial resources devoted to an expansion of the irrigation facilities. In the 1970s government investment in irrigation absorbed a large share of all state expenditures on rural development, but most of the projects undertaken were characterized by high costs, low rates of capacity utilization, and increasing inefficiency (see Chapter 10). It is estimated that less than 30% of the installed capacity under the major irrigation schemes and deep tube-wells, and only around 50% under the small pump system, is actually utilized.[6]

The poor development of water control and irrigation systems, and the low rates of utilization of the existing facilities, affect agricultural production in two basic ways. To begin with, cropping intensity is unnecessarily low; if the excessive flooding that occurs even in normal years could be avoided and the irrigation coverage expanded, there is no physical reason why Bangladesh could not raise its cropping intensity from the present 1.4 to, say, 2.0. This alone would increase the total cropped area by almost one-third. Production would thereby increase even more, since irrigated crops are more reliable, and give higher yields per acre. Secondly, the fact that the improved seeds and other Green Revolution inputs are not very well suited to deep flooding contributes to depress average yields considerably during the wet season, and many farmers are reluctant to undertake productive investments under the prevailing conditions of high risk.

Before leaving the question of the use of water resources, it should finally be noted that the abundant supply of water in Bangladesh could also be used to produce a considerable increase in fish production. The per capita consumption of fish, the main source of animal protein in Bangladesh, has declined steadily over the past decades. Inland fish yields are among the lowest in all Asia — slightly over 400 pounds per acre. Yet in rural Bangladesh there are over 600,000 acres of tanks and ponds, almost three-quarters of which are estimated to be silted up and derelict. If the tanks were reclaimed and maintained in good condition, every acre of tank water could yield up to 1,500 pounds of fish annually. In addition to fishing, the ponds could also be utilized for minor irrigation, duck raising, vegetable growing on the banks of the tanks, etc.[7]

Modern Inputs

Although the soil of Bangladesh is rich and fertile, it is nevertheless deficient
in certain important nutrients which have to be added in the form of fertilizer. Since the increased yields which would result from the use of fertilizer
would compensate to some extent for the inability to gain extra land for
cultivation, its use in Bangladesh is especially important.

In the early 1960s, the use of chemical fertilizers was practically unknown
to the majority of Bangladesh's peasants. Since then, consumption of
fertilizer has increased at a respectable rate (see Table 2.4), but on a per
acre basis it has remained far below that of most other countries. Thus the
use of fertilizer in 1978 was only around 25 pounds per acre, i.e. less than
one-tenth the recommended doses (for local varieties of rice; the high-yielding
varieties require even more fertilizer for optimal results).

Table 2.4:
Use of Fertilizer 1964–79 (annual averages)

	Fertilizer (Tons)
1964–65 — 1968–69	159,000
1969–70 — 1973–74	318,000
1974–75 — 1978–79	542,000

Source: Based on data from Bangladesh Agricultural Development
Corporation) and I.B.R.D.

The application of fertilizer still remains only a fraction of the recommended
doses, and the farmers also tend to use mainly nitrogenous fertilizer instead
of a balanced mixture. Furthermore the actual use is highly unevenly distributed, with a minority of farmers using, relatively speaking, considerable
quantities, whilst the majority use virtually nothing. Vast areas of land,
especially during the *aus* and *aman* seasons, are cultivated without any
fertilizer at all, and the same is true with respect to other modern inputs like
improved seeds, insecticides, and pesticides. The high-yielding varieties
(H.Y.V.s) of rice, for example, which were introduced in Bangladesh almost
fifteen years ago, still cover only around 15% of the total rice acreage.

The slow spread of the use of fertilizers, H.Y.V.s, and of other
ingredients in the technology of the Green Revolution, is a major
factor explaining the low crop yields per acre in Bangladesh. From
a technical point of view, an appropriate combination of irrigation
and modern inputs could easily double yields in all areas where
excessive flooding does not occur (although one would hope that
ecological considerations would ensure the usage of only those
chemicals which do not produce adverse side effects). With improved

methods of soil preparation (for which the small peasants' lack of draught animals is a serious restriction) and water control, output per acre could be increased even more.

Human Resources

The concepts of rural un- and under-employment are extremely difficult both to define and to measure, and the problems are particularly acute in Bangladesh where no reliable occupational census has been undertaken. The estimates of the rural employment situation therefore have to be derived mainly from farm management studies for different crops under different conditions, and the results extrapolated to the whole country. The size of the available labour force can then be compared with the number of person-years of employment that are needed, given the existing cropping patterns and techniques of production. To these estimates of the demand for labour in crop production one would add more or less informed guesses about labour requirements in transport and marketing, animal husbandry, fisheries etc.

There are, of course, many pitfalls in such calculations. The estimates of the total labour force are far from reliable, and different farm management studies often give contradictory results. There is also an almost complete lack of knowledge about many areas of activity which engage a large proportion of the rural population. For example, very little is known about women's and children's household work.[8] Officially, only 9% of the women in Bangladesh are economically active in the traditional sense, i.e. are included in the 'labour force'. But since we know that women work hard in Bangladesh, as in the rest of the world, this is rather a reflection of the male bias in statistical concepts than a proof of female inactivity.

There are, furthermore, no accurate estimates of labour requirements for important forms of work such as collection of food and fuel, transporting, processing and marketing, storage, etc. But even if data were available, many problems would remain. There is no consensus among economists regarding basic definitions, and concepts such as 'hidden unemployment', 'structural unemployment', 'underemployment' etc. are all very much open to criticism and debate.

There is also a tendency to reformulate the entire question of unemployment as a problem of poverty and low productivity. It is sometimes argued that the issue is not so much that people are actually sitting idle — those who can afford to do so are usually half-educated youths from the middle class — but that their incomes are so low in the activities they are engaged in — partly because they are exploited and partly because their productivity is too low to permit a decent standard of living.

The effects on labour mobilization and productivity of factors such as low motivation and malnutrition cannot be ignored.

More important, perhaps, than unemployment and underemployment

is the low productivity and occasionally low intensity of work arising
from the poor motivation, poor health and injustice that is found in
most rural areas. The exploitation and inequality to which the majority
of the rural population is subjected is demoralizing, engenders resent-
ment and stifles initiative and creativity. The effect is not only to
lower current output below its potential but to reduce the capacity and
willingness of the population to innovate.[9]

However, this should not hide the fact that, whilst lack of employment
opportunities for the rural poor is undoubtedly a real problem, a large number of people are both fully employed and extremely poor.[10]

Without taking a definite position in this controversy, we can safely conclude that the problems of poverty, low productivity, inequality, exploitation, and unemployment, which are all very much present in rural
Bangladesh, are intimately related to each other, and that they all contribute
to the perpetuation of a situation in which the full human potential is a far
cry from being realized.

Keeping these reservations in mind, and trying to refer only to strictly
measurable categories, about one-third of the human resources in rural
Bangladesh can be considered unutilized. In absolute numbers, this amounts
to between 7 and 8 million person-years wasted annually. By definition the
problems are particularly acute during the slack season, but, even during the
peaks of labour demand for crop production, there are clear signs of a
widening gap between labour supply and demand. In urban areas, the rapid
growth of the so-called informal sector, i.e. various low productive occupations in the service sector, bears eloquent witness to the incapacity of the
economic system to provide the people with productive work opportunities.

The wastage of educated manpower is also high. According to a report
published by the Planning Commission,[11] 44% of the educated labour force
(defined as economically active persons with at least a secondary school
diploma) were unemployed in 1973-74. Recently, Bangladesh has begun to
export tens of thousands of skilled workers, service personnel and technicians every year, mainly to the oil-exporting countries in the Middle East.
The fact that many educated people emigrate is a glaring illustration of the
abyss that separates the actual and potential usage of the human resources
of Bangladesh.

Our earlier discussion of land and water resources has shown that productive employment should not be lacking in the countryside. Tasks such as the
protection and improvement of the soils and the controlling of the rivers
require giant efforts of human labour. Other examples could easily be given.
Here is a tentative list:

Construction of dwellings, godowns, etc.; manual and semi-manual
irrigation; collection of human, animal and green wastes and producing
fertilizer therefrom; kitchen gardening and tree plantation; pisciculture;
cultivation of more labour-intensive high-yielding variety cereals in

place of traditional ones and following modern labour-intensive cultural practices traditionally absent; manual and semi-manual transportation; rearing of silk-worms — with easy-to-grow castor leaves and producing castor oil from the seed; spinning, weaving, knitting and other cottage industries of various kinds; participation in mass literacy programmes; family planning and health extension works; extension work in so many areas; and so on. Every developing country has its own combination of numerous, literally numerous, such works that can keep the entire population engaged with relatively small complementary inputs that should not be very difficult to produce. The gain in national product, and in capital formation simultaneously, could thereby be substantial.[12]

To conclude, there exists a variety of useful activities that could be undertaken. But the constraints are many, and difficult to overcome; the existing power structure and concomitant development policies are not, as will be shown in subsequent chapters, capable of achieving the necessary mobilization of human and other resources that alone is capable of bridging the gap between Bangladesh's great potentials and her actual levels of production and employment.

References

1. R. Dumont, 'Problems and Prospects for Rural Development in Bangladesh', The Ford Foundation (Dacca, November 1973), p. 71.
2. Discussed in J. Faaland and J.R. Parkinson, *Bangladesh: A Test Case for Development* (London, Hurst and Co., 1976), p. 132 ff.
3. The large differences with respect to topographical and climatic conditions that do exist between the different regions in Bangladesh are not discussed in this brief overview; as in the rest of the text, Bangladesh is assumed to be more homogenous than it actually is.
4. See S. Bose 'The Strategy of Agricultural Development in Bangladesh', B.I.D.S., mimeo (Dacca, 1973); and Agricultural Mission, 'Irrigation Policy', Working Paper No. VIII (1977).
5. See, for example, S. Biggs, C. Edwards and J. Griffith, 'Irrigation in Bangladesh: On Contradictions and Underutilized Potentials', Discussion Paper No. 22, University of East Anglia, February 1978.
6. Agricultural Mission, *Selected Policy Issues in Agriculture* (1977), p. 44.
7. The actual and potential uses of Bangladesh's water tanks is discussed in, among others, René Dumont, op. cit.; Agricultural Mission, 'Fisheries', Working Paper No. V (1977); A.M. Majumdar, 'Reclamation of Derelict Tank Project', B.A.R.D. (Comilla, 1978).
8. With respect to child labour, it is common that children of both sexes begin their economically active life around the age of five or six, when they start helping their parents in activities like gathering fuel, fetching water, looking after younger children, etc. Boys often assume

responsibility for the care of cattle when they are eight or nine, and begin agricultural work a couple of years later. The boys soon begin to give a net economic return to their families'. This study analysing the economic activities of children in rural Bangladesh, T. Cain, 'The Economic Activities of Children in a Village in Bangladesh', *Population and Development Review*, Vol. 3, No. 3, 1977, concludes that 'male children may become net producers (producing more than they consume) as early as age 12, compensate for their own cumulative consumption by age 15, and compensate for their own and one sister's cumulative consumption by age 22.' (p. 201). Cain's analysis clearly shows that it is almost an economic necessity for most families in rural areas to have many boys. Under such circumstances, it is not easy to convince the families of the virtues of family planning.

9. K. Griffin and A.R. Khan, 'Poverty in the Third World: Ugly Facts and Fancy Models', *World Development*, No. 3, 1978, p. 298.

10. Cf. also the discussion about rural poverty in India by Ranjit Sau, 'Growth, Employment and Removal of Poverty', *Economic and Political Weekly*, Special Number, September 1978. Observing that the percentage of the population living below the poverty line is usually several times higher than the rate of unemployment, Sau remarks, 'If poverty seems to be coexisting with a low rate of unemployment, it only means that the employment there is not worth the name' (p. 1280).

11. *Employment Market and the Educated in Bangladesh* (Dacca, 1964) cited in M. Alam, M. Alamgir and M. Chowdhury, 'Rural and Urban Unemployment: Concepts, Magnitude and Policies', B.I.D.S., mimeo (Dacca, 1976), p. 15 ff.

12. Anisur Rahman, 'The Utilization of Labour in the Strategy for Development in the ECAFE Developing Region', paper prepared for the ECAFE, United Nations, mimeo, n.d.

3.   The Urban Bias

This is not the place to analyse the impact of British rule on the Indian Subcontinent. To indicate the importance of this legacy for an understanding of the supremacy of the cities over the countryside, I will only quote an observer who, writing in 1925, described the British emphasis on urban dominance in the following way:

> The rapid growth of large urban centres like Calcutta and Bombay was regarded with holy pride, and everything was done to foster their development. A new intelligentsia arose and since the government recruited nearly all its officials from its ranks, the whole administration unconsciously assumed an urban complexion.[1]

The 'urban complexion' had no difficulty in surviving Independence in 1947. To the old British urban-based political control in the colonies was added a new element further accentuating discrimination against rural areas – the Karachi Government's obsession with rapid industrialization.

During the 1950s and 1960s, what was then East Pakistan was forced to follow the Pakistani Government's extremely discriminatory import substitution policy whose aim was to favour industry at almost any cost: subsidies to manufacturing; an over-valued exchange rate squeezing the agricultural export sector and favouring the import-intensive urban sectors; fiscal policies that mainly benefited industry and urban activities at the expense of agriculture, etc. The government consistently discriminated against agriculture, and against East Pakistan, while trying to achieve a rapid industrialization of West Pakistan. The disastrous effects of this policy in terms of exploitation of the East by the West, of agriculture by industry and of labour by capital have been dealt with extensively in the literature and will not be analysed here.[2] Suffice it to add that Bangladesh, when the new nation was born, had an appalling urban-rural income inequality.[3] These huge differences in average incomes were accentuated by the unequal access to subsidized food and social services such as education, health facilities, etc. which were – and are – heavily concentrated in urban areas.

Political Dominance of the Towns

After — and during — the war of liberation, the majority of businessmen and top government officials who had earlier controlled the small industrial sector in East Pakistan, and represented state power, packed their bags and left for Karachi. The new group of leaders that filled the resulting power vacuum in no way abolished the old policies and privileges, however: they merely took them over and invited some of their friends to help (according to a popular joke in Bangladesh, the twenty-two Pakistani families who used to rule East Pakistan were simply replaced by 2,200 Bangladeshi families). Thus, although the partition of the country had deprived the modern industrial sector of most of their powerful leaders, the majority of the influential Awami League politicians who took power in 1971 represented basically the same interests as their predecessors. All they lacked were their West Pakistani connections. In terms of educational and professional backgrounds, the differences were — and are still — only marginal, as is illustrated in Table 3.1.

Table 3.1:
Occupational Background of M.P.s in East Pakistan (1970) and Bangladesh (1973 & 1979) (%)

	Lawyer	*Businessman*	*Landlord/ Farmer*	*Teacher*	*Other*	*Total*
1970	29.5	26.9	16.9	9.3	17.2	*100.0*
1973	25.5	23.7	17.6	9.9	22.3	*100.0*
1979	25.6	25.2	21.7	5.8	21.7	*100.0*

Source: for 1970 and 1973: R. Jahan, 'Members of Parliament in Bangladesh' (1975); for 1979: *Statistical Pocketbook of Bangladesh 1979.*

The author of the study from which the 1970 and 1973 data have been taken, Professor Rounaq Jahan, comments:

> As expected, the majority of the Members of Parliament belong to urban middle class professions, i.e. law, business, teaching, and medicine. Lawyers are the majority. 29% of the Members of Parliament of 1970 and 25% of the M.P.s of 1973 were lawyers. Lawyers were the majority in the previous Parliaments also in 1951, 1962 and 1965. However, the decade of the 1960s saw the rise of the Bengali business class, and they were increasingly represented in the Parliament. In the 1970 and 1973 Parliaments, businessmen represented the second most important occupational group. 26% of the M.P.s of 1970 and 23% of the M.P.s of 1973 were businessmen. Surplus farmers were the third most important occupational group. . . . Land is the major source of occupation for only 17% of the M.P.s (as compared to over 50% of

their fathers).[4]

Rounaq Jahan also observes a tendency for leading politicians to be simultaneously engaged in several different activities of a both urban and rural character: 'Increasingly, the Parliamentarians are combining two or three occupations; law, business and farming being the most common combination. 50% of the Members of Parliament of 1970 and 66% of the M.P.s of 1973 recorded having more than one occupation'.[5] In recent years, the Members of Parliament have been asked by the President to publicly declare the size of their holdings. As a result, these trends to multiple interests have been confirmed by Bangladeshi newspaper reports, of which the following is typical:

> Syet Mohammed Qaisar (M.P. of the ruling Bangladesh Nationalist Party, BNP) has 13.54 acres of agricultural land valued at *taka* 202,500. The value of his share of building at his village home has been put at *taka* 100,000. He had a bank balance of *taka* 2,735,953 and cash in hand of *taka* 30,000 on April 15 this year. His wife has 100 tolas of gold ornament worth about *taka* 200,000. The ornaments were given by his parents, father-in-law and other relatives at the time of his marriage. The valuation of his household articles, including freezer, deep freeze, TV, camera with projector and air-conditioner has been shown as *taka* 290,000 approximately. Mr Qaisar is a co-sharer of a major rice-mill and a printing press at Noyapara, Sylhet. His wife has 30% shares in a joint-stock company and is an owner of a new Toyota Corolla Deluxe private car. He runs one life insurance policy for *taka* 1,500,000. He has 10,000 pounds sterling equivalent to about *taka* 420,000 in UK as his saving out of his earnings for seven years abroad. His wife has a dwelling house in London city valued at *taka* 400,000 approximately. She bought the house in 1976 out of her earnings in UK while she was there, the statement added.[6]

Thus what is significant is not so much the expected fact that the class origins of the political elite in Bangladesh are mainly in the rural and urban elites, but the economic and political fusion of rural and urban interests. More and more sons of big farmers tend to engage in business and in urban professional and political activities in general, and many urban rich – and quite a few not so rich – are busy buying up agricultural land. This strengthening of the links between the urban and the rural elites, is also present at the local level. Institutional changes in the countryside and, in particular, the introduction of the Green Revolution technology, have made the farmers increasingly market-oriented. Urban – and, to a growing extent, foreign – production techniques and consumption patterns are penetrating the remotest villages. The big farmers are diversifying their activities more and more, becoming not only landowners and moneylenders, but also traders, owners of electric rice mills, fertilizer dealers, government officials, etc. This trend is in part the result of the deterioration of the domestic terms-of-trade for farm products that has taken place since Independence[7] and which has made non-agricultural undertakings more lucrative than food production. But it is also the consequence of political and institutional transformations which have made urban professions more important in the economic and political life of rural Bangladesh.

In one study analysing the pattern of Union Parishad leadership, it was found that of 113 elected U.P. leaders in the district of Chittagong, only a minority of 49 had agriculture as their main occupation.[8] Another 49 of the local leaders interviewed stated business as their principal activity, the remaining 11 being mainly engaged in services. The great majority of the U.P. leaders were of rural bourgeois class origins, but had become distinctly more urban than their parents. They were appreciably better educated and wealthier than their voters; none of them were illiterate, their personal incomes were high, the average value of their declared personal belongings exceeded 100,000 *taka* (against a national average of around 13,000), and a majority also possessed modern household items like radios.

The elite character of the U.P. leaders is also highlighted in another study[8] which found that an elected U.P. leader spent on average 11,000 *taka*, or some U.S. $ 700 to finance his election campaign. By international standards this is not much, of course, but in rural Bangladesh, it is a fortune.

We will have occasion to return to the question of the class character of the leadership of different institutions several times in this study. What should be emphasized once more at this point is that the political leadership, both at the national and local level, tends to be not only economically much better off but also far more urban-oriented than the population as a whole. There is also, within the elite, a clear tendency for urban and rural interests to merge — with the former dominating the latter more and more. Let us now see how this is reflected in the actual development policies affecting urban-rural relations.

Allocation of Funds

In Bangladesh, where the rate of private capital accumulation for productive purposes is negligible, the public sector plays a role of paramount importance for the development of the economy. Through its control of foreign economic assistance, which accounts for the major part of the country's investible funds, the state can — subject to the restrictions imposed by the foreign donors — by and large determine the structure and direction of economic growth. Within the present agrarian structure, no rapid growth is conceivable without public investments in agriculture, and our first question must therefore be how the urban-rural inequality is affected by the overall allocation of state expenditures.

Superficially, it would appear that agriculture was a privileged sector in Bangladesh. The direct tax burden on agriculture is exceedingly light; in

1975-76, direct taxes on agriculture represented only 0.25% of total agricultural income, and agricultural taxes constituted no more than 2% of the entire state revenue.[9] The land tax is so insignificant that the revenue from it does not even cover the government's collection costs.[10] Furthermore, the agricultural sector is benefiting from state support of various kinds. Virtually all modern agricultural inputs sold to farmers are heavily subsidized, and government after government has declared its intention to give the highest possible priority to agriculture. Foreign donors and loan-giving agencies like the World Bank have also tended to emphasize more and more the importance of rural development.

Thus far the official picture. In reality, however, the treatment of agriculture, and of rural activities in general, is not as favourable as it might appear. With over 90% of the population living in the countryside, and almost 80% of the workforce directly engaged in agriculture, the character of the Bangladesh economy is overwhelmingly rural. The high share of agriculture in output and employment is not reflected in an equally high share in public and private development expenditures, however. 'Priority to agriculture, funds to industry and urban infrastructure' has, to borrow a phrase used by Michael Lipton,[11] been the *de facto* strategy adopted by successive governments both before and after 1971. The discrimination against agriculture in the allocation of funds is illustrated in Table 3.2.

Table 3.2:
Share of Agriculture in the Bangladesh Economy

Share of:	*% of total (averages 1973-77)*
Export earnings[1]	90-95
Employment	75-80
Gross domestic product	55-60
Public development expenditures[2]	10-15
Bank credit	9-11
Private investment	7-9
Current public expenditures	1-2

1. Including processed goods originating from the agricultural sector.
2. Not including water and flood control.

Source: Based on data from Planning Commission and Ministry of Finance.

If we include rural works, flood and water control and other items indirectly benefiting agriculture in the development budget, the share of public expenditures destined for the rural sector would increase to between 20 and 30% (see Tables 3.3 and 3.4).

Table 3.3:
Public Development Expenditure on Rural Development, 1976-79

| | *% of Total Development Expenditure*[1] | | |
	1976-77	*1977-78*	*1978-79*
Agriculture	13.4	13.1	13.1
Rural development	4.0	4.2	4.6
Water and flood control	7.3	11.8	10.0
Total Rural Development	*24.7*	*29.1*	*27.7*

1. 1976-78 from the Annual Budget, 1978-79 from the Annual Development Plan.

Source: Ministry of Finance.

Table 3.4:
Sectoral Allocation of the 1978-79 Development Plan

	Total *(taka in crores)*	*%*
Agriculture	192.6	13.1
Rural development and institutions	67.4	4.6
Flood control and water resources	146.9	10.0
Industry	253.3	17.2
Power and natural resources	209.5	14.3
Transport and communications	261.8	17.8
Physical planning and housing	113.8	7.7
Education	77.5	5.3
Health	54.2	3.7
Population control and family planning	44.1	3.0
Social welfare, public administration, miscellaneous	49.3	3.4
Total	*1,470.5*	*100.0*

Source: Ministry of Finance

Within the agricultural sector proper, a large part — over 40% on average during the last five years — of development expenditure is allocated to subsidies on fertilizer and pesticides, items which should rather be classified as current expenditure. These input subsidies have been essential for the strategy of increasing the use of the modern seed-fertilizer technology but they almost exclusively benefit the big farmers; to a large extent they can be regarded as constituting consumption subsidies enabling the rural rich to prop up their demand for urban-produced industrial goods. If these subsidies are excluded, then the share of development expenditures going to agriculture goes down to some 7 or 8%.

The other items in the development budget are predominantly urban-oriented. In the 1978-79 Plan, 17.2% of the funds is allocated to industry, mostly large-scale industry in the big urban centres. The post-liberation governments have, as will be discussed further in Chapter 6, continued with the same capital-intensive industrialization policies as their Pakistani pre-decessors. Another 17.8% of the 1978-79 Plan goes on transport and communications, and 14.3% on power, scientific research and natural resources. Each of these sectors thus received more than agriculture. Of the expenditures on education and health, only a relatively small part is allocated to rural areas, where the overwhelming majority of the sick, undernourished and illiterate people live. With respect to education it can, indeed, be questioned whether the present system actually helps or harms the rural communities. The content of schooling is largely irrelevant to the needs of the villages, and in practice its major function is probably to facilitate the brain drain from rural to urban areas.[12] The fact that only 13% of public expenditure on education is allocated to primary schools is a clear indication of the elite orientation of the educational system.

As for public and private banking, the disparity between urban and rural lending is startling. Many studies from different countries have shown that rural people are capable of saving a lot — they are, in fact, generally found to be better savers than the urban dwellers in corresponding income brackets — and this is equally true in Bangladesh. However, very little of their institutional savings are actually invested by themselves in their own villages. The entire credit system is designed as a kind of vacuum cleaner sucking investible surplus from the countryside to the cities. Exact data on the size of this urban appropriation are lacking but, as an example, we could quote one observer who, commenting on the ongoing 'relentless transfer of resources from rural to urban areas . . . spearheaded by the national banking service' gives the following figures: 'During 1977 *taka* 25 *crores* were deposited at different banks at Bogra when only *taka* 2.5 *crores* were sanctioned for the people in that district. Similarly, Pabna received *taka* 2 *crores* against 20 *crores* in deposits, and Rangpur received *taka* 2 *crores* against 30 *crores* in deposits.'[13]

There also exist a large number of other mechanisms by which investible surplus is extracted from rural areas. One such example, usually neglected in this context, is the vast amount of money that rural people spend on lawsuits, mainly disputes about land ownership. In a recent study[14] covering a sample of 52 villages in different districts, it was found that, in each village, an average of 6.5 suits were being heard in different formal and informal institutions. For each suit, the plaintiff and the defendant together spent an average of 3,144 *taka* per year; of this sum, the lion's share, or approximately 2,500 *taka*, went to urban dwellers (lawyers, hotel owners, etc.). If these villages are representative of all rural Bangladesh, an extrapolation of the findings would indicate that over 1,000 million *taka* is spent on lawsuits every year by rural people, of which 850 million *taka* is transferred every year to urban areas through lawsuits. The resources thus transferred represent over two-thirds of all public development expenditure on agriculture in 1977–78, when the study was made; the sums were 'a) equivalent to about 37% of the total value of H.Y.V. rice produced in 1977, b) equivalent to 30% of the total value of jute produced in the country, c) 25% higher than the sale value of all fertilizers distributed in 1977.'[15]

The Food Rationing System

The most important single example of the bias towards the urban population is the food subsidy system, which mainly benefits the middle class, and in particular the urban middle class. The system, originally introduced by the British after the severe Bengali famine of 1943, has been allowed to expand rapidly under successive governments of first Pakistan, then Bangladesh. The food distributed under the rationing system is mainly supplied by foreign donors; almost all the food aid is channelled this way. (See Chapter 4 for a discussion of the food aid system.) Additional quantities are bought on a commercial basis on the world market or, particularly in recent years when Bangladesh's harvests have been good, obtained from domestic sources. At present, about 2 million tons of grain, mainly wheat, are being distributed annually through the system.

There are several different categories of beneficiaries. A small minority in the so-called 'relief' category get their food free of charge in times of emergency. The food distributed under the food for work programmes is also included under this heading. On average, 'relief' officially receives somewhere between 5 and 15% of the total national grain, but in practice leakage is so big that the very poorest get appreciably less than this. Another category of beneficiaries are the holders of permanent ration cards under the so-called Statutory Rationing, which comprises all people who have been living in the six largest cities since before 1974 (in 1974, the government stopped issuing ration cards to new urban migrants, with the exception of government officials who were transferred to the cities). These urban residents are entitled to not only grain but also other foodstuffs such as edible oil and sugar once a week at prices that are about 50% lower than the free market prices.

Statutory rationing supplies some 3.5 million people with subsidized food, and accounts for approximately one-third of the entire ration off-take. Another one-third is allocated to 'priority groups' like the armed forces, the police, government officials and employees in large enterprises, students residing in student hostels, and a few others. These groups enjoy the same privileges as the city dwellers.

The 'Modified Ration System' operates outside the urban areas supposedly for the benefit mainly of the rural poor. But they are in fact only entitled to one-half of the ration received by the urban dwellers and 'priority groups'. Furthermore, and most important, even if the government wanted to reach the rural poor, there is no distribution system through which the grain could be channelled to the most needy. (This is also, although to a lesser extent, the situation in the urban areas, where many people never see the subsidized food.) Widespread corruption also makes heavy inroads on the amounts of food destined for rural areas. The result of all these factors is that 'the higher the income, the less one generally pays for food'.[16] According to official estimates,[17] only around 10% of the entire off-take through the ration system actually reaches the poor and destitute, and rural areas are particularly discriminated against. Thus, while 67% of Bangladesh's urban population was included in the 1978–79 ration system, the corresponding figure for the rural population was only 12%. A recent World Bank report concludes:

> The public food distribution system is not primarily designed to reach the poor . . . . That the rural poor are not the target of the present distribution system is clear from the fact that the average rural resident received perhaps 28 pounds of food-grains per year through the various forms of public distribution, including Food for Work, compared with averages of about 212 pounds per year for each resident of a statutory rationing area, and 321 pounds per year for each adult statutory rationing card-holder. If complaints of villagers about failure to receive Modified Ration Grain allotted to their Union Parishads are true, the actual per capita benefit to the rural poor is even less. It is likely that the present rationing system is also increasingly failing to reach the urban poor.[18]

The political rationale behind the selection of beneficiaries is quite obvious. The relief objective plays a very subordinate role — perhaps only enough to convince the foreign donors of the need for food aid. From the point of view of domestic political stability, it is far more important to keep food prices low for the small, but politically articulate, minority of urban residents and government employees. Or, in the words of a cable from the U.S. State Department Dacca Mission dated January 1976: 'There is no question of the extreme importance to Bangladesh leaders of a continued flow of imported food-grains to fuel the ration system, and above all to keep potentially active Dacca dwellers supplied with low-price foodgrains.'[19]

Since the costs of the ration system are mainly borne by American tax-payers — who thereby provide a considerable support to the relatively well-off minority of farmers in the United States — the direct expenditures of the government of Bangladesh are quite small, or less than 1 billion *taka* on average during the last few years.[20] This way of assessing the costs of the ration system is highly misleading, however, since without the food subsidies the government would be able to sell the imported food at market prices, thereby increasing the state revenues considerably.[21] If the costs of the food consumption subsidies were instead defined as the difference between the total value of food procured from both domestic and foreign sources at market prices and total receipts from the sales of subsidized food – with allowance for changes in stocks – the costs would increase several times. According to World Bank estimates, the true costs of the foodgrain subsidies have, when calculated in this way, ranged between 2.3 and 5.2 billion *taka* (see Table 3.5).

Table 3.5:
Estimated Nominal Foodgrain Subsidy, 1973-77 (million *taka*)

	1973-74	*1974-75*	*1975-76*	*1976-77*
Total expenditure	3,853	4,743	7,369	5,057
Total receipts	720	2,156	2,195	2,778
Deficit (nominal subsidy)	3,133	2,587	5,174	2,279

Source: I.B.R.D.

Table 3.5 thus gives a more accurate picture of the actual costs involved than the official expenditure data presented in the Budget. A comparison between these actual costs and the development expenditures on agriculture illustrates what is in practice given priority, and what is not (see Table 3.6).

Table 3.6:
Development Expenditure on Agriculture and Nominal Costs of Foodgrain Subsidy, 1973-76 (million *taka*)

	1973-74	*1974-75*	*1975-76*	*1976-77*
Development expenditure on agriculture	576	639	1,032	1,635
Value of food consumption subsidy	3,133	2,587	5,174	2,279

Source: I.B.R.D. and Ministry of Finance.

From the point of view of equity, we have seen that the costly ration system works heavily in favour of the urban upper and middle classes and the comparatively better-off strata of the population in general.[22] It serves, furthermore, as a disincentive to agricultural production: through the selling of large amounts of imported foodgrain at subsidized prices, the government reduces the market for domestically produced food while keeping food prices artificially low. It is one of the great paradoxes of Bangladesh's (and of many other Third World countries') development strategy that while the official *agricultural* policy is extremely production-oriented, with an almost exclusive emphasis on attempts to make the farmers adopt the Green Revolution package of modern inputs, the *food* policy is totally counter-productive in that it actually depresses agricultural prices, thereby reducing the farmers' investible surplus and discouraging the production of food. This apparent paradox can only be resolved if one assumes that it is low prices rather than high levels of production that interest the government most. For the Green Revolution in Bangladesh is, as will be shown in subsequent chapters, more efficient in lowering production costs for a minority of privileged farmers than in raising the overall production volume.

Concluding Remarks

We have seen how the government's discrimination against agriculture takes two basic forms: the allocation of state expenditures, with high priority given to industry and urban infrastructure, and the effects of the food ration system. In the next chapter, I will discuss how these policies are reinforced by the influence of foreign aid, which to a large extent is used to sustain the urban-oriented policies discussed above.

It should, however, be emphasized that the use of the expression 'urban bias' in no way means that the consistent class character of the policies should be overlooked. The neo-populist versions of the 'urban bias' concept currently in vogue even in World Bank rhetoric can be highly misleading, and may serve to obscure the fact that the basic contradiction is not between rural and urban residents but between classes — both in the countryside and in the cities.[23] The reasons why the rural rich — who, after all, constitute a vital source of support for the country's political parties and politicians — have been able to accommodate themselves to the successive governments' discriminatory policies are not too difficult to understand. They have, first of all, to an increasing extent diversified their economic activities in order to become more urban and less dependent on food production. Further, in their capacity as surplus farmers they have benefited in a variety of ways, mainly through the system of cheap credit and input subsidies which are supplied through various public and semi-public institutions in the rural areas. The strong coalition of urban businessmen and bureaucrats — all supported by the armed forces and by powerful foreign interests — that holds political power has been able to use its control over the state apparatus to provide extensive favours to the urban population, while at the same time giving selective benefits to the upper layers of the peasantry.

Today, it is difficult to foresee any major changes in this pattern of priorities. By and large, the country is run by urban people with urban interests, habits and friends, and who are in constant fear of discontent and unrest among politically volatile urban dwellers. The former Awami League Government probably depended more on support from the rural people than the present one. In the words of one Bangladeshi scholar:

The new rulers are basically supporters of urban interests and are determined to release resources from agriculture for industrialization. Towards that end they have withdrawn subsidies from agricultural inputs and have introduced measures to extract surpluses from agriculture. These measures, which mostly affect the poor and a section of the middle peasants, are manoeuvres aimed at siphoning off capital from agricultural production for investment in urban industrial growth and at more effectively controlling the powerful class of rich peasants and limiting their political power.[24]

Unless the present trends are drastically reversed, it will be even more difficult in the future to achieve the necessary mobilization of rural resources that alone can help to solve the problems of stagnating agricultural production, income and employment.

References

1. Sir Malcolm Darling quoted in G. Etienne, 'Bangladesh: Development in Perspective', Asian Documentation and Research Centre (Geneva, 1977), p. 130.
2. The standard texts on this subject are: K. Griffin and A.R. Khan (eds.), *Growth and Inequality in Pakistan* (London, Macmillan, 1972); I. Little, T. Scitovsky and M. Scott, *Industry and Trade in Some Developing Countries: A Comparative Study* (London/New York/Toronto, Oxford University Press, 1970); see also A.R. Khan, 'Employment in Bangladesh during the Second Five-Year Plan', ARTEP–I.L.O., (Bangkok, 1970); M. Masum, 'Technology and Employment in Bangladesh' in Report of I.L.O. Tripartite Symposium on Choice of Technology and Employment Generation in Asia (Bangkok, 1979) and Chapter 6 of the present book.
3. See M. Alamgir, 'Some Analysis of Distribution of Income, Consumption, Saving and Poverty in Bangladesh', *Bangladesh Development Studies*, No. 4, 1974.
4. R. Jahan, 'Members of Parliament in Bangladesh', mimeo (Dacca, March 1975).
5. Ibid.
6. *Bangladesh Times* 10 December 1979.
7. See, for example, A.M.A. Rahim and A.K.M. Hoque, 'The Terms of Trade of Bangladesh, 1972–76: An Analysis and Policy Implications', *Bangladesh Bank Bulletin*, April 1978. This study, which deals with the period up to 1976, shows that the terms-of-trade have moved against agricultural products throughout the post-Independence period, with the exception of 1974–75, when both world market and domestic prices of food rose drastically. After 1976, farmgate prices of rice have fluctuated widely without showing any distinct trend, while industrial goods as well as agricultural inputs, and in particular fertilizers, have

become dearer and dearer.

8. S.M. Nurul Alam, 'Pattern of U.P. Leadership — A Case Study of U.P. Leaders of Mathazari Thana of Chittagong District', Chittagong University, 1979 (unpublished): the data have generously been given in personal communication with the author.

9. Figures taken from M. Hossain, A. Rahman and M.M. Akash, 'Agricultural Taxation in Bangladesh', B.I.D.S., mimeo (Dacca, 1978).

10. Ibid.

11. Michael Lipton, *Why Poor People Stay Poor: A Study of Urban Bias in World Development* (London, Temple Smith, 1977), p. 347.

12. After having presented a wealth of material supporting the thesis that education in developing countries mainly serves to reinforce the urban bias in society, Michael Lipton (op. cit.) draws the drastic conclusion that 'the rural sector in almost every poor country would benefit from the termination of rural education' (p. 259). He is, however, careful to add that this conclusion should not be interpreted as a 'guide for action'. For a critique of Lipton's views on rural education — and of Lipton in general — see C.H.H. Rao, 'Urban vs. Rural or Rich vs. Poor?', *Economic and Political Weekly*, 7 October 1978.

13. A. Mukhopadhyay, 'Preparing for Parliamentary Polls', *Economic and Political Weekly*, 26 August 1978, p. 469.

14. M.A. Jabbar, 'Socio-economic Aspects of Lawsuits in Bangladesh' *The Bangladesh Journal of Agricultural Economics*, Vol. 1, No. 2, December 1978.

15. Ibid., p. 63.

16. Agricultural Mission, Working Paper No. II, (1977), p. 21.

17. Ibid. See also D.F. McHenry and K. Bird, 'Food Bungle in Bangladesh', *Foreign Policy*, No. 27, 1977; B. Hartman and J.K. Boyce, 'Bangladesh: Aid to the Needy?', *International Policy Report*, Vol. IV, No. 1, Center for International Policy (Washington, D.C., May 1978); R. Sobhan, 'Politics of Food and Famine in Bangladesh', *Economic and Political Weekly*, 1 December 1979, and various World Bank publications.

18. I.B.R.D., 'Bangladesh: Food Policy Issues', December 1979, pp. 27-8.

19. Quoted in McHenry and Bird, op. cit., p. 75.

20. This figure does not include interest and amortization payments on the foreign loans that are used to finance part of the aid imports.

21. If the ration system was abolished, less food aid might, on the other hand, be supplied to Bangladesh.

22. Cf., however, Chapter 4 below for a discussion of how the intrarural distribution of income is affected by a policy aiming at keeping down the prices of food.

23. For a vigorous critique of this tendency — and, indeed, of the entire notion of 'urban bias', see T.J. Byres' review article of Michael Lipton's well-known book (Byres' 'Of Populist Pipe Dreams: Daedalus in the Third World and the Myth of Urban Bias', *Journal of Peasant Studies*, Vol. 6, No. 2, January 1979). This critique of Lipton seems to me, however, as one-sided as Lipton himself; while Lipton interprets almost everything in terms of the urban-rural conflict, and in the name of equity suggests a number of policy measures which would actually benefit the rural rich at the expense of the urban poor, Byres refuses

to admit the very existence of a discrimination against agriculture, and against rural activities and people in general, in the Third World.

24.   J.K. Jahangir, 'Nature of Class Structure in Bangladesh', *Economic and Political Weekly*, 12 December 1977, p. 2065.

4.   The Foreign Bias

It is easy to underestimate the importance of the Bangladesh economy's foreign dependence. Most of the country's 65,000 villages exhibit few symptoms of the kind of foreign penetration that characterizes rural society in, say, Latin America and most of Africa. It is also true that the colonial heritage is less visible in Bangladesh than in India, where the economic, political and cultural impact of British rule is more conspicuous. The tourist's view of Bangladesh, however, as a comparatively 'untouched', traditional society little affected by the outside world, is very superficial. The colonial era had a decisive effect on the entire Bengali economy.

> The country's low level of industrial development is a legacy of colonialism. Before the British conquest in the eighteenth century, Bengal was one of the richest provinces in India. The fine muslin cloth produced by the weavers of Dacca was famous throughout the world, and both agriculture and commerce thrived in the area. To meet the needs of its industrial revolution, the British transformed East Bengal into an agricultural hinterland, producing raw materials for the Empire.[1]

Today, the signs of foreign influence are manifold. From a cultural and political point of view, Bangladesh's educational system and legal and administrative institutions have been very much shaped by the British tradition. The political elite, the urban leaders in Dacca and their followers are, like their Pakistani predecessors, quite outward-oriented and ready to import not only foreign commodities, technology and know-how but also foreign ideas and tastes, foreign economic doctrines, foreign military advisers, foreign T.V. programmes and magazines, and foreign experts. And, to use a phrase currently in vogue in the development debate, it is clear that many of these cultural and ideological imports 'trickle down' to the urban and rural poor at least as freely as the more tangible 'benefits' of trade. But to reduce the issue of foreign dependence to more manageable proportions, we have to leave most of these aspects aside and concentrate on rather conventional economic categories.

Foreign Aid: A Quantitative Assessment

Since Independence, Bangladesh has received more foreign aid than the whole of Pakistan received before 1971. There are today few, if any, countries in the world that are so heavily dependent upon foreign aid as Bangladesh. Officially, aid[2] now accounts for between 75 and 80% of all development expenditure. Since this category normally includes several items that are more properly regarded as current expenditure, the true figure would be even higher. According to World Bank estimates, in which corrections have been made for this and several other factors that distort the real size of both revenue and expenditure in the Bangladesh state budget, public savings have actually been negative during the last few years. This implies that external assistance has not only financed total public investment, but part of public sector consumption as well.

Taking the above adjustments into account, foreign aid, including loans, thus finances over 100% of public investment, or almost 10% of G.D.P. Or, to make another comparison that highlights the dependence on capital imports: foreign aid commitments in the latter half of the 1970s amounted to over twice as much as total export earnings during the same period. In absolute figures, the level of new aid commitments has averaged over one billion U.S. dollars annually in recent years. A summary of the 1979–80 situation is given in Table 4.1. Due to increasing problems in handling these

Table 4.1:
Foreign Economic Assistance — Actual Disbursements, 1979–80 ($ US millions)

	Food Aid	Commodity Aid	Project Aid	Total Aid
Opening pipeline	33	352	1,446	*1,831*
New commitments	309	655	904	*1,868*
Disbursements	187	472	356	*1,015*
Closing pipeline	155	535	1,993	*2,683*

Source: I.B.R.D. preliminary estimates.
Note: Opening and closing pipeline refers to undisbursed commitments at the beginning and end of the year respectively.

large amounts of aid, the level of disbursements has been appreciably lower than new commitments, in particular with respect to project aid. Looking at the aid actually disbursed under the different headings, Table 4.2 gives a picture for 1972–73 to 1978–79. Among the different donors, the United States stands out as the largest single source of external financing. Between 1971 and 1978, the United States contributed around one-third of all foreign aid to Bangladesh, the remainder being shared by a wide variety of

Table 4.2:
Foreign Economic Assistance, 1972–79 (US $ millions)

Type of Aid	72-73	73-74	74-75	75-76	76-77	77-78	78-79	Total
Food	183	233	373	306	112	182	187	1,576
Commodity and cash	289	107	379	378	247	352	472	2,224
Project	85	138	145	129	141	255	356	1,249
Total	558	478	897	813	500	789	1,015	5,049
Merchandise exports	340	362	358	380	420	497	603	2,960

Source: Planning Commission and I.B.R.D.
Note: Figures in current dollars; the value of aid to Bangladesh in 1978–79 was no higher in real terms than it was in 1972–73.

bilateral donors and multilateral aid- and loan-giving agencies. Of all the aid from the U.S., well over half has been given in the form of food aid.

The percentage of grants in the total aid package has been slightly less than 50% on average,[3] but the government expects this figure to rise to about two-thirds in the future. Most of the loans given have been soft, with low rates of interest and long repayment periods. The annual service payments are still only around 100 million U.S. dollars per year, i.e. only a small fraction of the net inflow of aid, but compared to the average export earnings of some 400–600 million dollars per year this represents a potentially heavy debt burden if capital imports begin to decrease. And while merchandise exports have risen only slowly, the foreign debt has, as seen in Table 4.3, increased at an alarmingly high rate, especially after the military take-over in 1975. Today, Bangladesh's foreign debt represents a sum which nearly equals the country's accumulated export earnings during its entire existence since 1971.

The Bangladesh Government is quite aware of the danger of a constantly rising foreign debt, and it is trying to direct more of the aid flow into directly productive activities and to increase and diversify the export sector. In the Two Year Plan 1978-80, the Planning Commission expressed its concern over the fact that most of the aid has been in the form of food and commodity aid. 'This pattern of aid absorption, while raising the debt burden of the economy, has failed to create necessary productive capacities for servicing debt. Debt burden has already started creating problems in the economy's capacity to finance imports'.[4] Such verbal recognitions of the excessive reliance upon foreign aid does not prevent the government, however, from constantly asking for more and more external assistance. To illustrate the prevailing attitude towards foreign aid among the present rulers, let me quote a letter from President Ziahur Rahman, dated 5 December 1979, to the Swedish

Table 4.3:
Outstanding Amounts of External Public Debt[1] (US $ thousands)

| Fiscal Year | Debt Outstanding at Beginning of Period | |
	Disbursed Only	Including Undisbursed
1972–73	36	130
1973–74	227	657
1974–75	490	1,081
1975–76	1,359	2,392
1976–77	1,806	2,759
1977–78	2,068	3,079
1978–79	2,581	3,898
1979–80[2]	3,005	4,653

1. Repayable in foreign currency and commodities.
2. Estimate.
Source: I.B.R.D.

Prime Minister, Torbjörn Fälldin:

Dear Mr. Prime Minister,
. . . Our country is a test case for ourselves and for the free world. . . .
We are projecting an aid disbursement in the tune of ten billion U.S.
dollars during Second Five Year Plan. This will warrant a commitment
of the level of some thirteen to fourteen billion U.S. dollars. . . . We
deeply appreciate the encouragement and support received from the
Government and the people of Sweden in our development programme.
We NEED AND ANTICIPATE AN ANNUAL COMMITMENT IN THE
ORDER OF U.S. DOLLARS 400 MILLION INCLUSIVE OF FOOD
AID FROM THE GOVERNMENT OF SWEDEN TO ENABLE US TO
MATERIALISE OUR MODEST SECOND FIVE YEAR PLAN.
. . . We would request your Government for a substantial upward
revision of food aid allocations for about three years beginning from
fiscal year 1980. . . . I would request you to please consider granting
us a BALANCE OF PAYMENT SUPPORT OF U.S. DOLLAR 50
MILLION FOR THIS YEAR AS A SPECIAL CASE. I would also avail
of this opportunity to put in a special request to place a deposit of
U.S. DOLLAR 50 MILLION in our Central Bank [Bangladesh Bank]
on mutually agreeable terms. . . . We need active and liberal assistance
from brotherly countries like yours, WHICH WE ARE CONFIDENT
WOULD BE FORTHCOMING. We need substantial increase in the
volume of your assistance to us, a part of which may be in the form of
LONG TERM EASY LOANS/CREDITS. . . . Only a fraction of your
national resources can put this nation on its feet to progress and
prosperity. . . . Mr. Prime Minister, I would request you to please give

personal direction to concerned agencies for special attention to and realisation of our development programmes in AGRICULTURE, OIL, GAS, MINERAL RESOURCES, DEVELOPMENT OF NUCLEAR ENERGY FOR ELECTRICITY, RURAL ELECTRIFICATION, POPU-LATION AND TRANSPORTATION SECTORS. For discussions with relevant agencies of your Government we would be prepared to send a high level delegation at any time of your choice. [capital letters in the original]

This letter reflects, among other things, an almost incredible confidence not only in the efficacy of foreign aid — 'only a fraction of your national re-sources can put this nation (of over 85 million) on its feet to progress and prosperity', etc. — but also in Sweden's generosity; the sums requested from Sweden represent well over ten times the present level of Swedish aid to Bangladesh.

The Effects of Foreign Aid
An attempt to summarize the complex economic, social and political impact of the massive flow of foreign aid into Bangladesh in a few pages is bound to be superficial. There is no shortage of opinions on the matter, for it is the subject of much debate by both foreign donors and Bangladeshi citizens; by a convenient selection of facts and arguments almost anything can be proved — or disproved. With these reservations in mind, I will nevertheless try to analyze some of the issues involved and indicate, albeit tentatively and without always being able to substantiate my assertions, the direction in which foreign aid is moving the country.

In the short term, there can be no doubt that foreign economic assistance has helped Bangladesh to overcome the various post-Independence crises. The relatively rapid rehabilitation of the economy after the war of liberation, the famine in 1974 and the political and economic dislocations of 1974–75 would have been impossible without the aid that was provided. The stabil-ization policy vigorously pursued after 1975 was also greatly facilitated by the continuous supply of aid in the form of food, commodities and foreign exchange.

As to effects upon the rate of growth, it appears that foreign aid has contributed virtually all investment resources. Domestic savings are estim-ated to amount to no more than some 3% per year, which clearly implies a negative rate of growth of G.D.P. per capita in the absence of external funds. Assuming a capital-output ratio of three or, put another way, assuming that an investment of three *taka* results in an annual increase in income of one *taka*) and a rate of population growth of 3% per year, the savings ratio would have to be raised to 12% just to make the per capita income grow by a modest 1% per year. The prospects for economic growth thus seem to be intimately related to the future size of foreign aid, which would have to continue at a rate of almost 10% of G.D.P. in order to make Bangladesh achieve even the 1% growth target. If, as is sometimes argued, the shortage of foreign exchange should be regarded as the number one economic bottleneck, then, logically, aid should be regarded as qualitatively superior to domestic savings in that it eases this fundamental constraint on economic growth.

But this way of looking upon the role of foreign aid is, in my opinion, highly misleading. The high share of loans included in the official aid estimates, the tied nature of much of the aid, and the constraints imposed by many donors on the use of the aid, contribute to making the true value of aid fall appreciably below the nominal figures. There is no way to quantify the overestimation of the value of aid arising from donor restrictions of various kinds, but the data in Table 4.3 showing the drastic increase in Bangladesh's foreign debt over the last few years illustrate the danger of exploiting the potential for future growth by relying too much on foreign credits today.

The quality of foreign aid is also reduced by the fact that leakage in the form of open or disguised corruption is likely to be particularly high when foreign aid is involved. This need not be the case, of course, and sometimes donor conditions may actually discourage this type of wastage, but by and large the following is accurate:

> International assistance is prone to waste and misappropriation even more than domestic resources, as they are less subject to accountability because of political sensitivities and as they are often given implicitly to strengthen the client's power balance and hence for distribution of patronage and the building of politically expedient white elephants.[5]

Perhaps the most serious factor reducing the positive impact of aid on the rate of growth is the fact that aid sometimes replaces, rather than supplements, domestic efforts to mobilize resources. For it is quite likely that 'the government of a developing country — particularly if the country is poor and politically difficult — *may voluntarily relax domestic savings efforts* wheb more aid is available than otherwise' (emphasis in original).[6] Observations with implications pointing in the same direction are, for example, Martin Bronfenbrenner's contention that 'the "demonstration effect" of American aid and aid personnel have worked the wrong way, inspiring more high-level consumption than high-level production'[7] and Ernest Gruening's affirmation, based on a study of the effects of foreign aid to Chile, that 'large-scale assistance vitiates the host country's initiative to attack basic problems'.[8] All these suggestions seem eminently applicable to the case of Bangladesh, and for these reasons, it would certainly be wrong to treat aid as a mere addition to internal savings and investments.[9]

More theoretical support for the above, rather intuitive, observations is provided by Keith Griffin[10] who insists that total consumption in a country is a positive function of total available resources, including capital imports, and that aid actually releases resources for consumption as well as for production. Especially when capital transfers are firmly expected they will be treated as part of total income when expenditure decisions are made. If this is accepted, 'it follows as surely as night follows upon day that — unless the marginal propensity to consume is zero — capital imports will raise total consumption and reduce domestic savings.'[11] Or, put another way, the fact that foreign aid has financed virtually 100% of all investments made in Bangladesh since 1971 does not imply that the rate of capital formation would have been zero in the absence of all aid; some savings and investments would certainly have taken place anyhow, and it is probably more accurate to say that aid to Bangladesh has helped to raise consumption more than production.

It is, of course, difficult to draw a clear line of demarcation between consumption and investment, especially in a country like Bangladesh where incomes are so low that many people's capacity to work is severely reduced for the simple reason that they cannot afford to eat enough. Humanitarian considerations apart, some consumption thus deserves to be treated as investment in human capital, i.e. investment that is a precondition for economic development. Several items of the government's current expenditure on health, education, etc., which in actual practice have been financed by foreign aid, should also be included in this category. But a large though unknown share of the aid is also used for less essential consumption; and the gigantic scale of corruption, bolstered by aid money, is an evident example.

Foreign aid not only affects the overall magnitude of economic growth but also its structure. Foreign aid can be used to sustain 'good' or 'bad' policies in the host country, but it is certainly not entirely neutral; it can, and does, exert a crucial influence on the choice of technology and on the sectoral allocation of resources; it can serve to reinforce or weaken various biases that exist in the domestic development policies; it invariably has consequences for the distribution of income, etc. Foreign aid plays, finally, an important political role in the recipient country, where its major impact usually is to help to support the groups actually in power and to strengthen the existing political and administrative institutions.

Let us now see how these, and other, aspects of foreign aid are reflected in Bangladesh. I will begin with a discussion of the role of food aid which, as shown in Table 4.2, has accounted for almost one-third of the entire foreign assistance to Bangladesh between 1972 and 1978-79.

Food Aid

Food aid can serve many useful purposes in a developing country.[12] Given for relief purposes, it can feed the hungry in times of emergency, and enable nutritionally vulnerable groups to survive and work. Food for work programmes, in which foreign donors provide the food, can complement domestic efforts to mobilize people in development projects. Food aid can also be used to build up stocks of foodgrains which, in addition to being a source of security in case of natural calamities, can also contribute to even out the large fluctuations and uncertainties that typically characterize a predominantly agrarian economy. In Bangladesh, where the seasonal variations in rice prices normally exceed 20% over the year, a reduction in these price fluctuations would be very important for the small and marginal peasants, who are almost always forced to sell their rice immediately after the harvest, when prices are low but debts have to be repaid. Very often, the same peasants have to incur new debts a few months later when they have to purchase grain on the local market at prices far higher than they received themselves.

All the above-mentioned benefits of food aid are, in theory, valid for Bangladesh. In actual practice, however, the food aid received has largely failed to meet these objectives, since virtually its only role has been to fuel the food ration system, the effects of which were discussed in Chapter 3. Less than 10% of the food distributed in this way has been channelled to relief, including the food for work programmes. Very little has been used to smooth out the seasonal price fluctuations through open market operations. We can thus conclude that food aid has only marginally contributed to feeding the hungry, mobilizing labour for development projects or serving as a weapon against the market forces which enrich the few while forcing the many to sell cheap and buy dear. It has, however, reinforced the already existing urban bias by making it possible for the government to expand its urban and middle-class-oriented ration system. Thanks to the food received free of charge, the government has been able to subsidize food prices at a very low cost in budgetary terms; the state revenues from the sale of donated food have in some years almost equalled the expenditure on commercially imported and domestically procured grain.

Let us now turn to the long-term development effects of food aid. In a food-deficit country, food aid can play a decisive role in relaxing an otherwise binding constraint on the growth of output and employment; it is certainly impossible to achieve a rapid expansion of the economy in a situation of chronic shortage of food. Food aid — or commercial food imports — may also be looked upon as an expedient way of reducing the inflationary pressures that are likely to arise in a rapidly expanding economy with a high income elasticity of food consumption. But one crucial question, however, is whether the food received complements or replaces domestic food production. In the short run, it is quite obvious that food aid adds to total supply: one ton of imported grain does not reduce domestic production by one ton. But the 'disincentive problem', which was touched upon earlier in connection with the food ration system — and also, in this chapter, in connection with foreign aid in general — cannot be dismissed so easily, and the issue is worth a brief digression.

Food Aid As A Disincentive

There are, basically, two different disincentive effects which we may call the 'price effect' and the 'policy effect'.[13] The former operates through the market mechanism: in the long run, if not necessarily in the short run, the deterioration of the domestic terms of trade for agricultural products that has accompanied the pumping in of imported foodgrains into the ration system in Bangladesh has undoubtedly worked as a strong disincentive to food production. The amounts involved have been far from marginal — between 1972 and 1979 Bangladesh received over 13 million tons, including commercial imports, of foodgrain, mainly wheat, or almost two million tons annually. This corresponds to around 15% of total domestic production or, perhaps, to over half the entire marketable surplus (the exact size — and even definition — of which is quite uncertain, however). It should also be observed that the value of food aid has almost every year exceeded total development expenditure on agriculture.

The effects of such huge injections of foreign grain on food prices are bound to be negative, although the increase in the overall purchasing power resulting from food (or from any other form of) aid on this scale in part offsets the decline in price. If the food aid had been channelled to the most needy, whose purchasing power is so low that they only marginally affect the market situation, the price depressing effects would not, of course, have been so serious, but from the earlier discussion about the working of the food ration system we know that it is mainly the urban middle and upper classes who actually receive the imported grain. The concomitant loss in domestic food production is extremely difficult to assess in quantitative terms, since no reliable estimates exist of the supply and demand elasticities of foodgrain in Bangladesh; all that can be said with certainty is that farmers do respond positively to price incentives and that the disincentive effects of low food prices are stronger in the long run than in the short run.

So much for the 'price effect'. The 'policy effect', understood as the disincentive impact of food aid upon the overall development policy of the recipient country, is, in my opinion, even more serious. A cable from the U.S. Embassy in Dacca in early 1976 illustrates this point neatly: 'The incentive for Bangladesh government leaders to devote attention, resources, and talent to the problem of increasing domestic foodgrain production is reduced by the security provided by U.S. and other donors' food assistance.'[14] Noting the 'pervasive relief mentality' characterizing government circles in Dacca, Donald McHenry and Kai Bird comment:

> Bangladesh officials are convinced that the international donors will not allow them to starve. Since it is much easier to order a shipment of food through the embassy in Washington than to spend time and money on a domestic procurement program, a definite complacency has settled over the bureaucracy. The technocrats who dominate the powerful ministries of finance, planning and food are resigned to continued reliance on American, Canadian, and Australian surplus of food grains. One symptom of the relief mentality is a reluctance to invest too much of the country's limited resources away from the more glamorous industrial sector and into low profile agricultural projects. 'Not only does food aid develop budgetary dependence,' says a U.S. official posted in Dacca, 'but it clearly reduces the political pressures

on the government to invest in the countryside'.[15]

Food aid has, in short, enabled the government to continue to neglect agriculture (and land reform), a policy which has 'forced' the government to rely more and more heavily upon imported food. Impossible to quantify, the losses in domestic production due to these rather subtle political mechanisms are likely to be very serious in the long run, when powerful vested interests fighting for the maintenance of the system have consolidated themselves. The more dependent a country is on imports of cheap grain, the more costly it becomes for the government to achieve self-sufficiency in foodstuffs. Today, it would be a budgetary disaster for the Bangladesh Government if domestic production increased so much that the foreign donors refused to supply food aid, leaving the government to assume the full costs of sustaining the food ration system.[16] The annual quarrels between the Bangladesh Government and the so-called donor community over the size of the food deficit illustrate the government's anxiety to prove how far from self-sufficiency the country is. We can safely assume that there is a strong political pressure against any policies which would completely eliminate the need for food aid.

However, it is not food aid per se that is the decisive factor creating urban bias in Bangladesh's development policies. It is the domestic power structure and the concomitant choice of strategy that, in the final analysis, determine how a particular country's resources are used — or not used. The fact that the Bangladesh Government has imported relatively large amounts of food each year on a commercial basis, in addition to the food aid received, clearly shows that the donors' major role has been to facilitate and cheapen the food imports. The 'foreign bias' in this case thus originates from domestic factors, but is reinforced by the donors' willingness to dispose of surplus grains and to support the prevailing power structure in Bangladesh.

Food Aid and Income Distribution
From the point of view of income distribution, food aid has had somewhat contradictory effects. Intuitively, a policy of cheap food would appear to be more equitable; poor people spend a higher proportion of their income on food than the rich, and in Bangladesh, land ownership data indicates that, even among the agricultural population, a majority of the people — including the very poor — have now become net buyers of foodgrain. Food aid and low food prices must then benefit the majority while harming only a limited number of surplus farmers. But this is to ignore the fact that any reduction in agricultural production resulting from a loss of markets to foreign suppliers, and a transfer of resources from agriculture to other sectors of the economy, has negative consequences both for the number of employment opportunities in crop production and for the amount of money circulating in rural areas (of which some may trickle down to the rural poor).[17] And while the rural rich can, and do, diversify their economic activities when food prices go down, it is not an option open to the poor, who are most likely to lose in employment opportunities what they gain from cheaper food. The net effect of all

these factors is very much open to speculation. Very little, for example, is known about how many of the rural population are net buyers and net sellers of grain, respectively; the large seasonal variations in rice prices, and the fact that many small farmers are both sellers and buyers of grain (although at different periods) also complicate the issue both theoretically and empirically. It nonetheless seems safe to conclude that a deterioration of the terms of trade for agricultural production resulting from food aid will tend to increase the urban-rural inequality, while it probably reduces the intra-rural income differences.

It should also be stressed that, under present conditions in Bangladesh, *no* price policy would be able to achieve simultaneously a rapid expansion of agricultural production *and* a reduction in rural class differences. As long as land ownership is concentrated in the hands of a minority, the bigger farmers simply have to be offered incentives in the form of acceptably high food prices (and/or input subsidies) if they are to invest in agricultural production – even if this implies rising costs of living for the rural poor. The conflict between the landowners and the consumers, and between food production and equity, can never be solved by price manipulations alone. The basic problems originate in the unequal distribution of assets and incomes, which creates rigidities on the supply side and an insufficient purchasing power among the undernourished majority on the demand side. The fact that the Bangladesh Government's present food aid/cheap food strategy acts as a disincentive to domestic food production and agricultural reforms does not mean that an alternative, autarchy/high price policy would solve the problem. In the absence of other, more fundamental, changes, it certainly would not. For the rural poor, the issue of high or low food prices can today best be summarized as 'tails you win, heads we lose'.

It should finally be emphasized that Bangladesh's heavy dependence on food aid entails a serious danger of political dependence as well. It has become increasingly clear to both donor and recipient countries that the 'food weapon' is a powerful political instrument in the hands of the major food surplus countries, most notably the United States. For example, in September 1974, the United States, in the midst of a famine in Bangladesh, threatened to cut off its entire food aid because Bangladesh at that time had agreed to export jute to Cuba. Bangladesh's extremely critical food situation weakened her bargaining power, and the United States was successful in forcing Bangladesh to cancel the exports. This example is far from unique – indeed, it is the rule rather than the exception that the food aid leverage is used for political purposes by the world's largest food donor – but in general 'food power' is of course used in a more subtle, but no less dangerous, way.

Commodity and Project Aid

Non-food aid has accounted for roughly two-thirds of all aid given to Bangladesh since Independence. In the short term this aid has played a decisive role in helping the post-liberation governments to overcome the most critical balance of payments and fiscal problems confronting the young nation. With respect to the long-term effects these are, again, more difficult to assess. Although the topic of foreign aid is intensively discussed in Bangladesh, there has been no systematic effort to review the hundreds of ongoing or finished aid projects, or the impact of commodity and project aid on the overall economic development of Bangladesh. Since foreign aid essentially plays a supportive role vis-à-vis domestic policies, allowing the recipient government to carry out its policies more easily, an analysis of the projects financed by foreign aid would have little purpose unless directly related to the general policy of the country in question. The high degree of 'fungibility' of funds naturally reduces the real influence of the donors, shifting the emphasis onto the marginal projects it has made possible.[18] For these reasons, this overview will be limited to a few general aspects of the 'foreign bias' in Bangladesh's economic policies that can be traced directly to the influence of aid. Lack of data on the use of commodity aid — i.e. aid given in the form of foreign exchange which enables the recipient country to increase its imports, usually from the aid-giving country — means concentrating on project aid, but the thrust of the argument should be applicable to commodity aid as well.

The pattern of sectoral allocation of project aid corresponds largely to the overall distribution of development expenditure, but with a higher concentration of funds to industry and infrastructure (see Table 4.4). This relatively high correspondence, of course, is hardly surprising, considering the dominant role played by aid in the financing of all development expenditures. But the figures nevertheless reveal that project aid has not been used to change the direction of economic growth in favour of agriculture and social services — on the contrary.

Table 4.4:
Sectoral Allocation of the Annual Development Plan and Project Aid, 1978–79 (%)

	ADP	Project Aid
Agriculture and rural development	27.7	22.6
Industry	17.2	23.9
Power and natural resources	14.3	21.6
Transport and communication	17.8	17.2
Other (education, health, welfare, etc.)	23.1	14.7
Total	*100.0*	*100.0*

Source: Ministry of Finance.

The effects of foreign influence are most pronounced within the different sectors and projects, however. It is in the concrete bargaining process over choice of technology and over how a particular project should be implemented that the foreign donors can most easily exert their influence; in this context, the 'fungibility' arguments lose most of their validity. The donors need not always use their leverage directly, by means of tying the aid to, say, the purchase of technology and specialists from the donor country. Rather, it is the indirect effect of the donor's economic power and (usually) superior knowledge of the technical options available that 'force' the recipient country to accept a project design that is not optimal from its own point of view. This process has been summarized by John W. Thomas, who studied an I.D.A.-financed irrigation project in Bangladesh:

> The availability of external aid to finance new investment in itself affects the choice of technology, for the preference of the aid given then becomes an important element in the decision-making process. The administrators in a developing country may very rationally accept technology that [it] considers second or third best if foreign financing is available only for that choice, since that may be the only way to receive this aid. Furthermore, the official may tailor his programme to the technology he considers most likely to attract foreign aid.[19]

The results of the Bangladesh Government's acceptance of foreign priorities are easily visible. Almost invariably, the aid projects in Bangladesh tend to be more large-scale, capital-intensive and import-intensive than would be desirable from the point of view of employment creation, income distribution and domestic resource mobilization. The rate of growth is also retarded by the unnecessarily high capital-output ratios typical of such projects.[20] This technological bias (to which we will return in Chapter 6) is seen in such different projects as irrigation (where foreign aid has financed huge investments in capital-intensive tube-wells with a high import content), in health (the expensive and sophisticated Cholera Research Laboratory, for example), in industry, in agricultural extension (where foreign aid has financed the construction of modern, well-equipped training centres, etc.).

In the agricultural sector proper, the most conspicuous examples of bias are found in the so-called Intensive Integrated Rural Development Programmes sponsored by the World Bank, the Asian Development Bank, Denmark and Holland.[21] In this 'rent-a-*thana*' approach to rural development, foreign donors have been invited to 'take over' a certain number of *thanas* — in an initial stage, seven *thanas* have been given to the World Bank, four to the Asian Development Bank, three to the Danes and four are scheduled for the Dutch[22] — in which massive amounts of money and foreign experts, equipment and agricultural inputs are poured. The foreign exchange component ranges between 23 to 37% of the entire costs of the programme, and despite certain differences between them, all four programmes represent a development which accelerates the foreign penetration of rural Bangladesh, making it further dependent on the supply of foreign technology, inputs and know-how.

But why should foreign donors tend to favour such misallocations of resources? Tied aid, and a limited knowledge of alternative, more appropriate technologies, are important and well-known parts of the answer. So are the economies of scale in the donor's administrative handling of the projects: 'If an agency is going to lend £40 million to a country it would normally prefer to finance one project costing £40 million that 40 projects costing £1 million each', argues Keith Griffin, continuing:

> By concentrating on a few large projects the agency can reduce the difficulties of supervising its projects and keep down its administrative costs. For this reason, aid programmes tend to sponsor large dams rather than small irrigation schemes, major highways rather than secondary schools, university buildings rather than village schools, etc.[23]

Another factor, also mentioned by Griffin and by several others, is the still common practice of allowing foreign aid to finance only the foreign exchange component of a project. This naturally reduces the effectiveness of aid – in Bangladesh today, many projects are stalled for lack of local *taka* financing, and the level of disbursement of project aid has, partly for this reason, been very low in recent years. A further consequence is the import bias in the selection of projects. So long as local costs have to be financed domestically, it is only natural that the Bangladesh Government will select projects intensive in foreign exchange and adjust the technology mix so as to make the foreign exchange component as high as possible. The implications of the distortions introduced – or, rather, strengthened – by the excessive use of capital-intensive technologies and commodities will be subject to further discussion in the chapters that follow. Before leaving the topic of foreign aid, however, a few final comments should be made.

The first observation is related to foreign aid's effects on Bangladesh's administration and development institutions. There are, today, several dozens of major bilateral donors and multilateral aid agencies and around 100 voluntary organizations working in the country, and vast amounts of time and money are being spent on meetings with the 'donor community', on the preparation of aid project catalogues, on feasibility studies and reports to serve the different donors, etc. Many people in Bangladesh are beginning to seriously question the high priority given to these activities supplying foreign donors with information, efforts to co-ordinate the different and often contradictory wills of the donors, etc. (not to mention the resources devoted to the provision of expensive housing and infrastructure for the expatriates residing in Dacca). The fact that so many of the country's skilled administrators and professionals are heavily engaged in these and similar tasks naturally means that they cannot direct their attention to the burning issue of mobilizing the country's domestic human and natural resources in a more self-reliant development strategy. This is not only a quantitative issue of time and money – the more harmful aspects of dependence on aid obviously do not arise only in the case of food. Thus, both commodity and project aid can substitute for rather than supplement domestic development efforts; they can create a relief mentality in the recipient country's administration; reduce political pressure to undertake necessary reforms; and support other institutions which constitute the most important obstacles to development. The main effect of aid may, in the final analysis, simply be to conserve a system which makes the aid necessary.

Political considerations apart, even if foreign aid is given in the form of grants, it often greatly increases the need for future imports. The import bias in foreign aid should be taken into account when we analyse the long-term economic dependency that has been built up in Bangladesh. Nor is the heavy import component limited to the construction period of a project, during which the requirements of foreign exchange are normally covered 100%. The need for imports of spare parts, fuel, technical assistance for maintenance purposes, raw materials and semi-processed goods, Green Revolution inputs, etc. grow and grow as more and more foreign-supported projects are completed. Already today, the Bangladesh newspapers are full of stories like this:

2,380 Pumps Idle in Kishareganj
A large number of power pumps are lying idle in Kishareganj for want of spare parts. Inadequate supply and exorbitant rates of prices of diesel and mobil have further accentuated the problem.[24]

50 Per Cent of Deep Tube-wells Not Working
Hardly 50 per cent of the already sunk tube-wells are operational now . . . . The country's DTWs are running at less than one-third of their operational capacity. Besides, over 50 per cent of the tube-wells are out of operation. The main reason is the sharp deterioration in maintenance and servicing facilities of the machines.[25]

To the public foreign debt of over US $ 3 billion, or some five to seven times the annual export earnings, Bangladesh thus must add another, invisible, foreign debt — the need for future imports that has been created with the help of foreign aid. If a factory, or a deep tube-well, cannot operate unless a certain amount of foreign exchange is spent on spare parts and maintenance facilities, then this figure could well be added to the official foreign debt to give a more accurate assessment of the degree of foreign dependence that all the aid has entailed. The Bangladesh economy is moving, and moving fast, towards a situation where foreign dependence will require a more or less drastic reorientation of the economy. There are already clear signs of a shift in the direction of more openness towards foreign investment and foreign trade.

Foreign Investment

Before Independence, almost all foreign investment was concentrated to the Western wing of Pakistan. Total foreign investment in what is today Bangladesh was confined to a General Motors assembly factory in Chittagong, some subsidiaries of pharmaceutic multinationals, and a few insurance companies and banks. The value of these investments is estimated to have totalled less then 30 million U.S. dollars.[26]

Today, the government wants this situation to change. The present regime has invited foreign capital to invest in the country on very advantageous terms, including guarantees of repatriation of profits, a tax holiday for manufacturing industries for a period of five years — which can be extended to ten if the investment is made in a 'less developed area' — from the date of commencement of production, tax exemption for foreign technicians for a period of three years, etc. There is no ban on foreign investment going into any industry or activity, and there is no limit on the proportion of foreign equity in a company. Although foreign capital is welcome anywhere, the government has made a list of activities in which it is 'particularly welcome'. The list includes many sectors for which the export potentials are regarded as particularly good. The foreign investors are guaranteed against nationalization of their assets without a 'just and fair' compensation to be paid in the investor's own currency.[27] In addition to these and other measures aimed at attracting foreign capital, the government has also decided to establish a so-called Free Trade Processing Zone in the district of Chittagong. Under this arrangement, foreign investors will enjoy even more privileged conditions.

It is still too early to tell whether these concessions to foreign capital will produce the desired results. The figures on new direct foreign investment remain low: 11.3 million U.S. dollars in 1978, 17.8 million in 1979.[28] Competition for foreign investment is fierce and, since most countries in Asia have established their 'free zones' long ago, Bangladesh is lagging considerably behind. The industrial tradition and infrastructure for foreign investment are, furthermore, comparatively weak in Bangladesh, which has also few resources other than cheap labour and natural gas to offer its investors.

Gas is important, however, and the main area of interest for foreign capital is likely to be the country's vast resources of natural gas and, possibly, off-shore oil. In the spring of 1977 it was announced in Dacca that the American company, International Systems and Controls Corporation of Houston, Texas, was negotiating an 800 million dollar investment to exploit these reserves, which have also attracted the attention of British and Japanese investors. The plans include the construction of a massive liquified natural gas complex to export gas from the Bakhrabad fields.[29] The deal has apparently not yet been concluded, but whatever the concrete outcome of the negotiations, it can safely be assumed that the exploitation of the gas deposits will signify by far the largest single foreign investment in Bangladesh and possibly on the entire Indian Sub-continent. The size of Bangladesh's total petroleum reserves is unknown, and discoveries have been poor so far, but six foreign oil companies have been engaged in off-shore oil exploration.[30]

The importance of private direct investment in Bangladesh should not be exaggerated. Foreign aid is, in the foreseeable future, certain to play a much bigger role than private foreign capital. But the energetic attempts by the government to make foreign investors participate more actively in the economy, and in particular in the export sector, are still worth observing for the trend they indicate.

Foreign Trade

Table 4.5:
Merchandise Exports, 1976–78 (U.S. $ millions)

	1976–77		1977–78	
	Value	*% of total*	*Value*	*% of total*
Raw jute	114	27.1	97	19.5
Jute goods	172	40.9	248	49.9
Tea	36	8.5	45	9.1
Leather	42	10.0	46	9.3
Fish and shrimps	22	5.2	21	4.2
Others	35	8.3	40	8.1
Total	*421*	*100.0*	*497*	*100.0*

Source: I.B.R.D.

As shown in Table 4.5, Bangladesh's export trade is quite limited. Imports are more diversified. In 1977–78, when merchandise imports totalled 1,347 million U.S. dollars, the largest items were capital goods (318 million dollars), foodgrains (236 million) and petroleum and petroleum products (166 million).

Jute and jute products account for roughly two-thirds of total export earnings. It is mainly due to the low prices of jute that Bangladesh's terms of trade have deteriorated considerably since Independence; if 1972–73 is set at 100, Bangladesh's terms of trade dropped to 67, 62, 56, 62, 75 and 79 in the subsequent six-year period. Jute production, competing with rice for land, is sensitive to the rice/jute price differential, and so declined as a consequence of low world market prices. Output is still below the levels of the late 1960s and early 1970s. If the recent recovery of jute prices continues, the share of jute and jute products in total export earnings is estimated to remain around 65-70% during the next few years. The government's intention, however, is to diversify exports by means of an increase in 'non-trad-itional' exports such as specialized textiles, onions, chillis, fruit and vegetables, etc. Through 'aggressive marketing', 'product improvement' and 'strict adherence to quality specifications and development of transport and storage facilities'.[31] new markets for Bangladesh exports are to be opened up. Eastern Europe and the oil-exporting countries in the Middle East are frequently mentioned as promising markets for agricultural products from Bangladesh. Potatoes, which were only relatively recently introduced in Bangladesh, have already begun to be exported to Holland, Singapore and the Middle East. The following quotation from the *New York Times* illustrates the present government's eagerness to increase Bangladesh's exports of proteins and vitamins:

> Although Bangladesh is chronically short of food for its own population, it has started a major programme to export high-value food items, mostly seafood and vegetables. Three shrimp and frogleg processing and freezing plants are currently in operation, and nine more are planned in joint ventures with private companies from Thailand, South Korea and Japan. Last year, Bangladesh exported 1,800 tons of frog legs and more than 2,000 tons of shrimp and prawns. United Nations fisheries experts say that Bangladesh, situated in the world's largest river basin in the Bay of Bengal, has barely begun to tap its fresh-water and salt-water food production potential.
>
> Government agriculture officials also envision Bangladesh becoming the truck garden for the Middle East. Last year, it exported about 300 tons of fresh fruit and vegetables. The United Arab Emirates, just six hours away by air freight, was the biggest customer.[32]

To the range of export potentials indicated above should be added the present drive to export skilled manpower. There are, at present, over 100,000 skilled workers and professionals from Bangladesh working in the Middle East, and the figure is rising every year. Deals are regularly being concluded in which the Bangladesh Government guarantees to supply a certain number of people with different skills in exchange for money and oil, for instance with Iran in November 1977, when Bangladesh promised to deliver 23,800 skilled Bangladeshis to Iran as a part of an agreement on 'technical co-operation' between the two countries. Commenting on the Iranian agreement in an editorial, the *Bangladesh Times* notes this 'positive achievement' and argues that there is 'room for still further improvement':

> It is hoped Bangladesh would be able to break new ground. For this, it is imperative that we work not only for the quantum, but also for the quality of the foreign employment. In other words, the skill and technical attainment of our prospective employees should be developed with a view to fostering the market potentials of our manpower export and also the price and prestige of our employment abroad. It is in this respect that the government decision to expand the training facilities for mid-level technicians should be viewed as a constructive measure for providing higher education and training facilities to diploma engineers

should also help the matter. For, it is these and other trained personnel who should form the bulk of our skilled manpower to find employment abroad.[33]

But those human exports are not in fact primarily the unemployed of Bangladesh. The categories of workers for which there is high foreign demand are experienced middle-level technicians and service personnel with very specialized skills, occupational groups which are quite scarce in Bangladesh. The effects of the emigration are beginning to be felt in many areas, and complaints are growing:

> Due to the unrestricted export of skilled manpower to Middle Eastern countries which the government has been encouraging over the last year, areas like Savar Thana are suffering from a shortage of carpenters, plumbers, blacksmiths and electricians, to name but a few.[34]

Remittances from Bangladeshis working abroad have already become an important source of foreign currency; in 1976, it accounted for *taka* 76 *crores*, or over 50 million dollars and more than 10% of total export earnings. In 1977, during the period January to June only, the foreign exchange earnings through this source rose to *taka* 70 *crores*, corresponding to almost 100 dollars per year or almost 25% of total export earnings. Next to jute and jute products, manpower is today Bangladesh's largest export good in terms of U.S. dollars, although it is still not classed under the heading 'merchandise exports'.

Concluding Remarks

In theory, foreign aid — and trade — could serve many useful purposes in Bangladesh. But, without denying the need for foreign aid (at least during a transitional period in order to avoid mass starvation), the main conclusion from the above overview must be that the aid actually given has largely failed to support any genuine development efforts, and that it has served to strengthen the present tendency towards a donor-oriented rather than self-reliant development strategy. In part the aid has competed with, rather than complemented and supported, domestic production and employment; this is especially true of food aid, in particular through its 'policy effect'. With respect to the other forms of aid, it is more difficult to make an overall assessment of their impact. Both commodity aid and project aid have undeniably helped to rehabilitate the economy and ease several constraints to economic growth, but they appear to have been less effective in supplementing the domestic mobilization of human and natural resources. Rather, the effect may well have been negative since it has increased both the passivity of the administration and the lack of co-ordination and consistency in domestic policies.

The income distribution effects of the aid have largely been negative in that most of the aid has failed to reach the poorest groups of society. But this is more the fault of the domestic economic, political and social structure than of the aid per se. By contrast, a direct influence can be seen in the neglect of agriculture and in the various biases, mainly of a technological character, that have been reinforced by the donors' preferences and by the nature of the project aid and tied commodity aid. The heavy indebtedness following upon the massive inflow of foreign loans and technical assistance should also be kept in mind. It is this indebtedness, with its concomitant debt service burden which, together with several other factors, has forced Bangladesh urgently to seek foreign capital and to increase and diversify its export of commodities, and even of skilled manpower. The process of increasing 'openness' of the Bangladesh economy is accelerating at a high rate, with important future consequences for the entire country — including the agricultural sector.

Finally the large amount of space here devoted to Bangladesh's foreign economic relations by no means indicates that external factors are taken to be determinant. The pattern of aid received and the 'donor community' in Dacca, chaired by the World Bank representative, certainly play a very important economic and political role. In the final analysis, however, it is the domestic class and power structure, and the concomitant choice of development policies, that determine both the structure of external relations and the impact on the national economy of whatever flow of aid (and trade) there is. Of course foreign donors must assume their part of the responsibility. The following remarks by Keith Griffin and A.R. Khan, referring to the time when Bangladesh was still East Pakistan, may be worth remembering today:

> An inflow of foreign resources inevitably strengthens established governments and enables them to carry out their policies more easily. If these policies lead to disaster, whether the donors like it or not, they are involved and are partly responsible. Donors cannot claim their part of the credit when things appear to be going well and then dissociate themselves when events turn out badly.[35]

References

1. B. Hartman and J.K. Boyce, 'Bangladesh: Aid to the Needy?', *International Policy Report*, Vol. IV, No. 1, Centre for International Policy (Washington, D.C., May 1978), p. 1.
2. Unless otherwise stated, foreign aid includes — incorrectly, but in accordance with current practice — both grants and loans.
3. 2.7 billion dollars in grants and 3.3 billion in the form of loans between 1971 and 1978. See 'Helpless Dependence on Aid', *Holiday*, (Dacca, 16 July 1978).
4. Government of Bangladesh, Planning Commission, *Two Year Plan, 1978-80*, Dacca, p. 22.

5. Anisur Rahman, 'The Utilization of Labour in the Strategy for Development in the ECAFE Development Region', Paper prepared for the ECAFE, UN, undated mimeo, p. 10.

6. Anisur Rahman, 'Foreign Capital and Domestic Saving: A Test of Haavelmo's Hypothesis with Cross Country Data', *Review of Economics and Statistics*, February 1968, p. 137.

7. Martin Bronfenbrenner, 'Second Thoughts on Confiscation', *Economic Development and Cultural Change*, July 1963, p. 271.

8. Ernest Gruening, 'United States Foreign Aid in Action — A Case Study', (Washington, D.C., U.S. Printing Office, 1966), p. 121.

9. Even the Asian Development Bank has drawn this somewhat self-critical conclusion. After having mentioned many important achievements of aid, the Bank observes: 'But unfortunately, the mere availability of foreign aid has not generally meant that it has performed its most basic function: that of adding to the overall level of investment in the developing countries.' *Asian Agricultural Survey 1976*: 'Rural Asia: Challenge and Opportunity', (Manila, 1977), p. 320.

10. See, for example, Keith Griffin, *International Inequality and National Poverty*, (London, Macmillan, 1978).

11. Griffin, op. cit., p. 75; see also Griffin, 'Foreign Capital, Domestic Savings and Economic Development', *Bulletin of the Oxford University Institute of Economics and Statistics*, March 1970; 'Discussion' in the same journal, May 1971, and K. Griffin and A.R. Khan (eds.), *Growth and Inequality in Pakistan* (London, Macmillan, 1972), Chapter 1; and M. Alamgir, 'Some Reflections on Below Poverty Level Equilibrium Trap: The Bangladesh Experience', mimeo, Institute of International Economics (Stockholm, 1977).

12. For a useful but, in my opinion, overly optimistic assessment of the gains from food aid for the recipient country, see P.J. Isenman and H.W. Singer, 'Food Aid: Disincentive Effects and their Political Implications', *Economic Development and Cultural Change*, June 1977. See also S.J. Maxwell and H.W. Singer, 'Food Aid to Developing Countries: A Survey', *World Development*, March 1979, where an attempt is made to summarize the theoretical issues in the debate over food aid, and to review some of the empirical evidence available.

13. Following Isenman and Singer, op. cit.

14. Quoted in D.F. McHenry and K. Bird, 'Food Hunger in Bangladesh', *Foreign Policy*, No. 27, 1977, p. 79.

15. Ibid.

16. The donors might, of course, replace the food aid with enough cash to make it possible for the government to buy the grain on a purely commercial basis. It is, however, most likely that some donors would be unwilling to do so, with the result that the total flow of aid would decrease.

17. These points are heavily emphasized by Michael Lipton who, obsessed by the idea that the whole peasantry must be supported against the bad guys in the cities, argues that food prices ought to be raised almost everywhere, and that 'the *whole* interest of the rural community is against cheap food'. *Why Poor People Stay Poor: A Study of Urban Bias in World Development* (London, Temple Smith, 1977), p. 67,

emphasis in original. For a critique of Lipton see Terry Byres, 'Of Neo-Populist Pipe-Dreams', *Journal of Peasant Studies*, Vol. 6, No. 2, January 1979; or C.H.H. Rao, 'Urban vs. Rural or Rich vs. Poor?', *Economic and Political Weekly*, 7 October 1978. According to Rao, the class struggle is far more important than any urban-rural conflict. Rao's more technical lines of reasoning are summarized as follows: 'Lipton's arguments assume a high responsiveness of agricultural supplies to prices. However, the available evidence for India shows that the aggregate supply elasticity is much less than unity, and since the employment elasticity to output is also less than unity, the derived demand for labour as a result of price rise would be much lower whereas, for any given rise in prices, the fall in real incomes of the rural poor would be much greater. It is clear, therefore, that for the rural poor, the negative real income effects of the rise in food prices outweigh the possible employment and income effects. Public investment in agriculture could benefit, at least proportionately, different sections of farmers whereas high output prices would essentially benefit the rural rich. Hence growth via the former would be more broad-based than from the latter.' (p. 1,701).

18. 'Fungibility' in this context means that, if a donor finances a particular project that has high priority in the recipient country, then the result of this aid is to finance something that would have been carried out anyhow, with domestic or other donor funds. In these cases the real effect of the aid is to release funds for other projects, and in order to assess the true impact of project aid one would have to analyse not the projects for which the foreign funds were earmarked but those marginal projects that were made possible thanks to the aid. It must be observed that the fungibility of aid is in no way restricted to choices between different investment projects but applies to choices between investment and consumption as well.

19. John W. Thomas, *The Choice of Technology for Irrigation Tube-Wells in East Pakistan* (Harvard, 1975) quoted in P.A. Ströberg, 'Water and Development: Organizational Aspects of a Tube-Well Irrigation Project in Bangladesh', SIDA (Stockholm, 1977), p. 43.

20. This is not to say that the choice of scale and technology would be socially optimal in the absence of foreign aid − only that it would be less biased.

21. For a further discussion of these programmes, see D. Asplund and S. de Vylder, 'Contradictions and Distortions in a Rural Economy. The Case of Bangladesh', SIDA (Stockholm, 1979), Chapter 4.

22. The Dutch project, which is appreciably 'softer' than the other three and which attempts to be designed exclusively for small farmers owning less than 2.5 acres of land, has not yet been approved by the Bangladesh Government, which has not been prepared to accept the 'target group' limitation suggested by the Dutch Government.

23. Keith Griffin, 1970, op. cit., p. 109.

24. *Bangladesh Times*, 2 April 1978.

25. *Holiday*, 2 April 1978.

26. 'N.M.J.', 'Murder in Dacca', *Economic and Political Weekly*, 25 March 1978.

27. For further information, see the article 'Bangladesh: Opening the Doors to Foreign Capital', *Economic and Political Weekly*, 15 April 1978, from which most of the information given above has been taken. Cf. also 'Bangladesh Lures the Investor' by S. Kamaluddin in *Far Eastern Economic Review*, 23 November 1979.

28. S. Kamaluddin, op. cit., p. 55.

29. 'Bangladesh: Opening the Doors to Foreign Capital', op. cit.

30. See Planning Commission, *Two Year Plan 1978–80*, p. 189 and M.A. Mansur, 'On Petroleum Sector', *Bangladesh Times*, 16 December 1977.

31. From the Planning Commission, op. cit., pp. 56–7.

32. James P. Sterba, 'Bangladesh Wooing Business', *New York Times*, 9 April 1979.

33. Editorial, *Bangladesh Times*, 5 January 1978.

34. Gonoshastaya Kendra, 'Progress Report No. 6', December 1977, mimeo p. 4. Cf. also 'Effect of Manpower Export on the National Economy of Bangladesh', *Illustrated Weekly*, Dacca, 13 August 1978, for a discussion of some income distribution effects of this policy. Referring to the Bangladeshis who work abroad for a couple of years, the article says: 'These people who have become rich almost overnight are purchasing huge agricultural land, residential land in Dacca and other towns, erecting magnificent buildings, collecting valuable immovable properties of modern civic life and thus they are leading a very sophisticated life in this poor country. . . . This is surely an economic injustice of a grave nature.'

35. Griffin and Khan, 1972, op. cit., p. 190.

5. The Bureaucratic Bias

The public sector plays an extremely important role in the overall development of the Bangladesh economy. This circumstance alone introduces a strong bureaucratic element in the economic life of the country. Or, rather, in the *dynamics* of the economy – virtually all the investible funds are channelled through the state, and in most areas involving growth and change, the government machinery is likely to be directly or indirectly involved. However, the vital role thus assigned to the state should not be confused with central planning, let alone with socialism. The Bengali state machinery was built up under British rule and still retains much of the old structure.

From our previous discussions about the class character of the state in Bangladesh it is clear that the existing state apparatus cannot possibly be used to foster socialist objectives. Nor does the fact that most of the country's development investments are allocated by the public sector mean that the *use* of these funds has a collective character; with private control over most of the means of production, and in particular of land, the most essential economic function of the state is to divert collective funds to private purposes.

But let us leave these more general aspects of the role of the state aside and concentrate on a few concrete issues connected with the actual functioning of the Bangladesh government administration in the development process. I will, to begin with, briefly indicate some of the technical and administrative deficiencies reducing the overall efficiency of the state bureaucracy, and the consequent impact on the rural community's use – and misuse – of resources. I will then proceed to a discussion of the 'bureaucratic bias' itself, the top-down, hierarchical approach to planning and implementation which has characterized most development efforts so far. Finally, some additional aspects of the interaction of the bureaucracy with different strata of the rural population will be considered, especially the role of corruption in this context.

Efficiency and Decision-Making

'The Public Administration System: An Aid or an Obstacle to Development?' was the title of a speech given in 1977 by a senior official with nineteen years of government service.[1] 'Too Many Doing Not Enough' is another reference[2] to the same topic — the inefficiency of the bureaucracy. No one would deny that the Bangladesh bureaucracy is weak and inefficient. Nor would anyone argue that Bangladesh is unique in this respect. What is remarkable about Bangladesh is that the multitude of foreign donors constantly interfering with domestic administrative affairs makes planning, co-ordination and implementation even more cumbersome in Bangladesh than in most other countries. Entire volumes could be filled with complaints about the functioning of the Bangladesh public administration, complaints from national newspapers, ordinary citizens and government officials themselves. The disillusioned former civil servant referred to above has compiled a representative list:

(i) Instead of encouraging private initiative, public administration system created more formalities and bottlenecks even when private initiatives were sought to be encouraged through specialized institutions.

(ii) The symbol of Government in the rural areas continues to be the police and revenue offices, though the declared intention of the development efforts of the past was to introduce new symbols like Thana Training and Development Centres. This by itself deters popular participation in development efforts.

(iii) The capacity to absorb development expenditure has remained inadequate because of the current system of public administration.

(iv) The morale of the Government officials dealing with development projects has remained low, because of the prevailing staffing pattern, wages and incentive structure of the Government Departments.

(v) Normally expected consequences of development efforts are not being realised due to inefficiency in the present public administration.

The net effect of these malfunctionings is a reduction in the rate of growth of the economy. Although private enterprise is officially very much encouraged, a host of controls limiting the scope for initiatives have been set up, and almost any undertaking requires permits, documents and state approval — a time-consuming and frustrating process which in practice bars 80% of the population, the illiterates, from many activities.

Within the public administration, development funds are often released only after a long processing of the projects by several different — and often competing — ministries and agencies. In the Ministry of Public Works, it has been calculated that there are 72 steps involved in the preparation of expenditure estimates, calling for tenders, issuing of work orders, etc.: if every official handling the matter works sincerely, the time needed to get a scheme approved and implemented would be over five years.[3] Although such anecdotal examples should perhaps not be taken too seriously, they do illustrate a phenomenon that is well-known to both Bangladesh officials and foreign donors. Indeed common knowledge has it that the low rate of disbursement of foreign aid is less due to the low absorptive capacity of the economy than the slow administrative handling of both commodity and project aid.

Incentives and Rural Attitudes

Even more important than the technical defects of the Bangladesh bureaucracy, is its effect on both private initiatives and attempts at collective self-
reliance. Both may be discouraged by excessive reliance on state funds and
development agencies. 'In the absence of private organization capacity for
innovation and change,' writes one observer of rural development in Bangladesh, 'all rural development becomes "governmentalized", assumed as a duty
of the government; this leads to reliance on the district gridwork to imple-
ment rural change.'[4]

Many studies of attitudes of the rural population confirm this impression,
for example: 'I observed a complete absence of any initiative taken by the
Swanirvar Committee to solve a local problem or undertaking a new project.
. . . About 75% of the people I talked with want the government to do more
things for them.'[5] In the S.I.D.A./B.I.D.S. survey of landlessness undertaken
in 1978, it was found that over half of the respondents — who were all
landless agricultural workers — answered 'if the government helps me' to the
question of how they thought their situation could improve. Another 25%
indicated that the formation of a co-operative could improve their lot. Only
in one village — a Swanirvar 'success story' — was there a significant proportion of the landless who mentioned alternatives like 'through our own
efforts.'[6]

This does not mean, of course, that the villagers look upon the government
and government officials as representatives of the poor. In the same Swanirvar
report referred to above, the author hastened to add: 'I observed a feeling of
desperation and frustration among the landless and small farmers. They feel
that their fate will not change in the future and all the benefits of "Swanirvar"
or government sponsored development projects will flow to the rich and
privileged few in the village.'[7] And in the S.I.D.A./B.I.D.S. study, the overwhelming majority of the respondents — 215 out of 301 — said that, in their
opinion, the Union Parishad leaders mainly represented the rich, and 238 of
them argued that the Thana officials represented either the rich or the
government. Only three respondents said they thought that the U.P. leaders
mainly represented the poor, and only one cherished this illusion with respect
to the Thana officials.

How can the rural population be so reliant on the government for support
when they have so little confidence in the representatives of the state? But
what alternatives are available? The following observations by Dr. Md. Yunus
probably give an accurate picture of the rural population's realism in this
respect:

> From their circumscribed existence, the villagers view the national
> government as a sort of foreign government in the colonial tradition.

> They consider the government as a wealthy, stupid, clumsy and
> forgetful outsider. . . . They make it a compelling occupation to out-
> smart the government in every way for fun and profit. Being honest
> with the government on any matter is regarded as a sure sign of im-
> becility. With the past performances of the government in terms of
> their policies, programmes, institutions for and dealings with the
> villagers, they perhaps have come to trust their own assessment of the
> government.[8]

Institutions regarded in this way can hardly become 'agents for change'
capable of mobilizing the rural population for development purposes. But
these institutions are, to repeat, the only ones available, and if the people
want something to be done — tube-wells, fertilizer, credit, etc. — the only
real possibility is to turn to a public agency, or to a co-operative fuelled
with state funds. This contradiction between dependence on and lack of
confidence in the state is likely to discourage individual and collective initiatives and to foster a mixture of cynicism and apathy rather than enthusiasm,
self-reliance and collective creativity.

   Thus the bureaucracy acts on the rural population in a way which parallels
the disincentive effects of foreign aid. This is not to say that the rural population would be better off in the absence of government aid, although this
aid is of dubious value for the poor. The share of state expenditure going to
agricultural development is, as we know, exceedingly low, and counteracted
by the variety of mechanisms producing a large capital and brain drain from
rural to urban areas. The observations made about excessive reliance on the
state rather serve to illustrate the more qualitative aspects of the role of
state development expenditures, i.e. their failure to serve as a true supplement to the rural community's own efforts to mobilize resources. There is
no way to estimate the size of these 'disincentive' and 'passivity' effects, but
this does not mean they should be ignored. All I suggest is that they do exist
in the socio-economic context of rural Bangladesh, and that they should be
considered. The fact that they are also likely to be accentuated by the
centralized, hierarchical character of the Bangladesh public administration
should not be ignored either.

The Top-Down Approach to Development

With the help of a growing body of statistics, literature and practical knowledge illuminating the failure of most past attempts at modernization *cum*
development in rural (non-socialist) Asia, more and more researchers and
practitioners have begun to question the entire basis of the conventional
approach to rural development. Much of the criticism has been focused on
the technocratic, 'diffusionist' view of rural development, against which are
offered concepts like 'collective creativity', 'mobilization', 'need-orientation',
'participation', 'de-alienation' and 'collective self-reliance'. Though not

entirely free of a tendency to obscure the class aspects of the rural society, these concepts do indicate the direction that the alternatives must take. The inspiration for this new approach to rural development has come not only from past failures but from positive achievements as well. The Chinese experiment has, of course, been extremely influential in indicating an alternative strategy; on a smaller scale, many village 'success stories' in different countries have also helped to give practical evidence of the development potential of Asian rural communities when the people themselves are motivated and mobilized.

This is not the place to review these experiments, or to analyse the new theoretical concepts that are emerging.[9] What is important for the purpose of this chapter, however, is the extent to which criticisms have centred on the role of the state and of public institutions in general. In Bangladesh, the thrust of this criticism is entirely valid: there is a tremendous contrast between the top-down, hierarchical way of planning and implementing development programmes in Bangladesh and a mobilization-oriented strategy aiming at releasing the full potential of the villages' human resources through 'collective creativity'. The following is a telling — and all too representative — illustration of the results of the present situation. The example refers to family planning, but the spirit it reflects can be found in many other activities as well:

> I talked with Mr. Badiud Alam who has been elected the secretary of the family planning sub-committee to find out the steps he had taken so far in his sphere. He told me that he didn't take any steps in the field. He further explained that he was not clear whether or not family planning method was allowed by the religion. Moreover he informed me that he didn't actually want to become the secretary of the family planning sub-committee.[10]

'The planning process should start at the local level, not end there,' argues Dr. Yunus, criticizing the whole approach to planning in Bangladesh. He continues:

> The Planning Commission has underscored the importance of decentralization but failed to suggest an institutional framework for a meaningful decentralization. . . . There is very little left for decentralization if the planning remains the reserve of the central planning authority.[11]

As it works today, the Dacca national headquarters of virtually all ministries and development institutions exercise an excessive control over the field offices and officials who, in turn, are relatively isolated from the ordinary villagers, and often ignorant of their needs. Noting the over-reliance on the central administration for steering the public works programmes in Bangladesh, Anisur Rahman describes how, and for whom, a centralized bureaucracy tends to work:

> Bureaucracy is a system of administration which is not directly
> responsible to the supposed beneficiaries; the chain of accountability
> is upwards rather than downwards, so that the system is not sensitive
> to lapses in the field; the ultimate accountability, in principle, to the
> people through the 'minister' or his equivalent is too indirect and
> diffused to contain much practical relevance, and even in principle this
> presupposes the practice of genuine democracy which is hardly the case
> in reality. In such a situation one needs a high level of personal commit-
> ment of the civil servants to deliver the goods in the field; but such
> commitment would essentially have to be of a *political* character, and
> career civil servants as a matter of principle are supposed not to cherish
> any political commitments.[12]

There is a caveat however: one should not put all the blame for the failure
of the state to 'deliver the goods', or to mobilize additional local resources,
on the bureaucracy per se. Neither should one expect fundamental changes to
flow from a reform of the bureaucracy to make it more field-oriented and less
centralized and hierarchical. What limits the scope for administrative reforms
is — apart from today's obvious lack of political will and commitment — the
fact that it is the political and socio-economic structures in the villages
themselves which by and large determine the outcome of public funds and
support.

Officials and Villagers

> Bureaucratic approach to rural economic change tacitly assumes that
> the rural people are passive, fatalistic, uninterested in initiating anything
> of their own, incapable of undertaking initiatives to change their
> lives, and therefore, need constant prodding, supervision, and spoon-
> feeding. While this view does not do justice to the reality, the opposite
> view, which seems to claim that the rural people are fully capable and
> willing to change their lives if only the bureaucrats would leave them
> alone, is equally unreal. The second view refuses to see the class struc-
> ture of the rural society and the exploitative process within it. Central
> intervention through institutional designs, legislations and appropriate
> policy measures must keep the exploiting class under check and let
> the dispossessed class have a fighting chance to free themselves from the
> instruments of exploitation.[13]

The crux of the matter is to try to avoid these two traps. Although it is easy
to criticize the overly centralized approach to development planning in
Bangladesh, it must also be remembered that, in the absence of control
from the government, all institutions at the village level are doomed to be
taken over and manipulated by the local vested interests as long as the rural

poor possess no viable organizations of their own. The following account of the relative success of the early Comilla co-operative model is revealing:

> Probably the most important factor was that somehow Akhter Hameed Khan and his associates were able to hit upon the right combination of control from above and participation from below, of supervision and autonomy. Supervision is needed to maintain the probity of administration, to prevent or, more realistically perhaps, to minimize the corruption that must be expected to occur in the absence of a firm and unwavering system of inspection from above. It is also needed to prevent a second danger that inevitably threatens local structures that become too free from higher direction — take-over by local elites. On the other hand, there are compelling reasons for having a high degree of autonomy at the local level. . . . If there is to be democracy at all in any significant sense in Bangladesh, it surely must begin at the local level in order to acquaint the people with its practice.[14]

In reality, however, it has been exceedingly difficult to 'hit upon the right combination of control from above and participation from below'. One reason is, as Gunnar Myrdal has put it, that 'the officials administering development programmes require co-operation of rural elites (if they are to get successful results). No wonder, then, that the evaluation studies invariably conclude that these programmes have helped mainly those in the rural population who were already well off.'[15] An official wanting to help the poor has to confront a powerful group of local leaders who more often than not accept neither participation from the ordinary villagers nor supervision from above (and far less from below). The result is, of course, that many well-intentioned officials become frustrated and give up their attempts to come to grips with the problems, trying instead to accommodate themselves to a system which is both inefficient and exploitative. A recent study of co-operatives in Bangladesh reports how an ambitious Thana Project Officer (T.P.O.), Waheed Ali, was almost physically chased out of the village of Dalalpur having fought, and lost, a battle against the corrupt leadership of a T.C.C.A.

> Waheed Ali, it seems, still has a bitter taste in his mouth from the whole Dalalpur experience. The former TPO frankly admitted his failure to check the Chairman and the other Directors in their improper activities and said with a tone of defeat in his voice: 'We gave up trying to fight them'. Waheed Ali says he felt 'Why should I die for this TCCA, which does not want to save itself? Let it go to hell.'
> Speaking now, however, he did not think the situation in Dalalpur was particularly unusual (unlike the new TPO who feels it is more extraordinary). Waheed Ali said the situation in Chandpur — where he is now posted albeit as an Assistant Director of the Chandpur Irrigation Project, not as a TPO any longer — is worse.[16]

The above example is exceptional in that the T.P.O. in question really made a serious effort to attack the local elite's corrupt and inefficient practices. Normally, there are very strong incentives for officials to seek co-operation with the rural rich, and not only for the reason given by Myrdal and partly illustrated by Waheed Ali's failure. There are also, as will be discussed further in connection with the 'landlord bias' in Chapter 8, very obvious economic factors that work in the same direction. Thus, extension agents achieve economies of scale in their work if they concentrate on large farmers, and for the officials responsible for the distribution of credit, fertilizer, improved seeds, etc., the very same mechanisms are operating. It is far easier, from an administrative point of view, to handle a few large farmers who borrow and buy in large quantities than to spread out the loans and sales to a large number of small peasants who might, furthermore, be regarded as 'bad risks'.[17]

The social, educational and cultural background of most civil servants in Bangladesh should also be considered. Most government officials come from the middle or upper class and have little sense of either the field or the poor. When they do leave their urban offices to make trips to the field, it is only natural that they find it easier to communicate with the rural rich.[18] The way the officials are trained also contributes to separate them from the ordinary villagers. Simply having formal educational qualifications immediately puts the officials in a different position from the rural poor. Once they have been recruited, they are then normally sent off to training courses in a town somewhere, to which they return now and then during their careers to take additional courses. Most of the literature they read is in English. Once installed in their offices, they often dream of moving to a bigger town. Even the civil servants who happen to be of more modest class origins soon pick up the urban and elite habits, and when they visit the villages as extension agents or senior development officers the people they relate to most easily are, of course, the influential, educated few. And it is also from these people the officials can expect most economic benefits.

Corruption

The purpose of this section is not to show that there is corruption in Bangladesh for this is beyond dispute. However defined, it is widespread — but impossible to quantify — and manifests itself in a variety of different ways. Rather my intention is to indicate, very briefly, some of the main causes of corruption in rural development programmes. I will also, for the sake of brevity and in order to avoid getting lost in a difficult conceptual discussion, concentrate on more 'modern' forms of corruption. This means setting to one side the role of traditional patron-client relationships, factionalism and family lineages, regionalism, etc. — all factors which are certainly important in the Bangladesh rural community but which cannot be put in the same category as corruption, although they may sometimes help to explain the form that the corruption assumes.

One explanation for corruption is the weakness and inefficiency of the public administration; the Gunnar Myrdal approach would see Bangladesh as a 'soft state', incapable of exercising its control functions. Now this is eminently true in Bangladesh, at least in the sense that interests us here,[19] and is reinforced by the lack of control mechanisms 'from below'. The poorer strata of the population are unorganized and economically too weak to be able to check the elite's misappropriation and corrupt practices in general. Since government officials tend to deal and communicate with the village leaders rather than with the poor and landless, this naturally also reduces the scope for supervision, be it 'from above' or 'from below'. All this is clear from our previous discussion.

Looking at the situation of the officials themselves, it is obvious that their formal power and position are not matched by equally privileged material conditions. Civil servants, at least at the local level, are poorly paid, and many of their beneficiaries enjoy visibly much higher living standards than they do. For the individual official, it must be tempting indeed to try to 'tax' the farmers for the services he renders them, and from an economic point of view, the entire system of low salaries plus bribes can be regarded as a means of shifting the burden of paying the officials from the state onto the rural population.

The main reason why corruption can arise in the administration of rural development programmes is the simple fact that the benefits that are distributed are 'cheap' (in the sense that it would be more expensive for a farmer to buy the relevant service on the open market — e.g. a tube-well or H.Y.V. seed) and scarce, and can accordingly only be handed out selectively. The limited supply of and heavy subsidies on irrigation facilities, fertilizer, improved seeds, etc. necessarily gives the official delivering the goods a key position, which can be used to his own — or to his friends' — personal advantage. There is always a good margin between the price the official is supposed to charge and the price many people are willing to pay, so in addition to open or disguised corruption we get the well-known side effects of shortages and black markets. 'The control of the powerful, rich peasants and leaders over the distribution and supply of fertilizers and insecticides is a critical feature of the village political economy', concludes one study, while registering that 'the method by which fertilizer is obtained usually involves some form of corrupt practices, maldistribution and other difficulties.'[20]

The landless or near landless lack both the economic means and the personal links with the government officials that would enable them to reap the benefits of the subsidy system. Even the small peasants with some land are often left out, especially in the distribution of agricultural inputs, whose prices tend to be higher on the black market than they would have been in the absence of public subsidies and control. 'The actual administration of input subsidies,' argues Michael Lipton in a general discussion of rural development policies, 'usually makes inputs *dearer* to the mass of farmers, and confines subsidies to the big farmers. . . . If fertilizers are scarce already, more will not be got into the field by subsidizing them.'[21]

This is not to say that the situation would be better if subsidies were abolished altogether. Without public price supports, the rural rich would be virtually guaranteed a monopoly on modern inputs; at least with subsidies, small farmers with limited economic resources get a chance to compete. But such a system inevitably opens the door for corruption; in order to be of any help for the poor, it requires a strict system of supervision which is absent in rural Bangladesh. It also seems to be the case that political influence and contacts with government officials are even more concentrated in the hands of the few than the distribution of income. If this is the case, as many studies of the local power structure in Bangladesh indicate, reliance on capitalist market forces may in fact be a less inegalitarian means of allocating scarce resources than the present system, which suffers from all the disadvantages of capitalism without enjoying any of the benefits of socialism.

Concluding Remarks

This chapter has dealt with a few aspects of the role of the state and, in particular, of public development institutions. The fact that a critical assessment has overshadowed the more encouraging achievements is not only due to the malfunctioning of the public administrative machine, however — it is also, and above all, the political and socio-economic environment in which the bureaucracy operates that makes it difficult or impossible to trigger off a process of self-sustained development with the help of the state.

If we look at a Bangladesh village in the same way that we view the country as a whole — as an economic unit which works much below its potential — we are also able to reformulate the role of the state and of development institutions. For true development to take place, the crucial function of outside funds and agencies must be to work as a catalyst for already existing resources; to undo material constraints and to supplement rather than displace the creativity and initiative of the people themselves. It would be necessary to get rid of the system in which external donors, responsible to headquarters far away, now and then let some funds, modern inputs and know-how trickle down in a patriarchal way to the grateful villagers.

We will return to several of the issues discussed above when we come to the 'landlord bias' and the 'private bias' in Bangladesh's development policies. Suffice it here to anticipate the conclusion: that any system of distribution of services and modern inputs in rural Bangladesh is bound to fail unless the poor are organized in order to receive and make use of the benefits in a collective way, under collective supervision by and for themselves.

References

1. A.M.A.M. Siddiqui, 'The Public Administration System: An Aid or an Obstacle to Development? An Expose Based on Personal Experience', mimeo (Dacca, January 1977).
2. *Holiday*, Dacca, 1978.
3. Siddiqui, op. cit., Appendix.
4. E.L. Tepper, 'The Administration of Rural Reform: Structural Constraints and Political Dilemmas' in R.D. Stevens, H. Alavi and P.J. Bertocci (eds.), *Rural Development in Bangladesh and Pakistan* (Honolulu, Hawaii University Press, 1976), p. 52.
5. Md. Alam, 'A Report on the Swanirvar Programme in Athiokhali, Lakshmipur, Noakhali', Report No. 19, Rural Studies Project, Department of Economics, Chittagong University, Chittagong, 1976. See p. 72.
6. Swedish International Development Authority/Bangladesh Institute for Development Studies, 'Landless Survey 1978', (unpublished). The 'Swanirvar', or self-reliance, movement was launched during the latter half of the 1970s as a special model for rural development in Bangladesh. Although officially emphasizing local self-reliance, the 'Swanirvar' strategy has, except in its populist rhetoric, little in common with local initiatives and popular mobilization. Today, the movement has lost much of the importance it once might have had. For a critical analysis, see D. Asplund and S. de Vylder, 'Contradictions and Distortions in a Rural Economy', SIDA (Stockholm, 1979), Chapter 5.
7. Alam, op. cit., pp. 12–13.
8. Md. Yunus, 'Planning in Bangladesh', Rural Studies Project, Department of Economics, Chittagong University, June 1976, p. 2.
9. Suffice it here to mention that, in the Bangladeshi context, researchers like René Dumont, Keith Griffin, A.R. Khan, Muhammed Yunus and Anisur Rahman — whom I have had occasion to quote several times already — have all contributed in different ways to giving theoretical guidance to the reorientation now under way. For a particularly clear formulation of the need for a break with conventional approaches to rural development, I would also like to refer to the works of a group of Asian scholars formerly connected with the United Nations Asian Development Institute in Bangkok: see, for example, Wahidul Haque, Niranjan Mehta, Anisur Rahman, Ponna Wignaraja, 'Towards a Theory of Rural Development', *Development Dialogue*, Vol. 2, 1977.
10. J.P. Dutta, 'A Report on Swanirvar Programmes in Shilkup, Monkirchar, Banskhali, Chittagong', Locally Sponsored Development Programme Series, Report No. 23, Rural Studies Project, Chittagong University, October 1976, p. 12.
11. Yunus, op. cit., p. 29.
12. Anisur Rahman, 'The Utilization of Labour in the Strategy for Development in the ECAFE Development Region', ECAFE Paper, undated mimeo, p. 3.
13. Yunus, op. cit., p. 51.
14. H.W. Blair, 'Institutional Change and Agricultural Wages in Bangladesh',

Bangladesh Development Studies, Vol. 4, 1976, p. 23.

15. *Asian Drama* quoted by Blair, 'Rural Development, Class Structure and Bureaucracy in Bangladesh', *World Development*, Vol. 1, 1978, p. 73.

16. A.C. Lindquist, 'Cooperatives, Rural Development and the State: A Bangladesh Case Study', University of Sussex, mimeo, May 1978, p. 82.

17. See also Blair, 1978, op. cit.: 'What is important is that the lower-level official should be able to tell his superior that he followed a "responsible" policy in making the loans, i.e. lent money only to those with a clear capacity to repay them' (pp. 73–4).

18. The somewhat absurd phenomenon that even those officials in Bangladesh who are supposed to work a lot in the field often receive a fixed salary but no *per diem* allowances to cover the extra expenses of travel, accommodation, etc. in the villages reinforces the officials' reluctance to undertake field trips and listen to the village people. To go to a village is regarded as not only cumbersome but also an economic sacrifice, and when the officials nevertheless do undertake such field trips they are most likely to try to arrange their accommodation as comfortably as possible – that is, in the house of a rich villager.

19. Though not necessarily in others: the famous label 'soft state' has many connotations that can be misleading. All those Asian states which Myrdal calls 'soft' have often shown a considerable strength and determination in dealing with the political opposition. When threatened, the ruling classes and their state machineries are seldom 'soft', and the real issue is not, as Myrdal's terminology may induce us to believe, lack of control, but control by whom? and for what purposes? It could also be mentioned in this context that the number of armed personnel in Bangladesh has almost doubled since the military take-over in 1975, to almost 100,000 today. According to Mosharaff Hossain, the increase in military and para-military expenditure between 1975 and 1977 was over *taka* 2,000 million, against an increase in total state expenditure on all other items of less than *taka* 1,000 million. 'Nature of State Power in Bangladesh', *The Journal of Social Studies*, Vol. I, No. 5, 1979. See also L. Lifschultz, *Bangladesh: The Unfinished Revolution* (London, Zed Press, 1979) and the discussion about the role of military aid in Michael Scott, 'Aid to Bangladesh: For Better or Worse?', Institute for Food and Development Policy/Oxfam–America, San Francisco, 1979.

20. G. Wood, 'Class Differentiation and Power in Bangladesh' in A. Huq (ed.), 'Exploitation of the Rural Poor', B.A.R.D. (Comilla, 1976), p. 179.

21. Michael Lipton, *Why Poor People Stay Poor* (London, Temple Smith, 1977), pp. 289–90, emphasis in original.

6.   The Capital Bias

Before liberation, Bangladesh was the exploited part of an unhappy marriage with West Pakistan, whose successive governments, as mentioned earlier, consistently favoured the West at the expense of the East, industry and urban infrastructure at the expense of agriculture, and capital at the expense of labour. It is this latter discrimination that interests us in this chapter. The 'capital bias' facilitated the accumulation of vast amounts of capital in the hands of a small minority of predominantly urban businessmen; this in part explains why both urban-rural and functional income differentials increased appreciably during the 1960s[1] Speaking in 1965, one observer noted:

> The rich have certainly become very rich indeed and persons and families which were worth millions a decade ago are now worth hundreds of millions. . . . The same family groups own industrial undertakings, banks, insurance companies, consultancy offices, construction firms, distribution trade, etc. etc., so that not only is there a horizontal but also a vertical concentration of wealth and a tremendous concentration of economic power.[2]

Most of these 'tycoons' were residing in the Western wing of the country, where the bulk of the investments were made. And if one looks a little more closely at the policies pursued, it is in a way a blessing for the majority of people in Bangladesh that East Pakistan was comparatively neglected; the high capital intensity distortion in both industry and agriculture that followed upon the choice of economic policies in the 1950s and 1960s is today more pronounced in Pakistan than in Bangladesh, and the economic and social costs of these distortions may be so high as to outweigh the higher rate of growth that was registered in the West. The labour-displacing effects of the mechanization policy have thus been more accentuated in the privileged West than in the neglected East. Within agriculture, for example, it was West Pakistan that was the main 'beneficiary' of the following tractorization programme:

> The government of Pakistan . . . has encouraged the use of large tractors and wheat combine harvesters through its policies of subsidizing interest

rates and the price of foreign exchange for imports of agricultural equipment. Even as early as 1964–65, over a third of all loans granted by the Agricultural Development Bank were for purchases of tractors and other mechanical equipment. Contrary to the expectation, or hope, that mechanization would increase the demand for labour, the widespread introduction of tractors in the Punjab and Sind has led to the eviction of tenants, a decline in employment on large farms and an attempt by big landlords to increase further the size of their holdings. In one study, in fact, it was estimated that increased use of tractors on large farms led to a reduction in the utilization of labour by as much as 50% per acre.[3]

Let us now see how the legacy from the Pakistani period has manifested itself in Bangladesh. I will also discuss whether the present policies serve to reinforce or weaken the 'capital bias' inherited from the past. For reasons of space my ambitions will be limited to giving a few illustrations of the phenomenon, rather than a theoretically and empirically rigorous treatment of the many different issues involved.

Manufacturing Industry

Bangladesh is characterized by an abundance of labour and a relative scarcity of capital. We should therefore expect the capital-intensity in Bangladesh industry to be rather low in comparison with countries where labour rather than capital is the scarce factor of production. This is not the case, however. If we analyze the technology of the Bangladesh industries, it is most perplexing to note that most of them are of a highly capital-intensive nature. In Table 6.1 the capital-intensities in a number of industries in East Pakistan in the 1960s are compared with the corresponding industries in Japan and the United States. The startling conclusion of Table 6.1 is that the capital-intensity in East Pakistan was higher than in Japan in all sectors except basic metals. In many sectors it was not very much lower than in the United States, and in one, paper, it was even higher. The exactness of the figures can certainly be questioned – the calculations are in fact quite difficult to make, and the conversions into U.S. dollars contain many pitfalls related to the choice of appropriate exchange rates – but there can be no doubt that the capital-intensity in the East Pakistan industry was amazingly high.

There are many factors that explain this phenomenon. There was, to begin with, the problem with the grossly over-valued exchange rate, making imports of foreign machinery and equipment exceedingly cheap. The domestic rate of interest was also kept artificially low, which encouraged the use of capital rather than labour. Several other measures aiming at a rapid industrialization also contributed to accentuate this capital bias: tax incentives were given to industries making investments in fixed capital, and the depreciation allowances were extraordinarily generous. The system of import licences

Table 6.1:
Capital–Labour Ratios[1] in Manufacturing, Selected Countries, late 1960s
East Pakistan = 1.00

	East Pakistan	*Japan*	*U.S.A.*
Cotton textiles	1.00	0.38	2.18
Leather goods	1.00	0.59	1.40
Paper	1.00	0.07	0.85
Rubber goods	1.00	0.32	4.43
Basic metals	1.00	4.04	13.60
Machinery	1.00	0.20	1.96
Wood products	1.00	0.40	—

1. Defined as value of fixed assets in U.S. dollars per worker.

Source: I. Ahmed, 'Employment in Bangladesh' (1973), p. 15. Cottage industry is excluded.

encouraged companies to import as much machinery as possible, since the granting of new material input licences — for which competition was intense — was largely dependent on the size of each industry's installed capacity. A whole set of policies thus distorted relative prices by reducing the cost of capital to an extent which in no way reflected its real scarcity. The highly uneven distribution of income in Pakistan served to reinforce all the distortions introduced by the government's own policies. With most of the purchasing power concentrated in the hands of a privileged elite, the ensuing pattern of effective demand, and hence production, was heavily biased in favour of import-intensive and capital-intensive commodities, while demand and production of mass consumer goods experienced a much less dynamic growth.

After Independence, most of Bangladesh's large-scale manufacturing industries were nationalized (many of these companies are now being returned to private hands). However the transfer of key industries to the public sector was not accompanied by any shift towards a new technology mix more suitable for society as a whole, although it did result in a massive increase in both investments and employment. But despite these efforts, output failed to respond; what actually happened was that more people produced less with the help of more machines. Not until 1977–78 did industrial production reach its pre-Independence level, and on a per capita basis, output has far from recovered even now. Labour productivity has dropped precipitately in most industrial sectors, the rate of capacity utilization remains low (around 50%), and labour's share of total value added has oscillated around one-third. In Table 6.2 some of the outstanding features of Bangladesh's manufacturing sector are summarized for the fiscal years 1960, 1970 and 1976 (excluding cottage industry).

The situation has, in short, become worse. Only one significant measure

Table 6.2:
Summary of Trends in Manufacturing, 1960–76

	1960	*1970*	*1976*
Value added (constant 1970 prices, millions of *taka*)	548	1,534	1,436
Employment (1,000s)	139	204	374
Capital (constant 1970 prices, millions of *taka*)	605	1,875	2,902
Output/worker (constant 1970 prices, *taka* per worker)	3,934	7,486	3,830
Average real wage (constant 1970 prices, *taka* per worker per year)	1,480	1,798	1,320
Index of total productivity (1960 = 100)	100	114	65

Source: I.B.R.D.

has been undertaken since 1971 to counteract the bias in favour of capital-intensive technology. This was the drastic devaluation in 1975, which gave the *taka* a more realistic value and helped to discourage certain capital imports. Other steps have been directly counter-productive, however. Among these one should first of all mention the heavy reliance on foreign aid. Without repeating all the previous arguments about Bangladesh's foreign dependence, we can note that the effect of the massive inflow of aid has been to ease the short-run (but probably not the long-run) foreign exchange constraint, thereby enabling the country to continue its large-scale imports of foreign machinery and equipment. Also, the forms in which the aid has been given — tied aid, restrictions on local *taka* financing, import bias in the selection and design of projects, etc. — have only served to accentuate the foreign and capital-intensive bias in overall domestic policies. The many privileges granted foreign private investors (see Chapter 4) — tax holidays, generous rules for depreciation of fixed assets, the 'Free Zone' concessions, etc. — work in the same direction. And it is explicitly stated by the new Minister of Industry that 'foreign investors . . . will be particularly welcome in capital-intensive units requiring sophisticated technology and know-how'.[5]

In domestic industrial policy, we can also see a clear return to the most extreme forms of favouring capital. The new Industrial Investment Schedule for the private sector 1978–80 emphasizes the importance of 'rapid industrialization' and gives private investors a variety of concessions which all contribute to make the use of capital goods of foreign origin as cheap as possible. A few excerpts from a presentation of the Investment Schedule illustrate the nature of the measures adopted:

Other fiscal concessions for the private sector industries, announced by

> the Industries Minister, include: a) Export-oriented industries . . . will be accorded the duty rate of 2½% irrespective of the machinery imports; b) The present concessionary rate of 5% on the capital machinery imported under the Wage Earners' Scheme will continue; c) No sales tax will be leviable on the import of capital machinery . . .Mr. Jamoluddin . . . said that the existing fiscal measures in the shape of a) tax holiday and b) accelerated depreciation coupled with investment allowance would continue in force up to June 1980 and June 1982, respectively.[6]

Prestige is very much involved, too; the more modern, and foreign, an industry is, the more attention it tends to get from the government. New, highly automated plants are often opened in the presence of ministers, or even of the President himself, and with much publicity – a clear indication of the present government's lack of interest in achieving a break with the earlier model of industrialization.[7]

The combination of government prestige, aid dependence, a still over-valued domestic exchange rate, artificially low rates of interest which in no way reflect the scarcity price of capital, and the various privileges given to foreign and national companies using imported machinery and equipment will guarantee that the 'capital bias' in Bangladesh industry persists, and is perhaps even reinforced. These policies will make it extremely difficult for Bangladesh's own small-scale industry to compete in virtually any sector in which the large (foreign) companies take advantage of the concessions granted them if they establish capital-intensive units. It should also be stressed that, if the measures described above are successful in the sense of leading to a high rate of profit in large-scale industry – and this is precisely what they are supposed to do – this will accentuate the drain of capital away from agriculture. For, as is well known, it is not the absolute, but the relative, level of profit that counts in investment decisions: if there is a rise in the rate of profit in the manufacturing sector, then agriculture is bound to lose even more investible surplus than in the past. Conversely, if the big farmers are to be persuaded to invest in the Green Revolution rather than in the urban bonanza, then the subsidies on agricultural inputs have to be made more and more generous for the beneficiaries.

From the point of view of income distribution, the 'new' industrial poli-cies affect not only urban-rural inequality but personal distribution of income within the towns as well. Of the fortunes that can be accumulated by the privileged handful of industrialists, little is likely to trickle down to the urban, and almost nothing to the rural, poor. The employment effects of capital-intensive investments in manufacturing will obviously be marginal, even negative in some cases, since modern food processing and textile fac-tories may take over markets from smaller units where employment per unit of output is much higher. Remember that less than 400,000 people, or around one-half of the *annual* increase in the labour force, are employed in the entire manufacturing sector. Even a drastic shift towards a more labour-intensive pattern of industrialization would thus contribute little to alleviating the employment situation in the short run, however massive the funds poured into large-scale industry. But the longer one waits, the more difficult the problems will become.

Agriculture

Since the ratio of capital goods to total output and employment is relatively low in agriculture, the effects of the 'capital bias' are not so pronounced in this sector as elsewhere in the economy. But the capital-intensive technologies which have been favoured have repercussions, particularly for irrigation techniques. Irrigation has a crucial role to play in Bangladesh; it can increase both the cropping intensity and average yields per acre. Irrigation, furthermore, affects labour use and creates jobs. The government does acknowledge the importance of irrigation but its investments have unduly favoured major capital-intensive works, and the subsidy structure has been described as 'nearly perfectly perverse' by the 1977 Agricultural Mission.[8] Table 6.3 is a good illustration of the perverse nature of investments and subsidies in the five-year period 1973–77.

Table 6.3:
Government Funding of Irrigation Schemes, 1973–77.

Type of Irrigation	Allocation in Five Year Plan (%)	% of Land Made Irrigable	State Subsidy as a % of Total Costs
Large-scale projects	53	5	100
Deep tube-wells	31	21	67
Low lift pumps	14	24	44
Shallow tube-wells	2	2	34
Hand pumps[1]	Nil	3	29
Traditional methods (dhones, swing baskets, etc.)	Nil	45	Nil

1. The hand pump scheme was initiated after the writing of the Five Year Plan.

Source: Based on Agricultural Mission 1977, I.B.R.D. and S. Biggs, C. Edwards and J. Griffith, 'Irrigation in Bangladesh', 1978.

We thus see that the more capital-intensive systems receive relatively more state funds and have higher rates of subsidy than the less capital-intensive ones. In terms of achievements, the pattern is the exact opposite. From the point of view of efficiency, the entire subsidy structure should rather be reversed. The indigenous devices, which are inexpensive and which cover almost one-half of the total irrigated area, receive no subsidies at all; yet with only a minimum of support, they could be expanded considerably. Over 50% of the state allocations went to the large-scale gravity schemes, subsidized to 100% but highly inefficient. The modestly subsidized hand pumps are much cheaper to install and to run per irrigated acre than the heavily subsidized deep tube-wells, etc.

Turning to the employment effects, we observe that the least subsidized methods are also the most appropriate. Mechanized irrigation, which is intensively supported, involves only a few working days per crop and acre, in contrast to perhaps over forty with traditional methods. Irrigation with capital-intensive equipment also counteracts the use of local manufacturing capacities for irrigation supplies, while increasing the dependency on imports of technology, equipment, spare parts, etc. Around one-third of all deep tube-wells are estimated to be out of operation at any given time due to technical problems. If simple domestic designs were encouraged instead, this would facilitate local maintenance and give rise to a derived demand for labour in construction, repair, etc.

Inefficiency it not the only problem with the present pattern of subsidies and priorities. The choice of irrigation technique also has important consequences for the distribution of income and political power in the villages, as the following reveals:

Normally there is a great demand for deep tube-wells in an area. The people in Government at central and local levels are well aware of this situation, and exploit it to their advantage. It is not unusual that a large amount of bribes will have to be paid to them by the rich people who start the co-operative. . . . One important consequence of this way of acquiring a deep tube-well is that linkages between urban and rural elites are strengthened, and that resources produced in the rural areas are transferred, in the form of bribes, to Government officials in the urban areas. The rich farmers who have had the expenses for the bribes inform the members of the co-operative of this, and demand compensation for providing water to the others. A normal way to collect payment from the members is to demand 150 to 300 *taka* for irrigating one *bigha* of land, or to ask for a certain percentage of the crop; 25% is common. In this way, the rich farmer(s) can more than recover their expenses, and the water from the deep tube-wells becomes a major source of income. . . .

A patron-client type of relationship can often develop between the controllers and the users of the water, where the users not only pay an economic compensation for the use of the water, but also have to show loyalty in other fields, for instance, to give political support in village and Union affairs. The more support shown, the more certain the client can be to receive other favours, including water supply, access to buy fertilizers and pesticides; goods which for poor people can be obtained only on the black market at high prices. . .

The organizational implications of the use of the pump are very different. There is no need to form and maintain a co-operative group around a manual hand pump. If credit is provided, even the poorest landowner could become owner of a hand-pump. The pump offers a good rate of return. Under normal price conditions, farmers using one hand pump to its capacity can regain their initial investment, and even a small net profit, during one *boro* crop season. Rich farmers feel threatened when poor farmers get hand pumps. The increased production which results from the additional winter crop is used to make the farmers more self-sufficient and independent of rich farmers. The rich farmers understand that as soon as farmers become self-sufficient and do not have to take up loans to survive, they will lose a chance for buying up land from the poor peasant. In several parts of Bangladesh where the hand pumps have been introduced, rich farmers have threatened poor farmers and refused them more loans if they start to use hand pumps for irrigation. While deep tube-wells often function as a means for strengthening the patron-client relationship type of social organization in rural areas, the hand pumps can function as a means to break up this pattern.[9]

The reasons for the apparently 'irrational', perverse subsidy structure described earlier can, against this background, be more easily understood; it is certainly not because government officials and the rural rich have a poor grasp of economic theory that they give priority to mechanized forms of irrigation.

Irrigation apart, the mechanization of agriculture has proceeded quite slowly in Bangladesh. The total number of tractors in use is reported to be only around 2,000,[10] and Bangladesh has one of the lowest ratios of tractors to agricultural workers in the world. A comparison with a few Asian countries in this respect is given in Table 6.4. Bangladesh is thus lagging far behind, although minor power tillers are becoming increasingly common in the countryside, but some attempts are being made to encourage the use of tractors. The Bangladesh Agricultural Development Corporation (B.A.D.C.) has thus prepared a 'tractor scheme' as part of a programme for 'mechanization of agriculture' aiming at 'modernizing the methods of cultivation'. The main reason why some support is given to the introduction of tractors is the acute shortage of draught power — and of grazing land for the oxen. But the small size of average landholdings in Bangladesh, and the fact that tractors are poorly suited to conditions of flooding, limit the scope for these labour-displacing vehicles. The danger of a rapid tractorization is therefore less imminent in Bangladesh than in most other 'Third World' countries, but there are less dramatic forms of innovation that tend to reduce employment. Weedkillers and other mechanical methods of weed control have begun to replace traditional, labour-intensive methods. With respect to the Green Revolution agricultural technology, there is, as will be discussed in Chapter 7,

Table 6.4:
Tractor Horsepower[1] Units per 1,000 Agricultural Workers for Selected
Countries, 1961–73.

	1961–65	*1973*
Bangladesh	2.2	4.0
Nepal	1.7	2.6
Vietnam	4.5	6.6
Thailand	6.3	28.4
India	8.4	36.3
Malaysia	33.7	82.3
Taiwan	20.2	89.7
Sri Lanka	97.7	111.1

1. A four-wheel tractor is assumed to have 30 hp.

Source: A.D.B. *Asian Agricultural Survey* (1976), p. 80.

always the danger that accelerated mechanization offsets the employment-
creating effects of the new technology itself.

The introduction of rice mills in Bangladesh has, in particular, entailed a
decrease in the demand for female labour. For millions of women, the
processing of rice is by far the most important source of income of their own;
for many, it is the only one. It is estimated that it takes approximately one
day for a group of two to four women to husk one *maund* of paddy – an
electric rice mill costing some 300,000 *taka* to install has, on the other hand,
a daily capacity of 135 *maunds* of paddy. One such mill, which requires
perhaps a dozen workers to operate, including office staff and mechanics, is
thus able to replace the work of around 400 women. Considering the present
drive, supported by the World Bank and by U.S.A.I.D., to achieve a large-
scale electrification of the countryside, it is very likely that investments in
rice mills will increase at an accelerated pace, with disastrous consequences
for all those women – and families – that are dependent on rice processing
for their subsistence.[11]

Concluding Remarks

This chapter has concentrated on the employment effects of a policy which
favours capital and capital-intensive technical change at the expense of
labour and more labour-intensive methods. The examples used were mainly
chosen from manufacturing and agriculture, but they could also have been
taken from construction, transportation, infrastructure in general, forestry,
etc. The conclusion was unambiguous: past and present policies of the kind
that have been discussed mean wastage, both of a scarce resource – capital,
which is used inefficiently – and of a resource in plentiful supply, namely
labour. Per unit of capital, far more employment – and growth – would

result from a reallocation of new investments towards alternative, less mechanized uses. Today's policies may be very rational from the point of view of the ruling classes, but not for society as a whole.

In no way should this argument be construed as a general hostility to technical change. Labour productivity in the Bangladesh economy is low and needs to be raised. Millions of people work extremely hard but are still unable to feed themselves and their families adequately; in part because they are exploited, but also because they simply produce too little. An increase in the productivity of labour is a necessary condition for all long-range development; without investments and innovations, poverty is bound to be perpetuated. Mechanization can be a blessing: it reduces the need for hard physical labour, it enables people to work less while producing more. It is a mixed blessing, however, and unless there exist mechanisms that guarantee that the benefits are shared, mechanization is likely to do more harm than good. Within the present socio-economic structure of Bangladesh, a policy aiming at modernization through generous subsidies for the use of capital rather than labour is bound to polarize the society further, to increase the excess of men over jobs, and to pauperize broader and broader sectors of the population. Such a policy militates, in the final analysis, not only against equity and justice, but against economic growth as well.

It should finally be emphasized once again that more appropriate technologies are available; the relevant alternative to mechanization of agriculture is not stagnation and backwardness but a different kind of technical change which utilizes both capital and labour more efficiently. 'Because of a total lack of interest in developing labour-intensive, low-capital techniques, there has arisen a notion that capital-intensive agriculture is the only way of increasing yields,' observes one student of agricultural technology in Bangladesh. He continues:

> As more and more highly productive, low-cost indigenous techniques spread of their own accord in Bangladesh and other countries (for example bamboo tube-wells, handweeders, multiple cropping practices, bullock drawn placement drills, to name just a few) it is increasingly realized that there are far more techniques and technologies available (or could be developed) — if only resources and national and international agencies were diverted in this direction.[12]

References

1. See, in particular, the collection of articles in K. Griffin and A.R. Khan (eds.), *Growth and Inequality in Pakistan* (London, Macmillan, 1972).
2. A.R. Ibrahim, *The Pains of Economic Development*, quoted in Griffin and Khan, op. cit., p. 40.
3. K. Griffin, *The Political Economy of Agrarian Change* (London,

Macmillan, 1974), pp. 53–4.
4. I. Ahmed, 'Employment in Bangladesh — Problems and Prospects', mimeo (Dacca, 1973), p. 13.
5. Quoted in *The Bangladesh Observer*, 10 September, 1978.
6. Ibid.
7. For an account of recent examples of government-supported capital-intensive technology choices, see M. Masum, 'Technology and Employment in Bangladesh' in Report of I.L.O. Tripartite Symposium on Choice of Technology and Employment Generation in Asia (Bangkok, 1979). Masum convincingly shows that even the companies belonging to the public sector tend to choose highly sophisticated, imported techniques of production.
8. Agricultural Mission 1977, Working Paper No. II, p. 12.
9. E. Jansen, 'Choice of Irrigation Technology in Bangladesh', *The Journal of Social Studies*, Vol. 1, No. 5, 1979, pp. 69–70.
10. Or, exactly 2,072 in 1977, according to *ADAB News*, Dacca, May 1977, p. 4.
11. For a discussion, see for example, S. Adnan and R. Islam, 'Social Change and Rural Women', B.I.D.S., Village Study Group Working Paper No. 7, mimeo (Dacca, May 1976) and Agricultural Mission, Working Paper No. XI, 1977. The Agricultural Mission concludes: 'There is qualitative evidence to suggest that the steady elimination of one of the major sources of female employment is occurring through technical change in rice processing. The traditional methods of rice processing . . . provided employment especially for widows, a major class of the rural poor. . . . In 1967–68 seventeen per cent of this work was taken over by rice hulling, and after another decade mechanical hulling has made further unknown inroads into this source of employment' (p. 24).
12. S. Biggs, 'Interaction between Technological and Institutional Development', mimeo (Dacca, 1975), p. 21.

7.   The Production Bias

Every reader of a Bangladeshi newspaper — or development plan — will be struck by the extraordinarily high emphasis the government places on a rapid increase in agricultural production. 'Production first' is an oft-repeated slogan, and 'self-sufficiency in foodgrains by 1985' is the most commonly stated objective today in the field of agriculture. The late President Ziahur Rahman had suggested even more ambitious goals; in late 1979, when launching his programme for a 'two-stage revolution' in Bangladesh, the President announced that the revolution's first step would be the doubling of food production in five years.

Our review of Bangladesh's agricultural stagnation during the last few decades has shown that an increase in food production is indeed essential. We also know, however, that the priority given to this objective, if seriously meant, should have been translated into a series of policy measures, such as a drastic reallocation of resources away from industry and urban infrastructure into agriculture, and a reduction in the reliance upon food imports — measures which have not been undertaken. The expression 'production bias' thus requires some necessary qualifications: I am not suggesting that agricultural production is excessively favoured over other activities — only that it is narrow production-oriented objectives that dominate the government's policies within the agricultural sector proper.

The purpose of this section is to assess to what extent the production goals have been achieved and to illustrate how the 'production bias', as defined above, has led to a relative neglect of other important goals, above all those related to employment and income distribution. Most of the aspects that should be considered in this context are related to the attempts to accelerate the use of the new High Yielding Variety (H.Y.V.)–fertilizer technology, which has been the cornerstone of agricultural policies for the past 15 years in first East Pakistan, and then Bangladesh. The analysis therefore will begin with some general technical and economic observations regarding the effects of this technology on output and employment. This introduction to the Green Revolution will also serve as a background to Chapter 8, on the 'landlord bias', where I will concentrate on distributional aspects.

The 'Green Revolution'

> The development of I.R.8 [the best known 'miracle seed'] and its dissemination throughout Asia is . . . literally helping to fill hundreds of millions of rice-bowls once only half full.[1]

> While India over the last few years has achieved impressive progress on its 'green revolution', the result in the countryside has been economic polarization with the few getting richer and the masses getting poorer. Many are being pushed off their land and losing their property.[2]

The research and literature about the so-called Green Revolution are today expanding at a far higher rate than the High Yielding Varieties themselves. Thus, while presently only around 30% of the Third World acreage of wheat and 20% of rice are covered by H.Y.V.s, virtually every book and article on agricultural development in Africa, Asia and Latin America written in the 1970s deals extensively with matters related to the use, and misuse, of the improved seed-fertilizer technology. In this discussion, almost all the natural and social sciences are involved in one way or the other, but the focus of attention has gradually been shifted from the biological-chemical-technical characteristics of the new seeds to the socio–economic consequences of the introduction of the entire package of modern inputs that accompanies the use of the H.Y.V.s.

Together with this shift in emphasis, the last decade has also witnessed a growing sense of frustration, nourished both by the dismal record of food production in many developing countries and by an increasing awareness of the dangerous, not to say disastrous, social effects of many attempts to modernize a traditional agriculture. The early euphoric descriptions of the 'miracle seeds' as the solution to the problem of world hunger — typified by the statement by Lester Brown quoted above — have to an increasing extent been replaced by appreciably less optimistic studies concentrating on the interaction between technological change and employment, economic and political power, ecological and cultural factors, and a whole host of other ramifications.

While not wishing to review this large and rapidly expanding literature, I do want to indicate its existence and to emphasize that there are many different, and multi-disciplinary, issues that should be taken into account in a thorough assessment of how green and how revolutionary the 'Green Revolution' really is.

H.Y.V. Technology

The H.Y.V.s require, as mentioned earlier, the simultaneous application of many different, complementary inputs. Like the 'Green Revolution', the term 'High Yielding Varieties' is a misnomer since, in the words of F.M. Lappé and Joseph Collins, it 'implies that the new seeds are high-yielding in and by themselves. The distinguishing feature of the new seeds, however, is that they are highly *responsive* to certain key inputs, such as irrigation and fertilizer.'[3] For this reason, I agree with Lappé and Collins in their suggestion that High Responsive Varieties (H.R.V.) would be a better label, and it must be said from the outset that what is of interest are the circumstances that make the new seeds realize their potential, rather than the seeds as such.

The core of the new technology is bio-chemical research. Although it has been going on for decades, this research is still in a relatively early stage of development, and it is more likely that many of the early limitations of the seeds will be overcome. There is, in this sense, much scope for optimism: we have every reason to believe that seeds with higher growth potentials than the existing ones, and in particular seeds that are better suited for local conditions, in Bangladesh and elsewhere, will be developed.

The local factor is important. The H.Y.V.s cannot, as was sometimes assumed a decade ago, be freely transferred to different countries and conditions. The highly sensitive biological components involved make it necessary to tailor the H.Y.V.s to fit each region's particular combination of soil, climate, hydrological conditions, local pests and diseases, cropping patterns, etc.[4] Even within Bangladesh, where conditions in these respects would appear to be relatively homogeneous, there are great local variations which make certain seeds very well suited to some parts of the country but virtually useless in other areas. Part of the reason why the Green Revolution has failed to achieve the expected results in Bangladesh is undoubtedly the relatively small efforts that have been made to develop domestic H.Y.V.s which meet different kinds of local requirements.

With these reservations in mind, and remembering that future research can make important contributions both in terms of improving the general quality of the seeds and in increasing the responsiveness of the H.Y.V.s to specific conditions in different parts of Bangladesh, we can now proceed to a discussion of some salient features of the H.Y.V.s that exist today.[5] I will mainly concentrate on rice — which still accounts for some 98% of total foodgrain production in Bangladesh — but much of what is said below is relevant for wheat as well.

The main advantage of the H.Y.V.s is, of course, their higher yield potential. Under ideal conditions, rice yields per acre are twice or even three times as high as for the local varieties. This higher yield potential is good in itself, but it should also be observed that this factor assumes a particular importance in a land-scarce country like Bangladesh, since it means that the size of a farm which can adequately support a family declines appreciably.

Some of the H.Y.V.s have also shorter maturation periods than the local varieties, a circumstance which, as well as enabling farmers to economize on water, also permits the cropping intensity to rise. Another advantage with the new seed-fertilizer technology is that it is, in principle — but hardly (as will be discussed further in Chapter 8) in actual practice — scale-neutral: both the new seeds themselves and most of the complementary inputs are, from a technical point of view, perfectly divisible, and can be applied with equal success on very small and very large farms.

Another basic quality of the new technology is that it tends to be conducive to more labour utilization. In addition to the higher employment required by the rise in cropping intensity and the increase in overall production made possible by the H.Y.V.s, the new seeds create more jobs than the local varieties since they need more careful cultivation, better seedbed preparation, more intensive disease control, more weeding, etc. Due to its higher production levels, and larger quantities of inputs to handle, the new technology also gives rise to a derived demand for labour in the service sector: transport, trade, storage, equipment maintenance, etc.

Such are the potential benefits. Let us now turn to some reservations and disadvantages. The modern rice is, to begin with, of inferior taste. People in Bangladesh prefer the traditional rice, and are willing to pay the higher price charged for it. The cattle also prefer the local varieties, whose straw content is appreciably higher than that of the H.Y.V.s.

However, the major disadvantage from the point of view of production potential is the fact that the modern seeds are poorly suited to conditions of drought and flood. In Bangladesh this makes reliable irrigation absolutely indispensable during the dry season, while the use of the H.Y.V.s for the monsoon crops is seriously limited by the lack of drainage and water control schemes. According to one estimate, only about 9 million acres, or about 40% of the land under monsoon season crops, is considered suitable for H.Y.V.s under rain-fed conditions.[6] But even these estimates are overly optimistic under the present conditions, since uncertainty and risk are major problems. The new technology requires substantial monetary outlays on seeds and other inputs, and the majority of poor and indebted peasants can ill afford to invest in the Green Revolution if excessive drought or flooding in one year may ruin them.

Another risky aspect is the fact that the new seeds tend to be more delicate than the indigenous varieties. They therefore require either ideal natural conditions or a great deal more skill and care in their cultivation. Often lacking the resistance of the local varieties, the H.Y.V. plants are, in particular, more susceptible to disease, while the greater use of fertilizers and irrigation results in more pest infestation — it is not only the rice plants that thrive, indeed the densely cultivated and genetically uniform H.Y.V.s provide an excellent environment for pests.[7] The climatic conditions of Bangladesh, with high humidity, abundant rainfall and high temperatures, also encourage the growth and multiplication of insects and pests.

The H.Y.V.s are, to repeat, not high-yielding by themselves; they need additional, and for the majority of farmers too costly, inputs. The application of a large and balanced dose of fertilizer is, above all, a precondition for the achievement of satisfactory yields. Modern varieties of rice are estimated to consume twice as much nitrogen and phosphorous and more than four times as much potassium as the local varieties, if they are to realize their potential. Once introduced, the H.Y.V.s tend therefore to generate a sequence of investment, often of a capital-intensive and import-intensive in character. 'Fertilizers,' writes Keith Griffin, 'are a *sine qua non* of the "Green

Revolution". Then comes irrigation. . . . Next, pest and disease control becomes essential and, lastly, mechanization.'[9] This last point leads to some
necessary qualifications to the employment-creating effects of the H.Y.V.
technology:

> The new seeds and their need for greater care and greater application of
> fertilizer have the potential to create more jobs. But in most countries
> the forces that started the "Green Revolution" also initiated a process
> of mechanization that reduces employment.[10]

Mechanization may be introduced at different stages before and after harvest.
During the cropping cycle, the activities most likely to become mechanized
are weeding and pest and insect control, operations for which labour-
replacing implements are available at relatively low costs. The more advanced
forms of mechanization, such as tractors, are used on a very limited scale in
Bangladesh; but the fact that the H.Y.V.s must be harvested more quickly
than the traditional varieties gives the timing of labour availability a crucial
role which, in turn, encourages mechanization during the peak season. The
delicate H.Y.V.s also need to be processed and dried more quickly after the
harvest to avoid deterioration as a result of pests and insects – a circumstance
which clearly favours the electric rice mills discussed earlier.

Considering the fact that techniques of production, and degrees of mechanization, tend to vary considerably, it is most difficult to isolate and
measure the effects of the H.Y.V. technology per se. The differences in
labour requirements per acre between the application of the whole H.Y.V.
technology with traditional, labour-intensive techniques on the one hand and
a highly mechanized cultivation of traditional varieties using few complementary inputs on the other are very large.[11] Between these two extremes there
are countless combinations of degrees of mechanization, amounts of inputs
applied, etc. all with different levels of labour requirement per acre.

Another factor which must be taken into account is the way the H.Y.V.s
fit into the particular crop rotation systems in use in Bangladesh. It must be
stressed that a shift from traditional varieties to H.Y.V.s is not merely a
switch from one kind of seeds to another; the entire cropping pattern is
changed, and one cannot assume that cropping intensity and employment
necessarily rise. It may very well happen, for example, that one safe, irrigated
boro crop with H.Y.V.s replaces two less secure, rainfed crops based on
traditional varieties, and in such cases the intensity of cropping may actually
go down with the introduction of irrigation and H.Y.V.s. Since the whole
issue of cropping patterns in Bangladesh is extremely complicated, and subject
to countless variations due to local climatic, hydrological, socio-economic and
other conditions, I cannot deal with this topic satisfactorily here. The interested reader is referred to various publications from agricultural research
institutes in Bangladesh or to the works by Hugh Brammer and Edward Clay.
In Table 7.1, estimates of labour requirements of a few of the many possible
combinations of crops and irrigation techniques are presented. The table,

which is a summary of a study made by Edward Clay, illustrates that the place of the H.Y.V.s in the rotation systems is of paramount importance for an assessment of the impact of the new rice varieties on overall employment.

Table 7.1:
Annual Crop Labour Requirements of Selected Traditional and New Crop Rotations

Rotations		Annual Labour Requirements (working-days/acre/year)		
'Traditional'	*'New'*	*'Trad- itional'*	*'New'*	% Change
Local+*boro*+fallow (traditional irrigation)	Modern+*boro*+fallow (low-lift pump)	111	109	− 1
	Modern+*boro*–fallow (doan irrigation)	111	144	+ 30
Boro +*aman*+fallow	Modern+*boro* (low lift pump)	85	109	+ 28
B.+*Aus*+B.+*aman* +lentils	Modern+*boro* (low-lift pump)	125	109	− 13
	B.+*Aus*+B.+*aman*+ Dwarf Wheat	125	156	+ 29
Local+T.+*aman* +fallow	Late *Boro* (low-lift pump)+Local T.+*aman*	64	173	+170
Local+T.+*aus*+ Local T.+*aman*+ fallow	Modern+late *boro* + modern T.+*aman* (deep tubewell irrigated)	142	215	+ 51

Note: T. = transplanted, B. = broadcast. *Boro, Aman* and *Aus* refer to the 3 crop season.

Source: Clay, 'Employment Effects of the H.Y.V. Strategy in Bangladesh', (1978), Table 6, p. 30.

The table shows that almost anything can happen to demand for labour. The impact of the H.Y.V. technology on employment depends on the nature of the crop substitution that takes place, and some changes actually have a negligible or even negative effect. We also observe that in absolute figures the differences between different rotations are very large. In general, however, employment does rise with the introduction of the H.Y.V. technology and the concomitant switch to a new crop rotation, and this is an important conclusion from Clay's study: the marked seasonality of crop labour requirements in Bangladesh is not affected to any major degree in the most common new cropping patterns.

Before finishing this general overview of the Green Revolution, a few final observations regarding the employment effects must be made. So far, I have only considered labour requirements per acre. Perhaps even more important is how the number of working days per unit of output changes with the introduction of the H.Y.V. technology. And here, the answer is unequivocal — the labour-intensity falls. 'Any innovation, whether biological-chemical or mechanical, reduces worker-hours of labour input per unit of output. The most drastic reduction is for mechanical innovation.'[12] This effect of the Green Revolution is well-known, although the actual size of the decrease in labour requirements per unit of output is subject to much discussion. Table 7.2 gives some relevant data, based on a study of labour changes in an irrigated low-land rice area in Orissa, India.

Table 7.2:
Labour Requirements on Irrigated Paddy Farms under Different Combinations of Technology and Technique, Orissa, India.

	Technology		*% Change*
	Traditional	*H.Y.V.*	
Estimated Yields			
(kilos of paddy per hectare)	1,500	3,800	+ 153
Worker-hours per 1,000 kg			
Traditional techniques	826	401	− 52
Mechanized techniques	358	164	− 24
Index of worker-hours per kg			
Traditional techniques	100	49	
Mechanized techniques	43	20	

Source: Based on Bartsch, *Employment and Technology Choice in Asian Agriculture*, (1977), Table 2.20, p. 39.

In order to get a convenient measure of the change in labour requirements per unit of output, the concept of employment elasticity is useful; it is defined as the percentage change in working time when output increases by 1%. Using the example given in Table 7.2 above, we see that the employment elasticity thus defined was 0.49 when H.Y.V.s of rice replaced local varieties while retaining the same traditional techniques. A shift from local varieties grown with traditional techniques to H.Y.V.s plus mechanization would give an employment elasticity of 0.20 — that is, output grows five times as fast as demand for labour. Or, put another way, a 10% increase in production implies only a 2% increase in labour requirements. I will return to this concept later. For the moment let us note that the employment elasticity in Bangladesh is generally assumed to be in the range of 0.5 for the switch from local varieties of rice to the whole package of H.Y.V. technology. Once this package has been introduced, however, the elasticity declines, which means that further increases in yield require proportionally smaller increases in labour input. Or, in the words of the 1977 Agricultural Mission:

> Cross-sectional studies indicate that variations in productivity within an established technology imply much lower employment elasticities of approximately 0.20. The implication is that, after an initial high rate of employment increase with the transition to the H.Y.V. technology, the rate of increase will fall sharply once this technology is adopted.[13]

Let us now return to the agricultural policies in Bangladesh. I will begin with a brief description of the main objective of the government's strategy, and then try to assess the concrete achievements in terms of growth of output and employment. I will, finally, briefly indicate the future implications of the strategy chosen.

The 'Production First' Agricultural Strategy

'Self-sufficiency by 1985' is the stated objective of the present government's agricultural policies. As to the question of how this goal is to be reached, the *Two Year Plan 1978-80* gives the following summary:

> The essential feature of the agricultural strategy is to increase the cultivation of the high-yielding varieties of foodgrains and other crops by using fertilizer, pesticides, water and agricultural credit in a package deal.[14]

The Green Revolution, in short.

There is nothing new about this strategy; it has, in fact, been the official policy in East Pakistan/Bangladesh ever since the H.Y.V.s were introduced in the late 1960s. Immediately after Independence, an Accelerated Rice Production Programme (A.R.P.P.), with the same ends and means as those described above, was launched. Since all the vital ingredients of the programme remain in force today, even though the name A.R.P.P. is officially buried, the following description from 1973 is still worth remembering:

> The A.R.P.P. aims to reach self-sufficiency in rice over five years (the enthusiasts now claim it to be two years) by the introduction of high-yielding varieties for all the three crop seasons, *aman, aus* and *boro*. The programme rests primarily on a coordinated promotion of controlled water supply, introduction of new seeds and subsidies for other inputs and the price of rice. Its emphasis is on production, utilizing subsidies, and on organizational methods to achieve rapid utilization of the new seeds. In contrast to the other Rural Development

Programmes, the organizational and disciplinary principles of cooperative and group efforts are given less weight; there is no special effort
to control farmers' participation in order to avoid disparities in benefits;
and there is little direct contribution to the income of the land-poor
and the landless. The major problem with the A.R.P.P. is that it
threatens to create [more correctly — contribute to a growing]
inequality of wealth and opportunity in the rural areas and lay the
basis for polarization of the landed and the landless.[15]

The above two quotations give, in a nutshell, the essence of what one may
call a production-biased strategy. And little or nothing has changed, in this
respect; the present government is equally obsessed with the growth objective, while very little attention is being paid to income distribution and
employment aspects, to the needs of the small peasants and landless, and to
institution-building. The cornerstone of the policy is still the provision of
subsidized Green Revolution inputs, and almost all state expenditure on
agricultural development is allocated to this end. The official 1977 subsidy
structure of the major inputs is shown in Table 7.3. The actual subsidies are
even higher, however, since the official estimates shown in Table 7.3 do not
include distribution and storage costs, administrative overhead costs, etc.
Also, the provision of cheap credit to facilitate the purchases of inputs is
another form of subsidy which is very important for those farmers who are
fortunate enough to have access to institutional credit.

Table 7.3:
Input Subsidies, 1977

Input	% Subsidy
Fertilizer	
Urea	32
Triple Superphosphate	71
Muriate of Potash	64
Irrigation	
Large-scale Gravity Schemes	100
Deep Tube-wells	67
Low-Lift Pumps	44
Shallow Tube-wells	34
Seed	
Imported Wheat	56
Rice	n.d.
Pesticides	50

Source: B.R.R.I., *Workshop 1977*, p. 263, and Table 7.3. above (irrigation).
Figures refer to 1977 except for irrigation, where average figures for 1973–77
have been used.

Given these substantial subsidies, and the high potential profitability associated with the new technology, one would expect the H.Y.V.s to spread rapidly. This has not been the case in Bangladesh, however, and one of the ironies of the government's strategy is that it has not been effective even on its own terms. Production has, as we know, failed to keep pace with the rate of population growth, and despite a few years of favourable monsoons and acceptable harvests (with the exception of the drought year 1979), the goal of self-sufficiency appears to be at least as remote as ever.

There are many reasons why output has not responded as positively as expected. Since the causes of agricultural stagnation in Bangladesh are the *leitmotif* of virtually all the chapters in this study I will, in this context, only provide a few illustrations to the more limited question of the relatively slow progress made in taking advantage of the potential of the H.Y.V. technology, remembering that this is only a symptom of other, more fundamental, political and structural problems of the entire economy.

Spread of H.Y.V.s and Modern Inputs
A quantitative assessment of the actual dissemination of the H.Y.V. technology, and the effects upon average yields, is given in Tables 7.4 to 7.11. The data on which the tables are based are all taken from official government sources, from publications of the Bangladesh Rice Research Institute or, occasionally, from World Bank estimates.

Table 7.4:
Rice and Wheat Areas Covered by Improved Seeds, 1971–77

| | *% of Total Acreage Covered by H.Y.V.s* | | | | |
| | | *Season* | | | |
	Aus	*Aman*	*Boro*	*Total Rice*	*Wheat*
1970–71	1.0	1.4	35.3	4.6	n/a
1971–72	1.6	4.7	36.4	6.7	11.8
1972–73	2.3	9.8	44.7	11.1	14.5
1973–74	4.3	14.5	56.0	16.7	23.6
1974–75	8.9	9.2	57.7	14.7	26.4
1975–76	10.3	9.7	55.9	15.0	58.8
1976–77	11.3	7.3	65.3	12.9	70.6
1977–78	12.2	4.0	53.8	12.0	83.4

After a relatively rapid spread of the new varieties the rate of adoption has stagnated (see Table 7.4). The highest rates of adoption have been achieved for wheat and for *boro* rice, crops which are almost exclusively cultivated under irrigated conditions. A summary of the relative importance of the improved varieties in terms of shares of total acreage and total production, respectively, is given in Table 7.5. It is also of interest to see how average yields per acre have developed over time for the H.Y.V.s and local varieties, respectively. Such information is provided in Table 7.6. From these tables it

Table 7.5:
Shares of H.Y.V. Rice and Wheat, 1971–77

Crop by Season	H.Y.V.'s % of Total Acreage	H.Y.V.'s % of Total Production
Aus	6.5	18.5
Aman	10.7	17.8
Boro	53.4	70.1
Total Rice	*13.9*	*28.1*
Wheat	37.7	59.4

Table 7.6:
Yields per Acre of Rice and Wheat 1967–77

	[A] *Local varieties*		[B] *H.Y.V.s*	
	Average Yield (maunds per acre)	Index	Average Yield (maunds per acre)	Index
Aus Season				
1967–71	9.9	100	34.3	100
1971–74	8.7	88	29.5	86
1974–77	8.7	88	26.9	78
1977–78	8.8	89	25.3	74
Aman Season				
1967–71	12.8	100	27.5	100
1971–74	11.4	88	28.6	104
1974–77	12.2	95	23.1	84
1977–78	13.1	102	25.3	92
Boro Season				
1967–71	18.0	100	39.6	100
1971–74	15.2	84	32.2	81
1974–77	14.7	82	28.4	72
1977–78	15.5	86	28.0	71
All Crop Seasons				
1967–71	12.1	100	38.7	100
1971–74	10.3	85	28.5	74
1974–77	11.1	92	26.0	67
1977–78	11.8	98	26.4	68

would appear as if aggregate rice yields per acre have declined. This impression is misleading, however, since the H.Y.V.s have increased their relative share of the total acreage. If we add the local varieties and the H.Y.V.s we get a picture of average yields for total rice production as set out in Table 7.7.

Table 7.7:
Rice Yields per Acre, 1967-79

	Average Yield *(maunds per acre)*	*Index*
1967-71	12.8	100
1971-74	12.4	97
1974-77	13.7	107
1977-79	13.8	108

Since the figures in Tables 7.4 to 7.7 by and large speak for themselves, I will limit myself to a few brief comments. The first observation concerns the impact on output of the H.Y.V.s. From the tables we notice that the H.Y.V. yields per acre have been, on average, between two and three times higher than the local varieties. This cannot, however, be interpreted as a measure of the relative superiority of the new seeds versus the local varieties, since much of the explanation of the higher yields per acre is due to the application of appreciably higher levels of complementary inputs in the cultivation of the H.Y.V.s.

As yet there exists no study in Bangladesh — outside the laboratory fields of the rice research institutes — which attempts to isolate the effects on yields of the H.Y.V.s per se, i.e. which analyses yields per acre of different seeds with equal doses of inputs and with identical methods of production. The hypothesis that the yield differentials in the tables to a large extent are attributable to higher levels of inputs — including labour — in the cultivation of the H.Y.V.s is, however, supported by all observations of farming practices in Bangladesh: everywhere, the H.Y.V.s receive more irrigated water, more fertilizers, more labour and attention, etc. than the local varieties (this is not to say that the H.Y.V.s get all that they need — in fact they do not). This reflects no doubt a rational behaviour on the part of the farmers; if the supply of, say, fertilizers, is limited, it pays to concentrate everything on the H.Y.V. acreage and neglect the local varieties. To this we should add that the category of farmers that grow the H.Y.V.s is not representative of the rural population as a whole; they are, on average, much better off than those who can only afford to grow the traditional rice. The fact that local rice yields have remained stagnant, or even declined, since the late 1960s confirms this pattern. What has happened after the introduction of the H.Y.V.s is simply that some of the farmers have diverted the best soils and most of the scarce inputs to the improved seeds, thereby producing a decline in average yields of the local varieties.

The reason why this point should be heavily emphasized is that many descriptions of the effects of the Green Revolution have been exaggeratedly optimistic in the sense that they have demonstrated the superiority of the H.Y.V.s by comparing their yields with those of the traditional varieties without asking any further questions. This is, however, a most myopic way of assessing the advantages of the new seeds, which absorb a disproportionately large share of all modern inputs. They are, in short, very privileged seeds; when fertilizers, irrigation facilities and other complementary inputs are scarce, a more relevant indicator of the impact of the Green Revolution is the development of yields per acre over the *entire* cultivated area of the country.

It is also clear that most of the inputs that have been provided have been concentrated on the *boro* season crop. In absolute terms, the levels of output of *aus* and *aman* rice have stagnated. Table 7.8 illustrates how the total increase in foodgrain production of about 1.5 million tons between 1965-68 and 1973-76 has been distributed between the different seasons. The contributions of *aus* and *aman* rice, and of wheat, have been quite marginal.

Table 7.8:
Increasing Production of Foodgrains by Season, 1966-76

	Average Production, 1965-66 (000 tons)	*Average Production, 1973-74 (000 tons)*	*Incremental Production (000 tons)*	*Contribution (% of total)*
Aus	2,887	2,964	77	4.7
Aman	6,510	6,580	70	4.3
Boro	854	2,253	1,399	85.4
Total Rice	*10,251*	*11,797*	*1,546*	*94.3*
Wheat	50	143	93	4.7
Total	*10,301*	*11,940*	*1,639*	*100.0*

The dramatic decline in average yields of the H.Y.V.s themselves — from 38.7 maunds per acre in the late 1960s to around 26 maunds per acre ten years later (see Table 7.6) also deserves a few comments. Although there are no studies analysing the phenomenon,[16] it is reasonable to assume that the H.Y.V.s during an initial experimental stage were mainly cultivated on the very best soils under almost ideal conditions. The more the improved seeds spread, the more difficult it was to maintain the good results registered in the beginning. Poorer soils begin to be utilized, less fertilizer is applied per acre, etc. Continued cropping with H.Y.V.s may also disturb the fertility of the soil because of inappropriate crop rotations, the use of unbalanced doses of chemical inputs, etc. The rise in the relative shares of *aus* and *aman* H.Y.V.s for which yields per acre are always lower than for *boro*, in itself also contributes to depress average yields, of course. A major reason for the disappointing performance of the new seeds is the simple fact that the supply of inputs has been quite insufficient. An indication of the poor rates of expansion of the major complementary inputs is given in Tables 7.9 to 7.11.

The Accelerated Rice Production Programme, and its different successors,

Table 7.9:
Area Irrigated, 1970–78

| | *Irrigated Area* | |
Period	Millions of Acres	% of Total Acreage*
1970–71	2.9	12.9
1971–72	2.7	12.0
1972–73	3.0	13.3
1973–74	3.2	14.2
1974–75	3.6	16.0
1975–76	3.5	15.6
1976–77	2.9	12.9
1977–78	3.7	16.4

* The size of the cultivated area is assumed to be 22.5 million acres each year.

Table 7.10:
Fertilizer Consumption, 1970–78 ('000 tons)

Period	Urea	Triple Superphosphate	Muriate of Potash	Total
1970–71	212	76	18	306
1971–72	170	60	14	244
1972–73	277	89	18	384
1973–74	261	94	18	373
1974–75	175	77	18	270
1975–76	312	110	22	444
1976–77	355	131	24	510
1977–78	375	157	68	600

Table 7.11:
Pesticide Use, 1970–78 (tons)

Period	Consumption
1970–71	4,000
1971–72	4,000
1972–73	7,000
1973–74	5,000
1975–76	2,040
1976–77	3,110
1977–78	2,690

have failed. Despite heavy subsidies, the new seed-fertilizer technology has made only marginal progress: the provision of modern inputs has been insufficient, and the growth of output has been equally sluggish. Average yields remain exceedingly low.

The 'production first' strategy has proved to be both ineffective and quite expensive. Today, input subsidies account for the major part of all development expenditure on agriculture. Fertilizer subsidies alone are estimated to absorb about 126 *crore taka* in the fiscal year 1978-79,[17] which can be compared to the total allocation to agriculture of 192.6 *crore* in the Annual Development Plan 1978-79. An attempt to achieve a satisfactory supply of fertilizers of, say, ten times the present level of consumption, would, under the present subsidy structure, signify a budgetary disaster for the Bangladesh Government, which would have to divert almost the entire development budget of the whole economy to this end alone. Although a drastic increase in the share of state expenditure going to agriculture is not only desirable, but an absolute necessity, such a reallocation of resources must also be accompanied by a shift in emphasis away from input subsidies — which, as will be discussed further, are almost inevitably syphoned off by the big farmers and often used for unproductive purposes. Other forms of support to rural development should be prioritized: institution-building, labour-intensive collective works to protect the lands and improve the soils, etc. The following remarks by Akhter Hameed Khan, the founder of the famous Comilla Academy, may give a clue to the change in emphasis that is needed and its likely reception:

> If we study closely the agricultural progress of Japan and Taiwan, we notice how carefully and persistently the physical and institutional structures and human skills were built up. Their progress was by no means like a one-day hike to the mountain top. The same careful persistence in three respects — development of land, institutions, and skill — is being shown in China since 1950. They, too, are beginning to reap the reward of their wise persistence. In a seminar of advisers I once advocated the importance of physical and institutional infrastructures for increasing productivity — the physical infrastructure of roads, drainage and irrigation, and the institutional infrastructure of local government councils, small farmers cooperatives, and training centres after the Japanese and Taiwanese pattern. A famous adviser listened contemptuously to our arguments. At the end he said, 'What you say may be true. I don't know. I only know that the boss wants more rice. I will get him more rice straightaway.' This was called the quick Mymensingh approach, in contrast to the tedious Comilla approach. Boss Munim Khan told me frankly: 'Your ideas are useless because you talk of twenty years. I want self-sufficiency in two years. I will show you how I get it.' Two years later the poor boss was tottering on his throne while the one and half million ton deficit was growing firmly.[18]

Let us now look at some further implications of the production-oriented strategy. Today 'self-sufficiency in foodgrains by 1985' is officially interpreted as the capacity to provide each citizen of Bangladesh with 15.5 ounces of foodgrains per day from domestic production. The achievement of this goal would require an annual increase in food production between 1980 and 1985 of over 500,000 tons of cereals, or around 4% per year. This is, in itself, an ambitious goal, considering the fact that the annual growth over the last ten years has barely exceeded 200,000 tons of foodgrains.

The major problem, however, is that even if the 4% per year growth target were reached, this would not be enough to reduce rural unemployment. Assuming an employment elasticity of 0.5 for the switch from local varieties to the entire H.Y.V. package, we see that the rate of increase in crop labour requirements would be in the range of 2% per year. If, as is more likely, the employment elasticity is lower – in part because a share of the increase in output would have to come from a more intensive cultivation of land where H.Y.V.s have already been introduced, implying an appreciably lower rate of increase in labour per additional unit of output – then even this figure is overly optimistic. According to estimates by Clay and Khan,[19] the growth of total crop employment would range between 1.4 and 1.9% per year for a growth rate of cereal production of 4.3%. Not even this latter rate of growth – which, if sustained for a number of years, would be unprecedented in Bangladesh's modern history – would be able to absorb the projected annual increase in the agricultural work force of around 2.1 per cent per year.

The dimensions of the employment crisis are even more alarming if we consider the fact that the number of landless has increased two to three times as fast as the agricultural labour force between 1960 and 1977. The structural change in the pattern of landholding, with more and more farmers becoming landless or near landless, signifies that the demand for labour would have to expand much faster than 2.1% per year in order to provide employment to the growing number of proletarianized peasants competing for jobs on the rural labour market.

The implications are obvious. The road chosen in Bangladesh is not a road that leads to an improved employment situation for the rural poor. Even if the goal of self-sufficiency is reached by 1985, the extent of agricultural unemployment is, according to calculations by the 1977 Agricultural Mission 'estimated to be around 9 million man-years in 1985 . . . compared to the 1975–76 estimate of roughly 7 million man-years.' The Mission concludes; 'Bangladesh's priority economic option of food self-sufficiency . . . cannot meet the country's broader social objectives.'[20] The Clay/Khan study, referred to several times earlier, is equally explicit:

> The available evidence points to the unambiguous conclusion that the agricultural employment situation has been deteriorating and that a production-oriented strategy even with the present largely non-mechanized technology will not improve the situation in the foreseeable

future. It is likely to deteriorate further unless priority is given to a strategy which is based on employment creation and the reduction of poverty rather than agricultural growth objectives.[21]

The emphasis here on 'employment creation *and* the reduction of poverty' is essential. For the elimination of unemployment, which is today no more than a dream, would still not be enough in itself; the fact that some four-fifths of the rural population are estimated to live below the poverty line, and over 40% are regarded as 'extremely poor', clearly shows that many people in Bangladesh are both very poor and fully employed. Employment must increase, true, but so must average incomes, and the latter can be achieved only through an increase in the productivity of labour or a decrease in the exploitation of the rural poor or, preferably, through a combination of the two. And this leads us to the question of equity.

Income Distribution and Effective Demand

The new seed-fertilizer technology can, as we have seen, under certain circumstances bring forth a relatively large increase in yields per acre. But what about equity? What are the effects of the Green Revolution on the distribution of wealth and income? This will be the topic of the next chapter which deals with the 'landlord bias' inherent in the present agricultural strategy. Suffice it here to make a few observations about the inevitable link between supply and demand. We cannot but anticipate the conclusion that any policy aiming at increased production must be connected with policies which create the necessary demand to absorb the increase in output, disregarding (as is legitimate in this case) the export potential. Or, put it another way, unless poverty is reduced, i.e. the purchasing power of the labouring masses is raised, no production-oriented strategy will succeed, for the very simple reason that the people who are supposed to consume the additional foodgrains will be unable to do so.

This is the Achilles' heel of the entire self-sufficiency strategy. Self-sufficiency, defined as so many tons of domestically produced foodgrains, is a meaningless concept unless it is related to the capacity of the people to purchase the growing quantities produced. Demand tends to generate its own supply, but the opposite is not equally true, and the key to success in a production-oriented strategy in Bangladesh is to concentrate on efforts to increase effective demand, i.e. to reduce the poverty of the masses. For the food problem is, above all, a problem of poverty. Of course this is not to say that demand generates its own supply without difficulties. It doesn't; especially not in rural Bangladesh, where institutional constraints of various kinds are abundant. But in the absence of adequate incentives and markets for the farmers, it will be all the more difficult to overcome the many rigidities that originate from the supply side.

If the crucial role played by the level of effective demand – i.e. average incomes *and* their distribution — is considered, then the past failures are more easy to interpret. Bangladesh has, during the past decades, witnessed a process of rapid dispossession of smallholders and a concomitant rise in the number of landless and underemployed agricultural workers. The per capita effective demand of the majority of the rural population has declined. Income distribution has become more unequal, and the prices of agricultural products have — in part because of cheap food imports — declined vis-à-vis other commodities. No amount of subsidized Green Revolution inputs have been able to counteract the disincentives to agricultural production originating from the demand side, and neither have the 'crash programmes' following one after each other increasingly rapidly.

From these observations it also follows that the employment effects of the Green Revolution should be formulated in terms of labour requirements per unit of output rather than per acre. If the lack of purchasing power is the ultimate constraint to a rapid increase in agricultural production, then the fact that labour requirements per unit of output inevitably decline with a switch to the H.Y.V. technology also means that overall employment in agriculture may actually fall as a consequence of an accelerated spread of modern seeds and inputs, even in the absence of mechanization. This 'perverse' result of a change to the H.Y.V. technology — which, to repeat, *is* labour-using per se on a per acre basis — will occur if the transition merely signifies a shift of production, and of income, between 'traditional' and 'modern' farmers. The overall effect will be to keep aggregate production levels more or less constant for lack of effective demand. Under such circumstances, total labour requirements in crop production will obviously be lower after the introduction of the Green Revolution than before — with horrifying implications for the rural poor in Asia, Africa and Latin America.

Concluding Remarks

In the attempt to assess the viability of the current production-oriented agricultural strategy, I have concentrated on a discussion of actual and potential effects on output and employment. It should, however, be emphasized that a global evaluation of a Green Revolution kind of development in Bangladesh would require further investigation of several aspects which for reason of space — and for lack of knowledge — have been neglected in this study. The ecological consequences of the spread of modern inputs would, for example, have to be analysed thoroughly. Questions of the following kind need to be answered: what happens to the quality of the soils when crop rotations are changed and modern inputs are applied? How is the inland water and the fishing potential affected by the use of fertilizers, pesticides and insecticides? What is happening to the Bay of Bengal, which has to absorb increasing amounts of chemical and other effluents? Will the delicate ecological balance of Bangladesh be seriously disturbed if the present type of development accelerates?

The policies should also be analysed against the background of Bangladesh's growing foreign dependence. Most of the modern inputs are imported and paid for with foreign aid. The road to agricultural modernization that Bangladesh has embarked upon is import-intensive and will most likely contribute to increasing foreign dependence still further.

But leaving these considerations aside the main conclusion is that Bangladesh's 'production first' policy fails to satisfy even its own limited objective, while the goal of reducing rural unemployment fares even worse. The situation is not new. There is no need to summarize the data and theoretical arguments presented earlier. Rather I will end this discussion about the 'production bias' by giving the last word to Akhter Hameed Khan, who is the right person to put the problem in its proper historical perspective:

> There was always plenty of optimism. Every year the government promised self-sufficiency within two years. After every crisis a final solution was announced with great fanfare. Between 1950 and 1960 these solutions ranged between the technological and the sociological. The technological solution emphasised immediate improvement of agriculture. The sociological solution emphasised community organisation. The technologist's panacea was the crash programme. Secretly the proponents despised each other. . . . The infighting never ceased till technology overpowered sociology . . .
>
> My old eyes have seen many crash programmes. When crisis caused anxiety, the boss demanded a permanent solution from the officers. If the officers hesitated, the democratic boss cajoled, the dictatorial boss blustered. In any case the underlings understood the steely look. Immediately the highest targets in the shortest time were fixed. If anyone urged realism, he has pushed aside. Pliant tools were always available. Working far into the night, the frantic officers compiled a spectacular plan. It was hugely publicised forthwith. Quickly the mood of anxiety changed into exhilaration. Ministers inaugurated 'Days' and 'Weeks'. The deputy commissioner and his minions summoned meetings without number. The determination to surpass the targets was declared again and again. Constant repetition worked like auto-suggestion. The boss came to believe that he was actually achieving what he was announcing. The future tense became the present tense. 'We will do it' became 'We are doing it'. Then euphoria erased all difference between the past, present, or future. The boss claimed, 'We have done it.' Small advances were magnified into great victories. Eager workers, mindful of the boss, sent glowing reports, out of which fantastic statistics were compiled. Jubilantly the crisis was declared dead forever. But like Shelley's cloud, it refused to die. It rose again 'like a child from the womb, like a ghost from the tomb'. Afterwards the officers complained that, shortchanged on resources and time, they were assigned impossible tasks. They could not move mountains by faith. Crash programming was as specious as suggesting that a good

hiker can reach Everest in one day because it is only six miles high.[22]

References

1. L. Brown, 'Seeds of Change: The Green Revolution and Development in the 1970s', Overseas Development Council (London, 1970), p. 4.
2. H. Munthe-Kaas, 'Green and Red Revolutions', *Far Eastern Economic Review*, 19 March 1970.
3. E.M. Lappé and J. Collins, 'Food First: Beyond the Myth of Scarcity', Institute for Food and Development Policy (Boston, 1977), p. 119.
4. For a discussion of these and related issues in the context of Bangladesh, see for example various examples in the Bangladesh Rice Research Institute, 'Workship on Ten Years of Modern Rice and Wheat Cultivation in Bangladesh' (Dacca, 1977).
5. For convenient summaries of the characteristics of the new seeds, see K. Griffin, *The Political Economy of Agrarian Change* (London, Macmillan, 1974); William Bartsch, *Employment and Technology Choice in Asian Agriculture* (New York, Praeger, 1977); B.R.R.I., op. cit.; Agricultural Mission, *Selected Policy Issues* and Working Paper No. I; E.J. Clay, 'Institutional Change and Agricultural Wages in Bangladesh', *Bangladesh Development Studies*, Vol. 4, 1976; E.J. Clay, 'Environment, Technology and the Seasonal Patterns of Agricultural Employment in Bangladesh', draft, mimeo (Dacca, 1978); B.H. Farmer, *Green Revolution? Technology and Change in Rice Growing Areas of Tamil Nadu and Sri Lanka* (London, Macmillan, 1977); Lappé and Collins, op. cit.; I. Palmer, 'The New Rice in Asia: Conclusions from Four Country Studies', U.N.R.I.S.D. Report No. 76.6 (Geneva, 1976).
6. Agricultural Mission 1977, *Selected Policy Issues*, p. 8.
7. These aspects are further discussed in W.H. Bartsch, op. cit., p. 14ff; and B.R.R.I., op. cit., p. 101ff.
8. B.R.R.I., op. cit., p. 137; see also H. Brammer, 'Costs of Production, Profits and Returns for Paddy and Wheat Cultivation at the New (July 1976) Fertilizer Prices', Soil Survey Department (Dacca, July 1976) for a detailed analysis of input requirements for H.Y.V.s versus local varieties.
9. Keith Griffin, *The Political Economy of Agrarian Change* (London, Macmillan, 1974), pp. 206–7.
10. Lappé and Collins, op. cit., p. 140.
11. For an estimate of labour requirements per acre with different combinations of techniques of production and seed/fertilizer techniques, see Bartsch, op. cit., especially Chapter 2; see also Table 7.2 in this chapter.
12. Bartsch, op. cit., p. 61.
13. Agricultural Mission, op. cit., p. 67.
14. *Two-Year Plan, 1978–80*, p. 75.
15. Obaidullah A.Z. Khan, 'Rural Development in Bangladesh: Problems and Prospects', mimeo (Dacca, 1973), p. 8.
16. Many useful comments are made in the B.R.R.I. Workshops, op. cit.

17. Data given by the Minister of Agriculture, quoted in *The Bangladesh Times*, 2 July 1978.
18. A.H. Khan, 'Three Essays: Land Reform, Rural Works, and The Food Problem in Pakistan', Asian Studies Center, Michigan, 1973, p. 9.
19. E.J. Clay and S. Khan, 'Agricultural Employment and Underemployment in Bangladesh: The Next Decade', Working Paper, mimeo (Dacca), June 1977).
20. Agricultural Mission, op. cit., pp. 3-4.
21. Clay and Khan, op. cit., p. 36.
22. A.H. Khan, op. cit., p. 6.

8.   The Landlord Bias

Adding together pieces of information from the preceding chapters, we know that the overall economic policies in both East Pakistan and Bangladesh have had a consistent bias in favour of the better-off sections of the population. In Chapter 1, we observed that during the last two decades real wages for agricultural workers have declined and income distribution has become more unequal. In Chapter 3 we saw that the urban upper and middle classes have been, and still are, grossly over-represented within the political leadership at different national and local levels, and that it is also these classes that have benefited most from the economic policies pursued. In Chapter 5 we saw that the role of the state has, by and large, been to conserve the prevailing power structure, and that government institutions and officials tend to interact with, and give their support to, the wealthier strata of the rural population. The economic factors which favour capital rather than labour were discussed in Chapter 6; it was concluded that both the urban-rural and personal income differentials have been accentuated by the capital-biased policies implemented both before and after liberation. In Chapter 7, finally, we observed how successive governments' production-oriented agricultural strategies neglect goals of increasing employment and reducing inequality.

Virtually all aspects of economic policy analysed so far have been connected with the issue of equity. What remains to be illustrated more concretely is the income distribution effects of the Green Revolution strategy. After a description of who has benefited most from the new seed-fertilizer technology, I shall then indicate tentatively how the surplus that has been accumulated in the hands of the major beneficiaries has been invested. Finally, I will draw some preliminary conclusions about the effects of the 'landlord bias' on the two, partly inter-related, questions of resource utilization and level of effective demand.

The Green Revolution — Who Benefits?

With the introduction of H.Y.V., the income from land has been increased manifold. But due to absence of equitable distribution of this income, the gap between the poor and rich has widened further.

106

The difference in the ratio of income between a landowner and a landless labourer has increased significantly. Besides, the well-to-do farmers are getting richer without rendering any labour and are becoming owners of more land. On the other hand, the small farmers are gradually becoming even smaller and at a certain stage are rendered landless with no employment.[1]

It has been estimated that the entire increase in production of 1.4 million tons of rice between 1968–69 and 1967-77 was generated by a minority of 15% of all farmers in Bangladesh.[2] Since these farmers also enjoy the most advantageous cost conditions, the distribution of net profits has therefore been even more unequally distributed. This is hardly an unusual pattern in countries experiencing agricultural modernization. In Mexico, where the Green Revolution has perhaps run its fullest course in the Third World, the production increase has been concentrated in the hands of an even more limited number of farmers, while the opposite appears to be true in countries like Japan, Taiwan and China, where land reforms have preceded the introduction of the H.Y.V. technology and where institutions that have been able to spread the benefits better have been gradually developed.

The above examples[3] illustrate that the gains from the new seeds and modern techniques of production can be very differently distributed in different political and socio-economic environments. And this is also exactly what we should expect. The neutrality as regards economies of scale of most of the Green Revolution inputs makes it possible for big and small farmers alike to take advantage of the new technology – if, and only if, the institutions that provide the credit, seeds and necessary inputs are also 'neutral'. And this is not the case in Bangladesh.

There are many different institutions that should be considered in this context. The local power structure at the village level is of obvious importance. Who decides, for example, on whose land a deep tube-well should be installed? To answer this question, both the traditional 'patron-client' kind of informal relationship and the control over 'modern' institutions like co-operatives, pump groups, Union Councils, etc. would have to be considered. In order to simplify the exposition I will, however, concentrate on a few key factors which are the main determinants of the unequal access to modern inputs. In particular, I will emphasize the imperfections that characterize the markets for credit and inputs, remembering that these imperfections are only the economic expressions of other, more basic, political and socio-economic factors related to the entire power structure of the rural – and urban – society.

By far the most important market is the credit market. To illustrate its importance, I will begin with a few numerical examples showing how the availability of cheap credit is a decisive factor for the profitability of the new seed-fertilizer technology.

Let us first consider the case when the farmer meets all his cash outlays from his own savings; no direct interest payments are therefore involved. If this is the case, and the farmer in question is able to get all the necessary inputs at the official, subsidized prices, the H.Y.V. technology reduces costs of production considerably. A few conclusions drawn from a sample of farm management studies may be enough to make this point clear. The quotations and data presented below are quite randomly chosen, and the results differ only in size from other similar field studies,[4] but the same general tendencies stand out clearly in all estimates of this kind:

> The production cost of H.Y.V. *aman* [rice] is higher (*taka* 1,866) than that of local varieties (*taka* 1,581) per acre. On the other hand, per acre profit of H.Y.V. *aman* is much higher (*taka* 1,227) than local varieties (*taka* 297) because the grain yield of H.Y.V.s is 40.12 *maunds* per acre whereas local varieties yield only 23.6 *maunds* per acre. . . . Per *maund* cost of production of H.Y.V.s is lower (*taka* 46.5) than that of L.V.s (*taka* 67). The profit per *maund* of H.Y.V. paddy is *taka* 30.6 (including value of straw) at the rate of *taka* 74.50 (government procurement price) per *maund*. The benefit/cost ratio is 1.65 and 1.19 for H.Y.V.s and L.V.s respectively.[5]

Or:

> In general, the levels of different input applications per acre in the production of H.Y.V.s were significantly higher than those of L.V.s. The result of the analysis indicated that the farmers with H.Y.V.s incurred larger expenses per acre, and also obtained a greater amount of returns per acre than the farmers with L.V.s.[6]

The data given in this latter study show that the per *maund* costs of production were *taka* 40.5 and 33.8 for two different H.Y.V. crops and *taka* 46.7 and 57.5 for the local varieties studied. This confirms what we would expect, namely that while costs of production per acre increase appreciably with the new seeds, the costs of production per unit of output actually decline. A shift from local varieties to H.Y.V.s would thus appear to be very profitable. The results from these and other studies also indicate, however, that the fact that the H.Y.V.s require much higher expenses than the local varieties signifies that their profitability is very sensitive to changes in paddy prices and to changes in the prices of inputs, which tend to vary considerably between different categories of farmers.

A simple example will illustrate under what circumstances it is profitable to apply the H.Y.V. technology. In Table 8.1 costs and returns of H.Y.V.s and local varieties are compared when two factors are allowed to vary: the cost of credit and the price of paddy. The figures used are hypothetical, but not unrealistic.

The assumptions underlying Table 8.1 are, of course, highly simplified, the amounts of inputs applied, for example, being regarded here as independent of interest rates and expected prices of paddy, whereas a more realistic model

Table 8.1:
Per acre Costs[1] and Returns of H.Y.V.s and L.V.s under Different Interest Rates and Paddy Prices (in *taka*)

	High Yielding Varieties Loan Interest Rate				Local Varieties Loan Interest Rate			
	18%	*30%*	*50%*	*100%*	*18%*	*30%*	*50%*	*100%*
a) Input costs (amount borrowed)	1,000	1,000	1,000	1,000	250	250	250	250
b) Interest, 6 months	90	150	250	500	23	38	63	125
c) *Total to be paid*	*1,090*	*1,150*	*1,250*	*1,500*	*273*	*288*	*313*	*373*
d) Yield (*maunds* of paddy)	30	30	30	30	15	15	15	15
e) Marketable surplus (10 *maunds* used for family consumption)	20	20	20	20	5	5	5	5
f) Income from Sales at Different Prices of Paddy Received								
50 *taka* per *maund*	1,000	1,000	1,000	1,000	250	250	250	250
60 ″	1,200	1,200	1,200	1,200	300	300	300	300
70 ″	1,400	1,400	1,400	1,400	350	350	350	350
80 ″	1,600	1,600	1,600	1,600	400	400	400	400
90 ″	1,800	1,800	1,800	1,800	450	450	450	450
g) Profit/(Loss) after Payment of Input Costs and Interest at Different Paddy Prices (f minus c)								
50 *taka* per *maund*	(90)	(150)	(250)	(500)	(23)	(38)	(63)	(125)
60 ″	110	50	(50)	(300)	27	12	(13)	(75)
70 ″	310	250	150	(100)	77	62	37	(25)
80 ″	510	450	350	100	127	122	87	25
90 ″	710	650	550	300	177	172	137	75

1. Excluding family labour and other non-cash expenses.

would allow for adjustments in these respects. The selling price of H.Y.V. paddy should also be slightly below that of the local varieties. The amount of paddy reserved for own consumption can, furthermore, be assumed to be a function of prices rather than a fixed constant; a poor indebted farmer who incurs losses may respond by squeezing his own consumption in order to increase the share of total production that is marketed when paddy prices are low; other better-off farmers may behave in exactly the opposite way. The example could be modified to take these and other factors into account, the only inconvenience being that the calculations are cumbersome and the presentation of the results equally tedious.

It should also be stressed that the example refers to owner-cultivators. For sharecroppers, whose situation will be discussed later in this chapter, the cost situation is more disadvantageous; only under very special conditions will it be profitable for a pure tenant – who, in addition to having to pay the full costs of all inputs is in practice excluded from all sources of cheap credit – to invest in the H.Y.V. technology.

Let us now turn to a few interpretations of the results obtained in the calculations made above. The first observation that can be made is that the price of rice plays a crucial role. If the price is low, all farmers, whether they grow H.Y.V.s or local varieties, and whether they have access to cheap credit or not, will make losses. The conclusion that follows is, of course, that when paddy prices are expected to be low, all farmers try to limit their use of inputs, and the most unfortunate farmers paying usurious rates of interest, had better avoid all cash outlays and restrict themselves to the purchase of seeds only. This is not to say, of course, that below a certain price for rice the farmers should stop all cultivating in order to avoid losses; poor farmers always have to grow their crop to get something to eat. What the example illustrates is simply that, if rice prices are low, it does not pay for the farmers to buy additional inputs to increase the marketable surplus. At paddy prices of 50 *taka* per *maund* in our example, the cultivation of H.Y.V.s is disastrous, since losses on H.Y.V.s are bigger than for the local varieties at any given rate of interest. The earlier observations on the disincentive effects of low prices for foodgrains are thus further illustrated – unless demand and prices are satisfactory, no production-oriented strategy aiming at accelerating the spread of the H.Y.V. technology will succeed.

The importance of the rate of interest also emerges clearly. It is primarily those farmers with access to cheap credit who can afford to use the new technology (whether they actually do so is, however, a different question). The break-even point for a switch to H.Y.V.s is, in our example, a price of paddy of around 55 *taka* per *maund* if the rate of interest paid is 18%. If, on the other hand, the rate of interest is 100%, the price of paddy has to be 75 *taka* per *maund* to make the switch profitable.

Access to institutional credit tends to be closely related to access to subsidized inputs as well. This circumstance was not considered in the example above, but it is an issue which we have touched upon earlier and to which we will return in connection with the role of the co-operatives. There are innumerable studies, from Bangladesh and many other countries, that confirm this pattern: when inputs are sold at subsidized prices, it is normally the economically and politically dominant groups that have the easiest access both to cheap credit and to irrigation facilities, fertilizers, and extension services of all kinds. The uneven allocation of deep tube-wells is particularly well demonstrated in the Bangladeshi context. But it is primarily the *subsidies* that are unevenly distributed; in many cases, the irrigation is in fact relatively more frequent on small units than on big ones, because of the amount of family labour applied in traditional, labour-intensive methods of irrigation. The heavily subsidized tube-wells of the big farmers often have such a miserably low rate of utilization that the acreage actually irrigated is proportionately *lower* than among the small subsistence farmers getting no subsidies at all.

But it is not always possible to compensate for the limited access to modern, subsidized inputs by applying more family labour. Certain things just have to be purchased on the market in order to enable the farmers to take full advantage of the H.Y.V. technology. Even small farmers using traditional varieties usually have some unavoidable cash outlays; the vast majority of all smallholders do not, for example, possess their own work animals, which have to be hired from someone else.[7] And since the price of credit affects the costs of all such inputs, including hired labour, the rate of interest paid constitutes the most important single factor accounting for variations in the costs of production between different categories of farmers. Let us therefore turn to the evidence that exists about the availability and cost of credit in rural Bangladesh.

Credit

Historically, the credit needs of the rural population on the Indian Subcontinent have been met from non-institutional sources: professional money-lenders, friends and relatives, tradesmen, market intermediaries, etc. More recently, since the overthrow of the colonial yoke, institutional sources of borrowing have been developed, but their role has remained supplementary, and non-institutional sources are still dominant. Thus, in 1956 it was estimated that institutional sources accounted for only 4.9% of all agricultural credit in East Pakistan, a figure which rose to 13.9% ten years later.[8]

Today, the new seed-fertilizer technology and the accelerated spread of market relations in the countryside have greatly increased the peasantry's need for credit. Although there is no extensive or reliable data on the extent of agricultural lending in recent years, any rough assessment of costs of production and availability of institutional credit reveals the inadequacy of the newly created institutions for rural credit. Thus, total institutional credit to agriculture amounted, in 1975–76, to 466 million *taka* (see Table 8.2), which corresponds to less than 15 *taka* per acre i.e. barely enough to pay for two days of hired labour or to purchase one-fifteenth of the recommended fertilizer dose per acre of H.Y.V. land.[9] Under such circumstances, it is hardly surprising that there are very few farmers who come even close to using the recommended levels of fertilizer and other inputs, including hired labour. On the other hand, there are, of course, a class of big farmers who have enough liquidity to pay the costs of all inputs without having to incur debt at all, and when these farmers borrow from institutional sources, it is often for consumption or for speculative rather than productive purposes: money-lending at exorbitant rates of interest, land purchases, etc.[10]

Of the total agricultural credit from institutional sources in 1975–76, the Bangladesh Krishi Bank accounted for almost 40%, and the commercial banks for another 27%. The co-operative banks, which in theory are supposed to benefit the small and medium-sized farmers, provided less than 10% of the total. The interest rates from these sources vary between 11% and 17.5%; they are all subsidized by the state. The exact number of persons benefiting

Table 8.2:
Agricultural Loans Granted by Institutional Lenders, 1975–76

	Target	Actual Dis-bursements	% of Total Disbursements
	(millions of taka)	*(millions of taka)*	
Bangladesh Krishi Bank	200	185	39.8
Bangladesh Jatiya Sama-baya Bank (B.J.S.B.)	340	106	22.8
I.R.D.P. (co-operatives)	205	45	9.7
Commercial Banks	90	129	27.7
Total	*835*	*466*	*100.0*

Source: Agricultural Mission 1977, *Agricultural Credit*, p. 5.

from this cheap credit is not known, but the Bangladesh Krishi Bank and
I.R.D.P. were officially granting loans to 67,000 and 231,000 farmers,
respectively. The average size of the loans was, in 1975–76, *taka* 2,700 and
200, respectively. If we somewhat generously assume that the B.J.S.B. and
the Commercial Banks, which all have weak financial structures, little capital
and few deposits, reached 50,000 farmers each, the total number of beneficiaries from institutional credit would be in the range of 400,000, or some
3.5% of the 12 million rural households in Bangladesh.

There are many reasons why the poor are excluded from these sources of
credit. The first restriction is that land ownership is a prerequisite for
agricultural credit; the landless or near landless, i.e. the majority of the rural
population, are thus automatically left out, even from the I.R.D.P. co-
operatives. In practice, literacy is another condition since few small farmers
are able to complete the necessary forms and documentation for getting a
loan. Influential friends are also important in dealing with bank officials,
co-operative leaders, etc. On top of this, all lending institutions are obliged
to meet some security requirements, which favour the wealthy and secure
(who, incidentally, are the biggest defaulters) at the expense of the poor and
insecure.

The income distribution effects of the instititional credit market are thus
similar to the effects of the food ration system: the higher one's income, the
less one pays for the food; similarly, the more wealthy one is, the easier it
is to get subsidized loans. And, we might add, the higher the income, the
lower the percentage of the credit actually used for productive purposes. It
has thus been found that the larger farmers in Bangladesh tend to use an
appreciably smaller proportion of their borrowed capital for improving
production than the smaller ones, and relatively more for speculative
purposes.

As a response to the disastrous credit situation confronting the vast
majority of the rural population, an ambitious and much publicized '100

crore credit programme' was launched in 1977 as a 'crash programme' with the rural poor as its target. If actually implemented, it would have more than doubled the entire volume of rural credit. The rate of interest was set to 12%. But the entire programme failed and according to one evaluation, for three main reasons:

> First, the main intended beneficiaries, the poor and marginal farmers, have not benefited. To quote an official report, 'the share of small farmers in the credit so far disbursed under the special agricultural credit programme is quite negligible and the main beneficiaries are farmers ploughing 3–9 acres of land . . . .' Second, there is a wide apprehension which, in the face of current operational practices, seems to be well founded, that, as usual, a large chunk of the credit disbursed under the programme has not been invested in productive purposes. Third, only 58 *crore taka* could be disbursed out of the 100 *crore*. . . . Against this disbursement, the rate of recovery was on average below 40% with one exception to a commercial bank with 49%.[11]

A U.S.A.I.D. study observes that the 100 *crore* programme only reaches the top 20% of all farmers, and during its initial stages these farmers evidently used the available credit for unproductive purposes.[12] The programme has now been suspended, leaving over 90% of the rural population still relying on non-institutional sources of credit, where the rate of interest often ranges between 50 and 300%. Loans from friends and relatives are cheaper, of course, but not necessarily simpler: they are often to be regarded as a kind of insurance scheme in which the credit provided today sets up an obligation to reciprocate in the future.[13]

Recalling the estimates in Table 8.1 of the costs and returns on the use of H.Y.V.s, we can now conclude that the present structure of the rural credit market prevents most small farmers from undertaking the necessary investments in the new technology. Unless cheap credit is provided on a massive scale — or the income and liquidity situation is so miraculously improved that the rural poor can free themselves from the clutches of the moneylenders — it will be impossible to spread the 'miracle seeds' to a significant proportion of farmers.

The high rates of interest prevailing outside the institutional sources affect the relative profitability of agricultural investments in two basic ways. First, the interest paid enters as a cost item in the borrower's budget, thereby reducing both his willingness and ability to invest. Secondly, moneylending as itself an alternative way of supporting oneself enters into the opportunity cost calculations of those peasants with surplus cash; the possibility of earning 150% or more on usury reduces, not the ability, but certainly the willingness of the rural rich to invest their money productively. Looking at the numerical examples given in Table 8.1, we observe that it is only when paddy prices are very high that a farmer comes even close to an equally high rate of profit on capital invested in H.Y.V.s and modern inputs. This point converges with what we found in Chapter 6 about the government's attempts to raise the profitability of large-scale industry: the more lucrative the alternative investment opportunities are, the more difficult it becomes to induce the rural elite to invest in food production.

The high incidence of usury in rural Bangladesh thus acts as a serious obstacle to agricultural growth by making both big and small farmers reluctant to undertake productive investments. The speculative element is omnipresent, and it is also very much reflected in the attempts by the rural (and, increasingly, urban) rich to get hold of the marginal farmers' lands. Or, in the words of a report on the rural market for credit in Bangladesh:

> Borrowing from non-institutional sources is either in cash or in kind, as is repayment. The interest rate of non-monetary loans could be 350–400%. In some cases it is even higher. Quite often the poor farmer loses his land because of his inability to repay the principal and the interest. As a U.S.A.I.D. study observes: 'Whatever the rate of interest, the main objective of landowners making loans of this kind is to acquire land, since the value of land — approximately *taka* 10,000 to 15,000 per acre — is far more significant to him than the returns in the form of interest.[14]

The informal rural credit market also serves other purposes for the creditors. A recent study[15] challenging the thesis that usury plays a predominant role in the relations between big farmers and the rural poor, argues convincingly that, although it is true that interest rates are often very high, and that some credit is advanced for purposes of land appropriation, a large amount of credit is in fact made available on relatively favourable terms in order to ensure the reproduction and supply of the debtors' labour power, and to maintain cohesion among the creditors' kin and local political factions.

Risk
The element of risk is not to be underestimated. With respect to the H.Y.V.s it has already been noted that these seeds are more delicate than the local varieties, more susceptible to disease, more sensitive to adverse climatic and hydrological conditions, etc. But even under perfectly 'normal' conditions, it has often been observed that there are much greater variations — between different farmers and between different years — in yields per acre of the H.Y.V.s. All these factors reduce the attractiveness of the new seeds in the eyes of small farmers, many of whom have learnt too late how dangerous the use of the new technology can be. As observed by the 1977 Agricultural Mission, the Green Revolution has created many new landless families:

> The irony is that the government's own programme of agricultural and rural development is tending to accentuate this process of dispossession

of the poorer farmers. First, the new technology combined with share-tenancy and the risks of farming make them more vulnerable to total indebtedness and forced sale of land. The government's liberal doses of credit and input subsidies to elicit the adoption of the higher-cost inputs have been syphoned off by the big landlords, who retail them out at higher interest/rentals to the smaller farmers, resulting in their further indebtedness and ultimately to the forced sale of their land. . . . If the poor farmer or tenant is to retain his land under such a system, he had better steer clear of the high cost of the new technologies.[16]

The supposed neutrality in terms of economies of scale of the Green Revolution clearly is highly dependent on a number of factors. In practice, the high risks associated with the H.Y.V.s, plus the unequal access to credit and modern inputs and the non-neutral character of government policies and institutions, are the main factors responsible for offsetting the 'technical' scale-neutrality and instead giving the H.Y.V. strategy a consistent bias in favour of the larger (and richer) farmers. This does not necessarily mean, however, that it is actually the big farmers, and they alone, who invest in the H.Y.V. technology. What it does mean is that when the big farmers do make such investment, they are able to do so on more advantageous terms than the less privileged sectors of the peasantry. This distinction is important. Big farmers are notoriously poor investors; productive investment as a percentage of surplus has been found to fall quite sharply with increasing farm size,[17] and the few studies that exist in Bangladesh about the rate of adoption of the new seeds indicate that it has rather been the middle-sized surplus farmers who have been the earliest adopters, while both the small marginal farmers and the very big ones lag appreciably behind.[18]

The poor performance of the big farmers is also illustrated by the inverse relationship that exists between farm size and land productivity Above a certain minimum farm size, yields per acre tend to decline, to become lowest on the very big farms, where neglect of productive investment and under-utilization of the soil are salient features. Average cropping intensity is also much higher on the small- and medium-sized farms than on the big ones. Indeed most findings from Third World countries confirm this pattern of land productivity. Table 8.3 illustrates this pattern for Bangladesh. It shows that the middle-sized peasants come out at the top, followed by the smallest units, while the biggest farmers have the lowest yields of all. This is also consistent with the main results from Mahabub Hossain's studies, which show that land productivity tends to be highest in the 2.5 to 5.0 acre size group, and then begins to decline quite drastically. Similar evidence is reported by S.A. Mandal, whose data indicate that yields go down on farms larger than approximately 4.0 acres.[20]

Bearing in mind the implications of the market imperfections discussed earlier, it should also be observed that the large farmers, with low capital costs, use relatively more material inputs and less labour than the smaller

Table 8.3:
Paddy Yields of Farms of Varying Sizes, Bogra District.

Category of Farmers (acres)	Average Yields Per Acre (maunds of paddy)
Small (0.01–2.00)	18.2
Viable (2.01–4.00)	19.6
Bigger (4.01–6.00)	17.8
Very big (6.01 and above)	12.0

Source: Md. Mustafizur Rahman, 'Land Distribution: Its Impact on Rural Development', *The Bangladesh Times*, 3 March 1978. Cf. also Mahabub Hossain (1974, 1977, 1978) who has provided a wealth of data confirming the tendency depicted in Table 8.3.

farmers. In a labour-surplus and capital-scarce country like Bangladesh, this signifies another form of misallocation and wastage of resources. It is reasonable to assume that the small, 'traditional' farmers come closer than the large ones to using human and capital resources in socially optimal proportions.[21] Figure 8.1 shows how the use of labour and material inputs tends to change with the size of the farm. It reveals the fact that the combination of capital and labour is quite different for different categories of farmers (if we use the measure 'per unit of output' instead of 'per acre', the differences would be even more striking). The small farmers without access to institutional credit compensate by using more labour (in general family labour, which does not involve any cash outlays), while the big farmer prefer, when there is a choice, material inputs to hired labour (which, though cheap, is not subsidized). Formulated in this way, it is easy to see that the 'landlord bias' in the present production-oriented Green Revolution strategy not only increases inequality but also leads to a less efficient use of resources than an alternative, 'small-farmer biased' promotion of the H.Y.V. technology. Another implication of the relationship depicted in Figure 8.1 is that a land reform which split up the largest holdings would have a positive impact on output, and an even greater impact on employment. (This is not to suggest, however, that such a land reform based on an equitable distribution of all land into petty subsistence holdings would offer a long-term solution for the peasantry and the country — it certainly would not).

So far, I have only considered the distribution of gains between different categories of farmers, using the admittedly vague distinction between 'small' 'medium-sized' and 'big' farmers. But, the title of this chapter notwithstanding, the groups that appear to have benefited most from the Green Revolution are not really landlords in the traditional sense — who hardly exist at all in Bangladesh where virtually all farmers are small by international standards. Rather it is the middle farmers, owning from three to eight acres of land, who have been most eager to take advantage of the H.Y.V.

Figure 8.1:
Relation between Farm Size, Yield, Employment and Material Inputs per Acre.

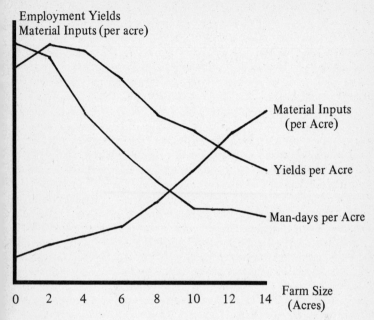

Employment Yields
Material Inputs (per acre)

Material Inputs (per Acre)

Yields per Acre

Man-days per Acre

0 2 4 6 8 10 12 14 Farm Size (Acres)

technology. This fact may seem to contradict the theoretical arguments about the 'landlord bias' presented earlier, but it can best be explained by reference to different behaviour patterns of, on the one hand, cost- and price-conscious, innovating middle farmers and, on the other, the largest, 'semi-feudal' landlords more interested in moneylending and similar activities. The evidence in this respect is not clear-cut, however, and in the present process of transition, such differences in behaviour may very well tend to level out.

Sharecropping and the New Technology

Even those small farmers who own around one acre of land, and for whom the application of modern seeds and inputs is a costly and risky business, are a comparatively privileged group in land-scarce Bangladesh. What remains to be discussed further are the implications of the Green Revolution for the 60% or so of the rural population who own no land at all, or less than one acre, i.e. the tenants and agricultural workers. Since the tenancy system is seen as an important institutional constraint on agricultural growth in Bangladesh, it should be examined separately from the general question of the effects of H.Y.V. technology on income distribution. Indeed there is a long tradition of neo-classical and Marxist argument linking the high incidence of share-cropping with agricultural stagnation. It will not be possible for us to do justice to the heated debate that has been proceeding for over two centuries.

The neo-classical approach, as systematized by Alfred Marshall and whose basic ideas date as far back as Adam Smith's discussions about the *metayer* system, usually argues that the use of agricultural inputs, and hence production, will be less than optimal under a system of share-tenancy. The main reason is that a profit-maximizing tenant will only produce up to that point where his own share of the marginal revenue will equal the marginal costs of production, which are assumed to be borne entirely by the tenant. If the tenant is a risk-minimizer, as is sometimes assumed, he is likely to produce even less. A profit-maximizing owner-cultivator, on the other hand, will apply the optimal amount of inputs since he will increase production until marginal costs and marginal revenue are equal to each other.[22] Similar arguments are applied to long-term investment, but here the case against sharecropping is even stronger: the tenurial insecurity that exists in most countries where sharecropping arrangements prevail makes a profit-maximizing tenant, who runs the danger of being evicted any time, extremely unlikely to undertake any such investments whatsoever. The disincentive effects are also present if the landowner assumes the costs of agricultural inputs, since he will then have to share the incremental output with the tenant; if the landowner does invest, it normally pays to evict the tenants and replace them with wage labourers.

In the Marxian tradition, sharecropping is often, but not always, depicted as a 'semi-feudal' remnant of a stagnant mode of production which is incompatible with agricultural growth. The role of usury capital in regions where 'semi-feudal' tenancy institutions dominate is frequently mentioned as a fetter on the growth of the productive forces. In the extreme versions of this approach, it is even asserted that the supremacy of usury capital as a form of exploitation tends to make the landlords not only uninterested in, but directly opposed to, agricultural innovation, the reason being that the heavily indebted tenants may become more independent of their creditors if they manage to raise output and incomes. In such a situation, the landlords may lose more in lost gains on usury than they gain by sharing the increase in production with the tenant.[23]

In Bangladesh between one-quarter and one-fifth of all agricultural land is estimated to be cultivated on a sharecropping basis. According to the Land Occupancy Surveys of 1977 and 1978, between 35 and 40% of all farm households are either pure tenants or part owners and part tenants. The extent of sharecropping differs widely between different regions, but it exists in all parts of the country. In one comprehensive study, it was found that almost two-thirds of all farms were involved in tenancy one way or the other — 14% as rentiers and about 50% as renters.[24] Sharecropping is not a marginal phenomenon in rural Bangladesh.

The average size of a parcel of land under tenancy is small — less than one acre. Most landowners renting out land have several tenants cultivating different plots of land. The majority of all tenants are also small landowners themselves, since totally landless workers usually lack the necessary draught animals, plough, tools, etc. to be accepted as tenants. Pure tenancy is often restricted to members of the same kinship group; the widespread existence of patron-client relationships within the same factions or kin groups makes hiring out of land — often on a long-term basis, in exchange for long-term loyalty — a rather common practice.[25] Apart from this, tenurial relationships are normally fluid and insecure, based on oral agreements; two-thirds of all tenants do not cultivate the same plot for more than three consecutive years.[26] This high rate of turnover of sharecroppers is partly explained by the fact that quite a few medium-sized farmers also rent land now and then for short periods. Presumably this is a response to emergency, e.g. in years following bad harvests, or when they have to meet some special obligations (marriages, etc.). For owners of very small holdings, the stability of the tenancy relationship is more important, but often difficult to achieve.

The terms of the tenancy relationship are utterly unfavourable to the tenant so that the average tenant hardly gets more, and sometimes even less, return on his labour than he would get alternatively by selling his labour power on the market at the prevailing wage rate.[27] According to the Land Occupancy Survey of 1978, the landowner takes 50% of the gross product in 93% of cases, and more than 50% in another 5% of cases. The tenant normally bears the full costs of production, and has to provide all agricultural implements himself. Since institutional sources of credit only accept land (or political influence) as collateral, it is virtually unavailable to sharecroppers, particularly pure tenants.

Under such circumstances, one should not expect tenants to be agricultural innovators. Even for the landowning peasant, who is entitled to 100% of his harvest, the H.Y.V. technology is, as we have seen, an undertaking which makes economic sense only when interest rates are low and/or paddy prices are high, and which may lead to disaster if the harvest fails. It takes a brave tenant to invest in H.Y.V.s. However, only some of the negative effects of sharecropping seem to be confirmed by the available empirical evidence. In Mandal's important study, the use of labour and other variable inputs was, as expected, significantly higher for the part owner part tenant on the land he owned himself.[28] Atiqur Rahman concluded, on the other hand, that the conventional arguments about the disincentive effects of sharecropping on agricultural investment were not, or only very partially, supported by his data.[29] Mahabub Hossain, also, has not been able to establish any significant difference in productivity between pure tenants and owner-cultivators, although his findings do show that the part owners part tenants do cultivate the hired land less intensively than their own fields.[30]

Such studies indicate that the situation is not as clear-cut as orthodox economic theory would suggest: neither do they lend much support to the hypothesis that usury capital is the dominant form of exploitation of tenants by landowners (although the phenomenon certainly exists). What they do show very convincingly is simply that productivity tends to be extremely low on all kinds of land. It is certainly true that owned land is cultivated more intensively (mainly due to a higher application of labour) than land rented *by the same cultivator*. The fact that *overall* land productivity does not appear to be significantly lower on land under tenancy is probably – but this remains a hypothesis – to some extent explained by the fact that part owners part tenants have comparatively better access to work animals and agricultural implements than do small farmers who do not rent in any land. The insecurity of the tenancy relationships also sets a lower limit to the productivity of the land that is rented; if a tenant does not produce the customary amounts of grain, he is simply evicted. The sharecropping system has, finally, some practical advantages over wage labour on large, but highly fragmented, holdings where problems of management and supervision reduce the profitability of 'capitalist' farming.

Considering the effects of share-tenancy on innovation and growth, there is some evidence that the landlords are quite aware of the disincentive aspects of share-tenancy. A new pattern in the landlord-tenant relationship seems to be emerging: in order to make the sharecroppers adopt the H.Y.V. technology, the landlords are slowly beginning to accept a rental arrangement involving a partial cost-sharing. Sometimes this cost-sharing simply assumes the form of a credit – the landowner provides all inputs, except labour, but deducts his costs from the gross harvest before output is shared. The tenant's risks are thereby reduced, but certainly not eliminated. In one study it was found that, in the case of irrigated crops, the costs of fertilizer and irrigation were generally shared equally, while in the case of non-irrigated crops, these costs were, in accordance with tradition, borne entirely by the tenant.[31] Similar observations, from different parts of the country, have been reported by M.R. Zaman, Hossain and Mandal.[32] The 'progressive' landlords who attempt to encourage investment in this way – and who, it should be recalled, constitute but a small minority of all Bangladeshi landlords – are thus behaving in a textbook way to reduce the negative effects of share-tenancy. The result of these new rental arrangements is, of course, an improvement in efficiency on rented land.

> It is interesting to note that while under traditional 'without cost-sharing' cases, significant differences in resource use and land productivity still exist between owned land and rented land, the difference narrows down in cases where partial cost-sharing for seed, fertilizer and irrigation was practised.[33]

Another tendency, which also conforms to the expected type of behaviour, is that tenants are often evicted and replaced by hired labour. A common effect of the sinking of a deep tube-well is that sharecroppers who worked the land before it was irrigated are evicted. With modern irrigation 'it is regarded as more beneficial to organize production on irrigated land with wage labourers, even if the sharecroppers would be willing to accept as little as 25% instead of the normal 50% of the crop.'[34] However, a major factor working against this tendency is the extremely high degree of fragmentation of farms; hence a land reform aiming at the consolidation of landholdings — which many people in Bangladesh advocate — would act as a strong incentive to replace tenancy with more modern forms of exploitation.

It is still too early to tell whether the sharecropping institution will be able to adapt itself to the new techniques of production. The spread of cost-sharing practices with the advent of the H.Y.V. technology may give share-tenancy a certain flexibility which increases its chances of survival in a changing environment; even an accelerated penetration of the agricultural sector by transnational agribusiness corporations may prove to be compatible, in Bangladesh as elsewhere, with modified forms of sharecropping relationships. Up until now, the percentage of the total acreage in Bangladesh under share-tenancy has remained relatively constant during the past two decades,[35] which indicates that there are factors — such as the rising share of land owned by absentee owners, who almost always rent out their land — that have counteracted the factors tending to erode the traditional share-cropping system.

The one thing that can be said with some degree of certainty is that the process of agricultural modernization that is slowly taking place will make it possible for the landowners to increase their share of total agricultural income. Unless share-terms for tenants are improved the income disparities between owners and tenants can only widen further with the use of H.Y.V. technology. Such an improvement in share-terms seems exceedingly unlikely, in view of the intense competition for land: the large and growing pool of landless workers exerts a downward pressure not only on agricultural wages, but on share-terms as well. We have already discussed the deteriorating employment situation of the rural poor at some length in preceding chapters; a few additional comments may be useful.

Wages and Employment

The employment elasticity of foodgrain production in Bangladesh indicated a decrease in the number of working-days required per unit of output with a shift to the H.Y.V. technology. If real wages are constant or falling, this automatically results in a decline in the share of output going to labour, and this is confirmed by farm management studies showing how labour benefits from the Green Revolution. Thus, from Hugh Brammer's data,[36] it can be inferred that the landowner's share in relation to that of the workers increases from a ratio of 2.4 to 1 for traditional varieties to 3.5 to 1 for H.Y.V.s.[36] In another study it was found that while the gross value of production increased by 100% per acre with a shift to H.Y.V. *aus*, total payments to labour increased by only 31%.[37] The numerical examples presented earlier in this chapter also illustrate that it is never the workers who benefit: if interest rates are high, the moneylenders gain the most; if they are low, it is the landowners.

In a balanced growth strategy, with both big and small farmers investing in agricultural production and where any tendency to a decline in crop employment was offset by a rise in demand for labour in other activities, it would be possible to take full advantage of the H.Y.V. potentials without impairing the workers' situation. Under such circumstances, the fall in labour requirements per unit of output would be matched by an increase in effective demand for foodgrains and for non-agricultural products, producing an over-all rise in wages. This has not been the case in Bangladesh where, on the contrary, rural unemployment has increased and institutional changes in the labour market[38] have depressed agricultural wages beyond the effects of the rise in unemployment. Hence, the decline in labour-intensity in additional foodgrain production is likely to aggravate the situation of labour more and more. The Green Revolution in Bangladesh has been much more effective in reducing average costs per unit of output for a minority of farmers than in increasing the overall level of production. The 'vicious circle' described by Erich Jacoby is frighteningly relevant in the case of Bangladesh:

> It is obvious that the increase in rural unemployment, which is not balanced by additional employment possibilities in urban areas, will have serious repercussions on the domestic market and price develop-ments. The multiplied supply of marketable food crops will be met by a declining effective demand for food due to the rising unemployment. This will cause declining food prices which ultimately will further impair the rural labour situation: on the one hand, the large producers will try to defend their profits by reducing labour costs through an increased use of modern farm machinery and often even by cutting down the actual area under cultivation; on the other, the small farmers, who cannot afford to rationalize, will be forced to market their surplus at prices which will reduce their main source of cash income, with the result that in the end they may have to sell their land cheaply and join the ranks of the unemployed.
>
> The vicious circle of unemployment, declining food prices and new unemployment must inevitably lead to a deterioration of the social stratification in the rural areas.[39]

Concluding Remarks

What is needed in Bangladesh, and indeed in most other countries, is a growth-plus-equity strategy. The present 'landlord bias' in agricultural policies mili-tates not only against justice, but against production as well. It does so in two basic ways: (1) By favouring larger farmers, whose utilization of land, labour and capital is less efficient from a social point of view than that of the smaller peasants, resources are wasted and both production and employment suffer; (2) By accentuating polarization and pauperization in the countryside, and hence reducing labour's share of output; real wages and effective demand for foodgrains lag behind, food prices are depressed, profitability in agriculture is deteriorating vis-à-vis other activities and, again, both production and employment suffer.

The achievement of the Green Revolution in Bangladesh is little more than a marginal increase in the use of the H.Y.V. technology accompanied by increases in yields per acre on the privileged units and declines in average yields on the remainder of the soils. A minority of richer farmers – though not necessarily 'landlords' in the traditional sense – have been the main beneficiaries; their costs of production have declined, while their share of total production – and, in particular, of the marketable surplus – has increased. The spread of the H.Y.V. technology has thus played a role similar to that of food imports: it has contributed to cheapening food consumption, which the urban population in particular has appreciated, while actually aggravating the position of the small and marginal producers. And this may, in the final analysis, be the main effect of any strategy for agricultural modernization which is not concerned with equity. To put this strategy in a broader perspective, I will conclude this chapter by giving the last word to Keith Griffin, who in fact coined the expression 'landlord bias':

> The introduction of high-yielding varieties of foodgrains . . . has enabled the marketable surplus to be increased, and the resource transfer [from agriculture] to continue, at a negligible cost in terms of investment in rural areas. The significance of the 'green revolution' is not so much that it has resulted in an improved livelihood in rural areas (although certain groups clearly have prospered) as that it has allowed governments to persist with industrial policies which had taken many nations to the brink of the catastrophe. . . .
>
> Given the needs of urban areas for cheap and abundant wage goods and for a continuation of the subsidy to industry from agriculture, the best things that could have happened, did happen: the 'green revolution' strengthened those in the countryside who were the natural allies of the urban ruling groups and it enabled these ruling groups to perpetuate the status quo essentially unchanged.[40]

References

1. Phani Bhusan Majumdar, Minister for Local Government, Rural Development and Co-operatives in 1975, quoted in Bangladesh Academy of Rural Development (B.A.R.D.), 'Socio-economic Implications of Introducing H.Y.V. in Bangladesh', Proceedings of the International Seminar (Comilla, November 1975), p. 9.
2. Agricultural Mission, Working Paper No. II, 1977, p. 2.

3.   There is an abundant literature analysing the interaction between technical change and output, income distribution and employment.

4.   H. Brammer, 'Costs of Production, Profits and Returns for Paddy and Wheat Cultivation at the New (July 1975) Fertilizer Prices', mimeo, Soil Survey Department (Dacca, July 1976); N.U. Ahmed, 'Cost of Paddy Production of Aus Paddy and Jute Cultivation per Acre', U.S.A. I.D. (Dacca, August 1976).

5.   Md. Shajahan, 'Cost and Return of Aman Cultivation 1976', mimeo, B.A.R.D. (Comilla, July 1977), p. 20.

6.   S. Murshed et al., 'Production of High-yielding and Local Varieties of Aman Paddy in Mymensingh', mimeo, Department of Agricultural Economics, B.A.U., Mymensingh, 1976, p. 20.

7.   When animals are hired, one commonly has to pay for the services of not only the animals but of the owner, who does the ploughing.

8.   M. Asaduzzaman and M. Hossain, 'Some Aspects of Agricultural Credit in Two Irrigated Areas of Bangladesh', B.I.D.S., Research Report Series, No. 18 (Dacca, 1974), p. 10.

9.   Based on the following doses and prices:

Urea: 2 *maunds*/acre at 60 *taka/maund*	=	120
Triple Superphosphate: 1½ *maunds*/acre, 48 *taka/maund*	=	72
Muriate of Potash: ¾ *maunds*/acre, 40 *taka/maund*	=	30
Total taka		*222*

10.   See for example, M. Mandal, 'An Economic Analysis of Resource Use with respect to Farm Size and Tenure in an Area of Bangladesh', unpublished dissertation, Wye College, University of London, August 1979; and Atiur Rahman, 'Rural Power Structure: A Study of the Union Parishad Leaders in Bangladesh', *The Journal of Social Studies*, Vol. 4, 1979. Mandal (p. 177ff.) found that the bigger farmers used around 40% of total borrowed capital for buying up extra land.

11.   *Economic Times* (Dacca), 30 June 1978.

12.   U.S.A.I.D., 'The Poor Majority of Bangladesh', undated mimeo, Dacca, p. 23.

13.   For a discussion, see A. Rahman, 'Usury Capital and Credit Relations in Bangladesh Agriculture', B.I.D.S., mimeo, March 1980, p. 51ff.

14.   Bangladesh Rural Advancement Committee (B.R.A.C.), 'Proposal for Bangladesh Rural Credit Trust', Dacca, 1977, p. 7.

15.   See A. Rahman, 1980, op. cit.

16.   Agricultural Mission, 'Selected Policy Issues', mimeo, Dacca, 1977, pp. 72–3.

17.   See A. Rahman, 1979, op. cit., whose data reveal a startlingly low level of productive investment among big farmers.

18.   See, for example, Md. Asaduzzaman and F. Islam, 'Adoption of H.Y.V.s in Bangladesh', Research Report Series (new) No. 23, B.I.D.S. (Dacca, 1976); M. Muqtada, 'The Seed-Fertilizer Technology and Surplus Labour in Bangladesh Agriculture', *Bangladesh Development Studies*, Vol. 4, 1975; and Mandal, op. cit.

19.   For a recent, comprehensive survey covering a large number of countries, see A. Berry and W. Cline, *Agrarian Structure and Productivity in Developing Countries* (Baltimore/London, Johns Hopkins, 1979).

20. Mandal, op. cit. The negative size-productivity relationship is, however, weakened or even reversed, if only those farmers who have adopted H.Y.V. technology are considered. See A. Rahman, 1980, op. cit. for a discussion of the (scarce) data available from Bangladesh.

21. Keith Griffin, *The Political Economy of Agrarian Change* (London, Macmillan, 1974), p. 46ff.

22. The traditional theory has, however, been challenged both by empirical evidence, to which I will return, but also, at the theoretical level, by that particular branch of neo-classical economics called the Chicago School. According to this school, the very fact that the sharecropping institution is based on contractual agreements which are mutually agreed upon by both parties under competitive conditions makes the tenancy system optimal; if it were not, it would be profitable for one party (or for both) to abolish it. For an overview, and a critique, of the Chicago School's views of sharecropping, see F. Jannuzi and J. Peach, 'Bangladesh: A Profile of the Countryside', U.S.A.I.D., mimeo (Dacca, 1978).

23. For a sophisticated presentation of this theory, see A. Bhaduri, 'Agricultural Backwardness under Semi-feudalism', *The Economic Journal*, Vol. 83, No. 1, March 1973.

24. Mandal, 1979, op. cit.

25. This and the following paragraph are closely based on M. Hossain, 'Nature of Tenancy Markets in Bangladesh Agriculture', *The Journal of Social Studies*, No. 3, 1979.

26. Jannuzi and Peach, op. cit.

27. See calculations made by Hossain, 1980, op. cit.

28. Mandal, op. cit.

29. Rahman, 1979, op. cit.

30. M. Hossain, 1979, op. cit.; and 'Foodgrain Production in Bangladesh', B.I.D.S., mimeo (Dacca, March 1980).

31. M. Raquibuzzaman, 'Share-cropping and Economic Efficiency in Bangladesh', Research Report No. 2 (New Series), Institute of Development Studies, Dacca, 1972, mimeo.

32. M.R. Zaman, 'Share-cropping and Economic Efficiency in Bangladesh', *The Bangladesh Economic Review*, Vol. 1, No. 2, April 1973; Hossain, 1979, op. cit.; Mandal, 1979, op. cit.

33. Mandal, 1979, op. cit., p. 254.

34. E. Jansen, 'Choice of Irrigation Technology in Bangladesh', *The Journal of Social Studies*, Vol. 1, No. 5, 1979, p. 76.

35. For an overview of available evidence, see Jannuzi and Peach, op. cit., pp. 16ff.

36. Brammer, op. cit.

37. N.U. Ahmed, 'Cost of Production of Aus Paddy and Jute Cultivation per Acre', U.S.A.I.D. (Dacca, August 1976).

38. See E. Clay, 'Institutional Change and Agricultural Wages in Bangladesh', *Bangladesh Development Studies*, No. 4, 1976; and Chapter 1 above. A micro-perspective of the same tendencies is provided by J. Arens and J. van Beurden, *Poor Peasants and Women in a Village in Bangladesh* (Birmingham, Third World Publications, 1977). The following observation, which illustrates how the process under way is eroding

the old patron-client type of relationships, also shows how real wages may decline when the labour market assumes the characteristics of a *market*: 'As to labour, it is more and more exceptional that a labourer is employed because he and his employer are members of the same *bangsa* [kinship group]. We only know of a few such cases. Rich landowners are more inclined to select able-bodied, hard-working men to whom they have no other obligation than to pay their daily wages.' (p. 93). From the point of view of income distribution and security, the old system might have had some advantages.

39. E.H. Jacoby, 'Effects of the "Green Revolution" in South and South-east Asia', *Modern Asian Studies*, Vol. 6, No. 1, 1972, p. 260.
40. Griffin, op. cit., p. 128. He is not explicitly talking about Bangladesh in this passage.

9.   The Rice Bias

An Expensive Crop

'All agricultural and rural departments are now I.R.R.I. rice minded,'
observed René Dumont when he visited Bangladesh in 1973. 'All credit is
available for I.R.R.I. rice, H.Y.V., but nothing for other crops like vegetables,
fodder, and animal husbandry.' The high emphasis put on an acceleration of
the spread of H.Y.V. rice was severely criticized by Dumont, who argued that
the preservation of the semi-monopoly of rice was 'completely out of the
question', the main reason being that:

> With the amount of water needed for one acre of rice, you could irri-
> gate 3 acres of wheat, 4 or 5 acres of vegetables. Wheat gives 50% more
> protein than rice per *maund*. Young shoots of legumes give much
> more protein in less time, etc.[1]

Similar observations were made by the 1977 Agricultural Mission, which
advocated:

> the extraction of the maximum nutrition from the scarce land available
> This requires the cultivation of marginal ricelands with other crops with
> higher yields of calories and proteins per acre. One acre of sweet
> potatoes, for example, provides more than three times the calories and
> about twice the proteins that one acre of rice produces under present
> yield levels in Bangladesh. Its vines [leaves] further provide a source of
> vitamin A, in which this country is greatly deficient. In disaster-prone
> Bangladesh, it has an additional role to play as a famine-reserve and
> disaster-recovery crop. The same applies to sorghum. In the context
> of land scarcity and malnutrition, sorghum can be grown on marginal
> lands where paddy production is presently hazardous. In the present
> Bengali diet, the displacement of rice at the margin with more
> nutritious and less hazardous crops could have a considerable nutrit-
> ional impact. The obvious objection is that the consumer preference is
> for rice. But in times of hunger, the real choice is not between rice and
> sweet potatoes, but between sweet potatoes and hunger.[2]

The 'rice bias' in Bangladesh's agriculture is often explained by tastes and habits. And although it is true that people in Bangladesh prefer rice to any other foodgrain, it is also true that wheat has become much more acceptable in recent years, in particular in urban areas. And the fact that wheat, thanks to food aid and huge wheat imports, now accounts for over 10% of total foodgrain consumption but only 2% of production shows that the Bangladeshis are more willing to diversify their consumption that their production.

The heavy concentration on rice (see Table 9.1) is an old, controversial and complicated issue in Bangladesh. The purpose of this brief section is not to attempt to prescribe an 'optimal' mix of crops and crop rotations for Bangladesh — only to indicate the nature of the debate and to point out that there seem to exist vast, but largely untapped, potentials for a diversification of the virtual monoculture of rice that characterizes today's agriculture in Bangladesh.

Table 9.1:
Total Area of Major Crops, 1975–76 ('000 acres)

	Acreage
Rice	25,525
Jute	1,277
Oil Seeds	769
Pulses	754
Chillies, onions, garlics, minor spices	380
Wheat	371
Sugar cane	329
Tobacco	122
Tea	106

Source: Based on Bangladesh Bureau of Statistics, *Statistical Pocket Book of Bangladesh, 1978*

When considering the possibilities of diversifying food production, it must first of all be stressed that the issue under discussion is not the abandoning of rice in favour of some other crops; no one has suggested anything like that. Bangladesh's soils, climate and topographic conditions make the country eminently suited for paddy cultivation, and during the wet season, when jute is the only serious rival to rice, the supremacy of paddy is not likely to be threatened. The appeal for diversification is strongest during the dry season, when rice has a variety of good competitors. The choice is limited to marginal shifts, mainly between *boro* rice and other crops, a choice which involves minimal reallocations of land, labour, material inputs, research resources, etc. In many cases, it would not be necessary to reduce rice production at all; much land remains unutilized during part of the year, and it is therefore perfectly possible to expand the production of wheat, millet,

sorghum, potato, fruit and vegetables, etc. without having to encroach upon
the acreage available for rice.

As to the question of choice of alternative crops, it is clear that this
depends on a wide range of economic, nutritional, ecological, climatic and
other factors which vary substantially between different regions of Bangla-
desh.Opinions also differ between different observers and, since both tropical
and temperate crops can be grown in the country, it is not surprising that
there are a number of good substitutes for rice. Virtually all crops have their
defenders: René Dumont is, for example, an ardent advocate of sweet
potatoes (for their high nutritional value), of sorghum (for its drought-
resistance) and of legumes (for their nutritional qualities and short maturation period). The 1977 Agricultural Mission, in addition, suggests millet (for
its short maturation period and low water requirements), pulses (for their
high content of protein) and several others. Jute is often recommended for
its high employment potential — jute is appreciably more labour-intensive
than both rice and wheat — and for its role as Bangladesh's major earner of
foreign exchange. Fruit and vegetables have a strong case for their vitamin
content and export potential, while the cultivation of tobacco, cotton, oil
seeds and sugar can easily be defended on import substitution grounds.

Limiting ourselves to the winter (*boro*) crops, we should observe that all
the recommended alternatives to rice have one thing in common: they
require much less water per acre — and per unit of output — than rice. Lack
of irrigation is the major bottleneck during the dry season, so it would appear
to be sensible to economize on water by reducing the cultivation of *boro* rice.
Most of the foodgrains suggested are also superior to rice from a nutritional
point of view, and since their maturation periods are almost invariably
shorter, a substitution of other crops for rice would also enable the cropping
intensity to be raised even in areas where the availability of irrigation would
permit the growth of a crop of *boro* rice. To illustrate this logic, let us briefly
compare rice and its main competitor among the cereals, namely wheat.

An Example: Wheat and Rice

It is only under certain circumstances that wheat can be regarded as competitive with rice. Rice is absolutely superior to wheat under conditions of
flooding, when wheat cannot be grown at all. On the other hand, on upland
soils too permeable for a rice crop, wheat can be grown without competing
with rice, and during the winter season wheat, but not rice, can be grown
without irrigation on some soils with particularly high water retention
capacity. For these reasons, the example below is only relevant for the
choice between wheat and *boro* rice under irrigated conditions.

Yields: Average yields of rice and wheat in Bangladesh were, in 1976–77,
approximately the following (in *maunds* of wheat and paddy per acre):

Boro H.Y.V. Rice	All H.Y.V. Rice	H.Y.V. Wheat	Local Rice	Local Wheat
29.9	25.7	20.4	11.7	8.3

Since one *maund* of paddy provides only about two-thirds of a *maund* of rice, while the milling loss for wheat is less than 10%, the relevant yield results of rice and wheat are not too different from each other — as a rule of thumb, we could say that *boro* H.Y.V. rice gives perhaps 10% more than H.Y.V. wheat.

Water Requirements: On a per acre basis, wheat requires only about one-third of the amount of water needed for the cultivation of rice. Per unit of output, water requirements for wheat are somewhere between 35 and 50% of the corresponding rice figures.

Nutritional Value: H.Y.V. rice is nutritionally inferior to modern wheat, but not as inferior as René Dumont suggests. The protein content of the best new varieties of rice is still below that of wheat, but the difference has been reduced considerably.

Maturation Period: Wheat is distinctly superior to rice from this point of view. The maturation periods are 3.5–4 and 4.5–6 months respectively, which means that yield per acre and per month of cultivation — which should be the most relevant yield measure in land-scarce Bangladesh — is actually slightly higher for wheat. After harvesting the winter crop of wheat, the same land can be replanted with other crops, preferably broadcast *aman* or jute — this is not possible on land planted with *boro* rice. With wheat instead of rice during the dry season, the cropping intensity can thus be increased.

Risk: Wheat is appreciably less susceptible to pests than rice. The fact that wheat is generally harvested in March–April, before the cyclones and hailstorms have normally started, also means that wheat is a relatively disaster-free crop, although the rains may start too early, before the harvesting and threshing period is over; late November rains may also damage the recently planted wheat. Wheat is also much more drought-resistant than rice.

Storage: Wheat is more difficult to store than rice during the humid months. This is the most important 'technical' disadvantage of wheat; while milling losses are lower, storage losses are higher. As a result many farmers without access to good storage facilities of their own are forced to sell their wheat surplus almost immediately after the harvest, when prices are the lowest.

Costs: Wheat requires smaller doses than rice of all relevant inputs — water, fertilizers, pesticides, insecticides and human labour. Costs of production — per acre and per *maund* — are thus lower for wheat than for rice. In actual practice, the size of the cost differential is of course determined by both the amounts of inputs actually applied and by the prices paid for these inputs (and for credit).

In a numerical example used by Brammer,[3] a comparison was made between the costs of production of H.Y.V. *boro* rice and irrigated H.Y.V. wheat when the recommended doses of all inputs were applied and all farmers had equal access to cheap credit and subsidized inputs. According to these estimates, the per-acre costs of production were *taka* 2,208 for rice and *taka* 1,586 for wheat, figures which, by and large, are corroborated by other similar calculations.[4] If fewer inputs are used, the cost — and yield — differentials are levelled out, while they increase if the prices paid for obtaining credit and inputs are higher than the official, subsidized prices.

When subsidized inputs are purchased the social costs are appreciably higher than the private costs. One clear example of a misallocation of resources in favour of rice is the huge subsidies given to irrigation; the users pay, as we recall, only a small fraction of the total costs of tube-wells and large-scale irrigation schemes. Consequently the beneficiaries waste valuable water on *boro* rice when other, less water-consuming, crops would have been preferable from a social point of view.

Employment: The lower costs of production of wheat are not necessarily a blessing. Rice is a relatively labour-intensive crop and this does make it expensive to grow, but it also gives more employment than most alternative crops. Thus, while H.Y.V. *boro* rice grown under ideal conditions, i.e. with the best methods of cultivation and with the application of the recommended levels of all inputs, requires about 117 working days per acre, irrigated H.Y.V. wheat would only need 67 working-days.[5] Even if we adjust for the rise in cropping intensity made possible by the substitution of wheat for *boro* rice, overall employment in crop production is likely to decline with a shift from rice to wheat. Labour's share of total production costs also tends to be lower for wheat than for rice; according to Brammer's estimates, a daily wage rate of *taka* 7 would give labour a share of 36 and 49% of the total costs of production of wheat and rice respectively (labour's share of value of output is of course appreciably lower in both cases). From the point of view of employment and income distirbution, it would thus appear that rice is the superior crop.

Prices: In order to assess the profitability of different crops from the farmer's point of view, we also need to consider the prices received for the sale of the crops. And here, rice has its major advantage; despite its slightly higher food value, wheat will fetch a lower market price as long as the consumers prefer to eat rice. The price differential has varied considerably since the introduction of wheat in Bangladesh. As a rough estimate we could say that the price of wheat received by the producer has tended to be around two-thirds of the farmgate price of rice. It is, under the circumstances, perfectly understandable that most farmers prefer to grow rice when irrigated water is available and there is a choice between paddy and wheat. The rapid expansion of wheat cultivation during the 1970s has taken place mainly at the expense of other crops than rice.

Tentative Conclusions: There are few safe conclusions that can be drawn from the above, superficial analysis of the relative advantages of rice and wheat. I have simply listed a number of factors that should be taken into account when assessing the relative merits of the two crops under consideration, neglecting local variations in soils, rainfall, etc. and not pretending to provide any quantitative estimates of costs and benefits in private versus social terms. The conclusions are therefore admittedly vague, and can best be summarized in the following way: a) If nutrition values are to be maximized, wheat is preferable to rice; b) If output per acre is to be maximized, rice is slightly superior; c) If output per acre and per month of cultivation is to be maximized, wheat seems to yield the best result in view of its shorter maturation period; d) If output per unit of water during the dry season is to be maximized, wheat is definitely superior; e) If output in terms of gross value of production is to be maximized, rice will produce the most when there is plenty of water available; f) If farmers net profits are to be maximized, rice will probably give the highest profits per acre (but not per unit of invested capital) if the necessary credit and inputs are available at subsidized prices — if not, the disadvantage of wheat will disappear at some levels of interest rates and/or input prices; g) If employment is to be maximized, rice is the better crop even if adjustments are made for the higher cropping intensity made possible if wheat instead of rice is grown; h) If workers' total incomes are to be maximized, rice will normally be preferable; i) From the point of view of risk minimization, wheat is easily the best.

The successive governments' policy of cheap food imports have played a double role in relation to the price of rice and wheat. It is only thanks to the huge injections of mainly American wheat that wheat has become accepted at all by the Bengali consumers. But these imports have, while stimulating the consumption of wheat, also played a discriminatory role vis-á-vis the production of domestic wheat in Bangladesh. Wheat has accounted for some three-quarters of total food imports, including food aid, and a comparison between the ratio of domestic and import retail prices of rice and wheat respectively, seems to indicate that the food and price policies pursued in recent years have been relatively discriminatory against the producers of wheat. Thus, according to one study, 'the domestic-import price ratio of rice has remained consistently and substantially higher than the domestic-import price ratio of wheat. This would imply that government price policy has tended to depress wheat market prices more than the rice market price.'[6]

Other Crops

The example discussed above referred only to rice and wheat. Since *boro* rice and wheat are competitive with a large number of other crops such as sugar cane, tobacco, vegetables, potatoes, millet, sorghum, sweet potatoes, pulses, etc., the analysis should ideally be extended to cover these and other alternatives as well. Although I shall not undertake this here, it seems safe to assume that a diversification away from both rice and wheat could have a large and positive impact on, above all, the nutritional content of agricultural produce in Bangladesh. Rice is, as we know, a very uneconomical crop from this point of view, especially when water is scarce, and in a country where some four-fifths of the rural population are unable to meet their minimum food requirements, and where the per capita intake of both proteins and vitamins has been going down drastically, a prime goal for agricultural policies should be to stimulate the cultivation of cheap and nutritious food rather than to reinforce the existing rice bias. A system of high and stable procurement prices for such alternative crops — which, among other uses, could be distributed for relief purposes and stored as disaster reserves — is one possible way to encourage their production and consumption.

The major advantage of rice — besides its taste — is its labour-intensive character. There are, however, a variety of crops such as pulses, vegetables, etc. that require even more labour per acre of cultivation and which are preferable to both rice and wheat from a nutritional point of view. Much could also be achieved by encouraging the cultivation of these crops on homestead land – which now often lies idle – through, say, the provision of extension services and subsidized seeds and fertilizers. As it is today, virtually all research resources, extension services and subsidized inputs go on rice.

It should also be observed that an increased production of crops other than cereals would give rise to a higher derived demand for labour in small-scale food industry. In terms of linkage effects to the rest of the economy, both rice and wheat have quite limited potentials, and if agriculture in Bangladesh is to support a domestic food-processing industry of any importance in the future, diversification of agricultural production will be necessary.

The Role of Foreign Trade

So far in this chapter Bangladesh has been assumed to be a closed economy without any foreign trade. This is, of course, a gross over-simplification, and the existence of trade changes the relative superiority of different crops in important respects. Central to this foreign trade calculation is the possibility that Bangladesh could engage in what we might call a 'calorie bargain'.[7] One way to reduce the country's food deficit could be to export rice, which normally commands a high price on the world market, in exchange for cheaper cereals. For every ton of rice exported, Bangladesh could buy two tons of wheat or three tons of sorghum; in calorie and protein terms, the gains could be even larger (recent trends towards increased self-sufficiency in rice in several Asian countries, and mounting rice surpluses in Japan, may however, reduce the scope for rice exports).

A simple example illustrates the point. Suppose that the goal of self-sufficiency in foodgrains by 1985 requires an annual growth of domestic production of some 500,000 tons of grain, i.e. two and a half times the growth that has actually been registered during the last ten years. A nutrition-oriented trade policy would make the self-sufficiency goal appreciably less utopian, however, considering that a modest growth of rice production of 200,000 tons per year could be used to import 400,000 tons of wheat or 600,000 tons of sorghum. Jute, which is already exported, could naturally be used in the same way, although the semi-monopolistic position of Bangladesh on the world market for jute makes it difficult to expand production substantially without having to lower prices (which have already been quite depressed during most of the period since Independence).

Similar arguments have been put forward by, among others, the 1977 Agricultural Mission, which strongly advocated an exchange of rice for cheaper grains at the margin. 'Bangladesh,' writes the Mission, 'would then be exporting rice *not* because it is *surplus*, but because it is *deficit* in food grain.'[8] The fact that Bangladesh has a natural advantage in rice makes such trade attractive; almost a textbook case of Ricardo's old theory of comparative advantages. This still leaves unresolved the problem of the distribution of benefits from trade – under the present ration and distribution system food imports reach, as we know, mainly the middle and upper classes in urban areas, and cheap food going to these categories has price-depressing effects which hamper domestic production. The potential gains from an appropriate 'calorie bargain' are considerable, but in the absence of a re-distribution of economic and political power, foreign trade may actually do more harm than good, as it has done in so many parts of the world.

Concluding Remarks

In theory, it would be easy to solve Bangladesh's food and nutrition problem, even within the existing methods of production, with the help of a diversification of production and consumption. During the dry winter season, rice could be replaced with other, more nutritious and less water-consuming crops; in terms of calorie and protein content, such a reallocation would perhaps be enough to bridge the entire gap between required and actual nutrition levels. Taking the possibilities of foreign trade into account as well, the food problem could – theoretically – be solved even more easily. If only one million tons of rice, i.e. less than 10% of total production, were exported in exchange for 2–3 million tons of wheat and sorghum, the food gap could also be bridged. Since Bangladesh is very well suited for rice production during most of the year, we thus see that it is a diversification of consumption rather than of production that is potentially most rewarding from a nutritional point of view.

But all such speculations simply part company with reality. In actual practice there is, to begin with, a huge obstacle in the form of a strong consumer *and* government bias in favour of rice that prevents the necessary diversification from taking place. And, most important of all, the food and nutrition problem is, to repeat, essentially a problem of poverty. The majority of people in Bangladesh remain poor, desperately poor, and landlessness, lack of employment opportunities, low labour productivity and exploitation continue to be the basic factors responsible for the perpetuation of the misery of a growing number of people. Under these circumstances, and as long as the distribution of income determines what is produced, and for whom, no diversification measures can offer any easy solutions – only marginal improvements for a limited number of people. It is only in a society in which the satisfaction of all people's basic needs is the over-riding objective that elaborate calculations about 'optimal crop mixes' and 'calorie bargains' assume their full practical relevance.

References

1. R. Dumont, *Problems and Prospects for Rural Development in Bangladesh* (Dacca, Ford Foundation, November 1973), p. 55.
2. Agricultural Mission, 'Selected Policy Issues', mimeo (Dacca, 1977), pp. 16–17.
3. H. Brammer, 'Costs of Production, Profits and Returns for Paddy and Wheat Cultivation at the New (July 1976) Fertilizer Prices', mimeo, Soil Survey Department, Dacca, July 1976.
4. See, for example, R. Ahmed, 'Foodgrain Production in Bangladesh', International Food Policy Research Institute, Washington, D.C., 1976, p. 100ff.
5. Brammer, op. cit.
6. Ahmed, op. cit., p. 106.
7. The expression was coined in relation to China in the early 1960s: when severe drought had affected the country for three consecutive years, China sold large amounts of rice on the world market in exchange for wheat and sugar. Through this pattern of trade, China took advantage of the international price differential between rice and other crops in order to buy more calories than she sold.
8. Agricultural Mission, op. cit., p. 21.

10. The Private Bias

In Chapter 2, when discussing the appalling under-utilization of Bangladesh's human and natural resources, we observed that there is plenty of productive work to be done in rural Bangladesh. This has been further confirmed in subsequent chapters, where we have seen time after time that there are a variety of things that need to be undertaken, while at the same time resources are being wasted, or used in a socially inefficient way. The potentials are great. Construction of capital projects by hand and with simple implements could give work to millions. To tame the rivers, to irrigate the lands that lie idle during the dry season, to protect and improve the soil, to construct roads, embankments and drainage channels, to excavate the silted tanks, etc. – all these tasks call for giant efforts by human labour, and the millions of hands now remaining un- or under-employed could achieve miracles, if properly mobilized and organized. On a smaller scale, cottage industry, fishing and many other activities could form the basis for a badly needed expansion and diversification of rural employment outside crop production.

Most of these undertakings are of a collective character and would require the co-operation of many people, possibly many villages, to be successfully implemented. In other cases, it might be enough if only a handful of individuals got together in order to, say, rehabilitate a derelict tank and start a fishing co-operative. But co-operation is a difficult thing in an essentially competitive, hierarchical society where those who have the most to gain from co-operation lack the necessary means to set the projects in motion, and where those who do have the means find it more rewarding to channel the investible surplus in other, more individualistic, often speculative, directions.

Contradictions: The Case of Water

Irrigation

About one-third of the deep tube-wells in Bangladesh are estimated to be out of order at any given time. In the village, there is no organization and no technical competence available that can handle the repair and maintenance of the tube-wells: while the crop dries up, the farmers have to wait for the arrival of an outside technician, who generally attends to those farmers who offer him the highest rewards. Inefficiency, corruption and crop destruction are the results. Of the tube-wells that are actually working, the irrigated area covered is often 50% or more less than the potential area. One of the main reasons for this under-utilization is the fact that very few landholdings in Bangladesh are large enough to be able to take full advantage of even the smallest low-lift pump. Within the relevant area of a deep tube-well, there can be hundreds of separate fragments of land with up to 100 different owners.[1]

Mechanized irrigation is thus an example of a 'lumpy' kind of input which — unlike, for instance, fertilizer — is imperfectly divisible.

> In Bangladesh not only are the landholdings small, but within the individual landholdings the plots are fragmented; thus, the mechanized methods of irrigation require, for high rates of utilization, a high level of co-operation between users. But the level of co-operation necessary to bring out a high level of utilization of the mechanized methods (particularly the large-capacity 2 cusec methods: low-lift pumps and deep tube-wells) is difficult to achieve. Consequently, there is a funda-mental contradiction between the highly fragmented landholding structure and the indivisible technology of mechanized irrigation. The government responded to this problem by introducing village level credit co-operatives. However, most empirical studies have shown that these co-operatives have merely reflected existing rural power structures and that smaller farmers have not received water from this type of institutional structure. One way to resolve this technological-cum-institutional problem would be land consolidation through the form-ation of co-operatively-owned or collective farms, but this is highly unlikely at present given the political structure.[2]

Derelict Tanks

Fish provide around 80% of the animal protein in the Bangladesh diet. Despite the importance of this source of nutritious food, fish consumption has declined 50% per capita between the mid-1960s and the mid-1970s.[3] Of the annual catch from inland fishing, only around 10% is estimated to come from the 660,000 small ponds that are found all over the country. Some two-thirds of these ponds are said to be in such poor shape that they are useless not only for fishing but for most other purposes as well. Many of the ponds have been polluted by industrial or agricultural activities — the increased use of pesticides and insecticides has in particular destroyed much valuable water — but the overwhelming majority of them are simply neglected and have become silted and/or covered by water hyacinths.

Most attempts to reclaim these derelict tanks have been opposed for one main reason: multiple and/or uninterested ownership. The landowners them-selves are notorious for their neglect of their tanks, and the rents demanded are almost invariably in excess of what a group of landless workers wanting to form a co-operative but lacking all access to institutional credit can mobilize. The result is a tremendous gap in employment opportunities in fishing – and in ancillary activities like net-making, boat-building, trade, etc. – and of valuable protein.

The problem with the water hyacinths is a glaring illustration of the inability of the existing system to provide incentives for people to engage in socially useful, collective work. The water hyacinth has been described as a 'pernicious weed', 'an ornamental plant that turned into an international menace'.

> In Bangladesh it covers most of the low-lying areas, choking tank waterways and ponds all over. It impedes the flow of water, obstructs irrigation and navigation, chokes the ponds and tanks making them unfit for drinking, harbours insects, pests and their larvae, causes high degree of evaporation (four or five times more than normal) and leads to losses in fish life through eutrophication.[4]

It has often been suggested that nationwide campaigns based on voluntary efforts by all citizens should be launched in order to eradicate the water hyacinth and rehabilitate the choked tanks and channels. It has also been pointed out that the 'pernicious weed' that now threatens most inland waterways can be very useful as fodder, manure, fuel, etc. But no people can be properly motivated and mobilized to give their free labour services to activities whose fruits accrue to others, and with private ownership of the ponds and channels and a virtually complete absence of credit facilities for the poor, the situation is hardly likely to improve. As in so many other instances, productive work for which the social costs are small and the benefits considerable meets with insurmountable private obstacles.

Water and Flood Control

The need for co-ordination in the field of water control is quite obvious. Appropriate embankments and drainage channels require, from a pure technical point of view, much co-operation between different landholders, villages and districts. In the case of major storage dams and river control schemes, the co-operation would even have to be extended to the neighbouring countries; Bangladesh's extremely flat topography dictates that the dams necessary to store the abundant water during the monsoon season would have to be located outside the country's borders, in India or Nepal.

Today, however, competition is the rule, and co-operation the exception. The struggle for control over water resources is intense: landowners compete with each other, as do kinship groups and political factions, villages, Union Parishads, and districts (and, certainly, countries as well, as witnessed by the long drawn-out conflict between India and Bangladesh over the regulation of the Ganges). The administrative boundaries are usually quite arbitrary, and rarely correspond to the limits of the water systems. Embankments are often constructed in a way that helps some landowners in one village while actually harming people in other areas, whose lands may suffer from excessive flooding when the land of their neighbours is protected. The lack of co-operation between the government's Water Board and the various rural development agencies further reinforces the basic contradiction between the need for large-scale planning and implementation and the privately determined and scattered nature of most of the water control projects that are carried out.

The Need for Organization

The emphasis in most of this study has been on crop production, while relatively little attention has been paid to the overall question of the expansion and diversification of the rural economy. The desirability of such a development must however be stressed: no long-term solution to the problems of rural poverty and unemployment will be found unless expansion takes place outside crop production proper, a development that must be supportive to, rather than competitive with, traditional agricultural production. The alternatives are many — livestock, fishing, small-scale industry, transport and services of various kinds. But what is required is, above all, organization and co-operation. And, we may add, adequate markets and incentives.

The need for organization is also clear if we look at today's approach towards savings and investments. Under the present system, rural development policies are not based on the mobilization of the rural community's own potential but are almost identical to — or, rather, mistakenly identified with — resources 'given' by the state to individual beneficiaries. These resources are, as we know, often wasted on speculative, unproductive activities. They are also hopelessly inadequate amounts and represent but meagre compensation for the much larger losses in investible surplus suffered by agriculture through the constant transfer of funds to urban areas. Total development expenditures on agriculture amounted, in 1977-78, to less than *taka* 15 per household engaged in agricultural production. As for credit, in recent years the total agricultural credit supplied by institutional sources has been in the range of *taka* 15 per acre of cropped land.

Even so these are average figures which hide the fact that most farmers in a normal year receive absolutely nothing at all; the coverage of both development expenditures and institutional credit is, in terms of number of beneficiaries as a proportion of all rural households, exceedingly small. But these simple calculations nevertheless serve to illustrate an equally simple fact: to extend the existing system of input subsidies and cheap credit to the entire agricultural population with a minimum of funds per family is completely out of the question. Today, a farmer who manages to buy the recommended fertilizer doses at the official prices receives a state subsidy of over 100 *taka* per acre. To replicate this form of subsidy alone to cover all acres cropped in Bangladesh would cost the Treasury over 340 *crore taka* per year, i.e. more than twice the size of the annual development budget for agriculture. No amount of increased taxation or foreign aid is likely to enable the government to get even close to satisfying the demand for state benefits. And this has, in fact, never been the intention: the system has been created to provide selective, not general, favours.

Even from a strictly practical point of view, the present, individual-oriented strategy is therefore unlikely to be able to solve the problems. It will be virtually impossible for the government – even if it wanted to – to make credit, modern inputs, extension services, training, etc. available to all farmers on an individual basis. The public development agencies will simply have to co-operate with organized groups of people in order to reach a significant proportion of the peasantry. The only viable solution lies in an altogether different strategy, based on the collective mobilization of man-power and savings 'from below', supported 'from above'. Such a strategy – which, of course, would require a whole range of political and socio-economic changes – would also make it possible to overcome the fundamental contra-diction that exists between the need for collective effort and the private control that continues over capital and land.

The creation of rural co-operatives may appear to be the ideal means to overcome these contradictions and constraints. Through a viable co-operative structure, it might be possible to mobilize local resources, to distribute government services to peasant organizations rather than to individual far-mers, to take advantage of indivisible technology, to give incentives to invest-ments that serve the community as a whole, etc. But, unfortunately, co-operative ideas require – just like the High-Yielding Varieties of grain – extremely favourable conditions if they are to take root and prosper; if disseminated in a hostile environment of competition and unequal access to political and economic power, co-operative ideas and institutions are likely to be absorbed by the prevailing power structure. They can easily be turned into instruments for individual gain rather than for co-operation for social benefit. Rural co-operatives can therefore never be a substitute for other political and socio-economic reforms; rather such reforms are the prerequi-sites for the success of co-operative institutions. In order to see this argument in action, we must look to the story of the rise and fall of rural co-operation in Bangladesh.

The Comilla Model

Background
The Comilla co-operative programme, pioneered by the well-known founder of the Pakistan – now Bangladesh – Academy for Rural Development in Comilla, Dr. Akhteer Hameed Khan, was started in Kotwali *Thana*, Comilla District, in 1961. The programme was gradually expanded and, by the late 1960s, covered all *thanas* in Comilla. In 1970–71 it was decided to spread the Comilla model to the rest of the country and, under the title of Integrated Rural Development Programme (I.R.D.P.) the co-operative structure developed in Comilla was replicated in a large number of districts and *thanas*. After the independence of Bangladesh, the diffusion of the

co-operatives through I.R.D.P. was accelerated, and today the I.R.D.P. co-operatives have around 700,000 individual members and cover some 50 of Bangladesh's 411 rural *thanas*.

Organization was the cornerstone of the programme. The small and medium farmers, for whom the early Comilla model was primarily designed, were urged to organize themselves in co-operatives in order to mobilize savings, accumulate capital and become more independent of the local moneylenders. The co-operatives were also supposed to bring a new sense of collective responsibility and discipline to the farmers. Or, as the advantages of the co-operatives were summarized by A.H. Khan himself:

> Co-operatives can overcome the constraint of impoverished little holdings. They can make credit, machines, fertilizers, pesticides and other modern inputs easily available. By promoting habits of thrift, savings and investment, they can start the process of capital accumulation. They can widely diffuse new technical and managerial skills. Above all, rural co-operatives can create a healthy social consciousness and a desire for harmony and order.[5]

Other ingredients in the Comilla approach, such as the *Thana* Irrigation Programme and the Rural Works Programme, also served to reinforce the collective, integrated character of the model. The simultaneous development of physical infrastructure and of skills and institutions was heavily emphasized:

> Evidently, the foremost constraint in Comilla *thana* was a very defective physical infrastructure. Increased production was scarcely possible without link roads, flood control and irrigation. However, this fundamental network of roads, drains, embankments and irrigation could be constructed and maintained only through vigorous local institutions. Hence, the absence of such institutions was the second serious constraint. Improvement of the physical infrastructure was dependent upon the improvement of the institutional infrastructure. Each was linked with the other. This perspective of interlinked priorities differed from the viewpoints of the old rural reconstruction, community development and agricultural extension. It rather conformed to the Chinese view of the priority of land improvement through local organization.[6]

The Comilla approach can thus be seen as an attempt to tackle the basic contradiction discussed earlier between the need for collective work and the private ownership of land and capital. This by no means equates the programme with a subversive threat to private property, however. The originators of the programme clearly recognized that they, in the words of Akhteer Hameed Khan, 'were the servants of a conservative government whose political, economic and administrative orientation we could scarcely change.'[7]

Khan personally — and, presumably, the majority of his collaborators — was, in fact, deeply committed to individual farming. 'There was,' Khan explains, 'no intention of putting an end to private possession. On the other hand, we cherished the qualities of family farming. We admired the Japanese family more than the dispossessed commune workers.' The basic objective was, as formulated by Khan, to 'organize the peasant proprietors for production as well as protection', while the strategy — or rather, tactic — vis-à-vis the big farmers was the following:

> Initially, we worked quietly around them, suggesting not that they should be excluded from the co-operatives, but that they should not be allowed to dominate, as they had dominated the old co-operatives. It was no easy job. We saw that the struggle would be long and bitter. The rural elite, hand in glove with the urban elite, wielded great economic and political power. It was going to use that power to defend its privileged position.[8]

Achievements

What made the Comilla model so famous as a 'success story' in the 1960s was, above all, the spectacular agricultural improvement registered in Kotwali *Thana* after the introduction of the programme. Rice production more than doubled in ten years, and average yields of rice increased from 14.7 *maunds* per acre in 1963-64 to 23.3 in 1969-70 and 31.3 in 1973-74.[9] When the H.Y.V.s of rice were introduced in Bangladesh in 1968, the farmers in Kotwali were the most enthusiastic adopters in the country, and already by 1970-71 over 40% of the total acreage was covered by the improved varieties.[10] The expansion of irrigation facilities was also impressive: the percentage of the total acreage that was irrigated rose from 2.2 to 32.1% between 1964-65 and 1973-74. This expansion, in combination with the rapid spread of Green Revolution inputs, resulted in a particularly drastic increase in *boro* rice yields, which rose by over 200% in ten years.

Even more striking, perhaps, than these production records was the fact that small farmers seem to have benefited very much from the programme. In the early Comilla years it was, in fact, mainly the small and middle farmers who joined the co-operatives and took advantage of the H.Y.V. technology, while the big farmers looked upon the experiment with much suspicion, adopting a cautious wait-and-see attitude. Apparently, they were initially more interested in quick returns on moneylending than in introducing new methods of production. Once the benefits of the credit and input programmes were demonstrated, however, the big farmers also began to engage in the co-operative movement. Table 10.1 gives a rough indication of how different categories of Comilla farmers benefited.

It would thus seem that the Comilla experiment was quite successful in spreading modern agricultural techniques, including the H.Y.V. technology, without the adverse distributional effects generally associated with a Green Revolution type of agricultural development. But landless labourers gained

Table 10.1:
Increases in Rice Yields of Comilla Co-operatives by Size, 1963–70

	Rice Yield (maunds per acre)		% Increase
	1963–64	*1969–70*	
Under 2 acres	28.5	50.6	78
2–3.5 acres	22.1	49.8	125
Over 3.5 acres	17.3	38.8	124

Source: S.A. Rahim, 'Rural Cooperatives and Economic Development of
Subsistence Agriculture', (1972) p. 36.

Table 10.2:
Real Agricultural Wages in Comilla and Bangladesh, 1967–72

	Comilla District (taka per day[1])	Bangladesh (taka per day[1])
1967	2.71	2.60
1968	2.65	2.76
1969	2.96	3.01
1970	3.38	3.03
1971	n.a.	n.a.
1972	2.15	2.16

1. At 1967 prices .

Source: A.R. Khan, 'The Comilla Model and the I.R.D.P. of Bangladesh'
(1978), p. 27.

little or nothing, however, while agricultural wages developed in almost
exactly the same way in Comilla as in the rest of Bangladesh. But overall
employment did increase. The cropping intensity rose, and the Rural Works
Programme also increased employment somewhat. The latter Programme
brought, in the words of Akhteer Hameed Khan, 'gainful employment to
large numbers of landless labourers during the dry winter months — the slack
farming season. It resolved the tragic paradox of thousands of sturdy men
sitting idle while essential work remained undone.'[11] But it was, as usual, the
landowners who benefited most: 'In fact better drainage, link roads and
irrigation substantially enhanced the value of land and its rent. The unearned
increment of the landowners was a hundred times more than the wages
earned by the labourers. Even an elementary student of economics should
know that it would be so as long as ownership is not transformed.'[12]
   With respect to organizational achievements, the Comilla Academy

managed to build up a relatively wide network of village co-operatives. In
Kotwali *Thana*, almost 40% of the 35,000 rural households had become
members of primary societies by 1973–74. The most rapid expansion took
place in the early years, and enrolment stagnated after 1967. Although the
small farmers did very well in terms of production, they were grossly under-
represented among the co-operative members. Thus, while 41% of the
Kotwali agricultural population had below 0.8 acres of land, in the early
1970s, only 14% of the farmers who had joined the co-operatives belonged to
this category. The landless or near landless were in actual practice excluded
from the co-operatives since they could not obtain any credit, which required
land collateral.

These and other shortcomings of the Comilla experiment must be discussed and will be later in this chapter. However nothing can hide the fact
that considerable progress was made. Among the reasons for the substantial
achievements, the enthusiasm, dedication and honesty of the originators of
the programme should perhaps be singled out; in particular, as one observer
has put it:

> the guiding and sustaining influence of Akhteer Hameed Khan himself.
> Virtually every analysis of the Comilla project points to his charismatic
> style of leadership, and it cannot be denied that his continuing presence
> was a *sine qua non* of success during his stewardship over the years
> 1959–71.[13]

Earlier I mentioned the importance of 'hitting upon the right combination
of control from above and participation from below', in connection with the
early period of the Comilla experience. A.H. Khan and his colleagues appear
to have been very successful in this respect. And when one travels in Comilla
and asks the peasants how they feel about the present situation, a common
answer is still: 'Things are not as good as when Akhteer Hameed Khan was
here', or 'If only Dr. Khan had stayed . . . .'

When all this is said and recognized, it must still be stressed that the most
important single factor responsible for the agricultural development in the
Comilla District in the 1960s was the huge inflow of foreign and domestic
human and material resources into the project area. The spectacular increase
in rice production that was registered was only to a minor extent the result of
a successful mobilization of the local communities' own resources. Indeed,
the 'basis of the programme was a massive concentration, by Bangladesh
standards, of modern inputs (e.g. pesticides, and training) which were heavily
subsidized.'[14] Or, in the words of Harry Blair, 'Massive and seemingly un-
removable subsidies have been at the very heart of the Comilla program, and
after the first few years have become more and more a drain rather than a
channel for agricultural development in Bangladesh.'[15]

In short, virtually everything was free, or at least drastically subsidized.
Instead of relying upon the members' own savings and deposits, the Comilla
co-operatives became increasingly dependent on outside resources. It has

even been questioned whether the progress made in Comilla actually had much to do with the co-operatives at all. A.R. Khan, for example, argues that the significant gain in production that took place 'seems to have owed little to the co-operative organization itself. The credit is more appropriately due to the concentration of resources made available by the government.'[16]

Growth and Stagnation

As long as almost all resources and attention were devoted to Kotwali *Thana*, the progress there was quite remarkable. The programme was soon expanded to other *thanas*, and in 1965–66, co-operative federations had been set up in seven new *thanas* in Comilla District, and by the late 1960s, the remaining 13 *thanas* in Comilla had become integrated as well. The programme also began to be replicated, on an experimental basis, in a few *thanas* outside Comilla.

The expansion preserved the shortcomings of the original model — in particular, the lack of benefits accruing to the landless and the inadequate mobilization of internal savings — while adding new defects to the old ones. The administrative attention and uncorrupted guidance that had character-ized the Kotwali experiences deteriorated, particularly as the programme expanded. This process has been observed by many students of the rise and fall of the Comilla model:

> Supervisory capacity fell off markedly in the late 1960s, at precisely the time of the program's most rapid growth and, indeed, largely because of that growth. . . . Worst of all, in terms of the long-term implications, the inspection cadre became corrupted. The inspectors are the key figures in the Comilla program, and the seepage of venality into their ranks has had a severe impact on the whole experiment. . . . Many of the inspectors, especially in the growth period of the late 1960s when there was in effect an emergency recruitment of personnel to administer the growing program, were themselves big borrowers from the primary societies that they had been managing. When they became inspectors they were in a position to cover up their own loan defaults . . . . Partly because of this subversion of the inspectors and partly, perhaps, because of the administrative impossibility of keeping close watch on more than 300 primary societies, another perversion set in, that of takeover of the co-operatives by local elites.[17]

By the early 1970s, the Comilla co-operatives had ceased to represent the small farmers' interests — if they ever had. Their management was increas-ingly taken over by farmers who were large by Comilla standards. Some of the traditional village leaders, who initially had stayed out of the co-oper-atives also began to join the movement, but the most successful group appears to have been the category of modern, profit-oriented farmers-cum-business-men.[18] A study of the Managing Committee of the federation of co-operatives in Kotwali *Thana* (A.C.F.) thus concludes that 'the Managing Committee of

A.C.F. is attracting more and more educated, young and rich persons who have membership of other local councils and have some non-farm occupations in addition to farming.'[19] The study observed that 'gradually the percentage of persons having farming as their only occupation began to decrease. A new occupational group known as contractors (who also had their own agricultural farm) began to join the federation in increased number.'[20] In the last Managing Committee that was studied, only two out of twelve managers had agriculture as their only occupation. The representation of bigger landowners was significantly larger than the average of co-operative members, and with respect to the privileges enjoyed by the Managing Committee members, it was concluded that these co-operative leaders had 'demonstrated their tendency to issue more loans, allot more tube-wells, borrow more from its financing bank and to get their own men appointed in the federation.'[21]

Such was the situation in the very birthplace of the Comilla model, the 'laboratory' Kotwali *Thana*. Studies from other areas corroborate the conclusion that the management of the co-operatives has become dominated by the better-off sectors of the rural population, and that the benefits have become increasingly concentrated in the pockets of the few and powerful.

The capture of the co-operatives by the local elites was facilitated by an administrative reform directed at the appointment procedures of the Managing Committees of the T.C.C.A.s.[22] Carried out in 1972 and announced as a step towards a decentralization and democratization of the co-operatives, the new provisions specified that all twelve members of the Managing Committees were to be elected locally by the primary co-operative members; in the original Comilla model, between one-third and one-half of the members were *thana* officers or agricultural experts appointed 'from above'. But this seemingly very democratic reform in fact made supervision of the co-operatives largely illusory, and the big farmers, who had come to dominate the primary co-operatives, could now more easily become the undisputed leaders of the T.C.C.A.s as well. The reform thus upset, in the words of Lindquist, the 'delicate balance in Akhteer Hameed's model',[23] and its effects serve to illustrate once again that the issue of centralization versus decentralization is, indeed, a delicate one.

The low rate of growth of deposits, and the deterioration in the co-operative members' repayment discipline that took place, made the entire co-operative structure resemble a leaking bucket rather than a vehicle for the mobilization of local savings. Instead of becoming self-sufficient, the credit system became totally dependent on larger and larger injections of state funds to cover the deficits. By 1970–71, accumulated overdue loans in the co-operatives of Kotwali *Thana* reached *taka* 5 million, or more than three times the loans issued that year, and two and a half times the accumulated value of savings and share capital in the co-operatives. The number of co-operative members getting loans declined drastically,[24] in part as a consequence of the financial crisis that affected virtually all primary societies and T.C.C.A.s in the early 1970s, in part because of the takeover of the co-operatives by a small number of big farmers. The co-operatives' own savings represented but a tiny fraction of the resources that were poured into the project area. In the mid-1970s the annual average accumulation of savings in the Comilla co-operatives was less than *taka* 11 per member, i.e. about one-tenth of 1% of the annual income per member household.[25] The average size of loans, on the other hand, increased from about *taka* 200 in the mid-1960s to over 400 ten years later.

Considering the problem of overdue loans in particular, Akhteer Hameed Khan himself was very well aware of the dangers:

> The problem of wilful and mischievous defaulters is specially alarming. Historically the old co-operative system was captured by influential people and they castrated it by wilful default. The same sort of people want to perform the same operation on the modern co-operative system. They are powerful and well informed. They know that the old sanctions (certificates, notices, pressure by officers) are now dead, and they can repudiate them with impunity. If the new co-operatives are to be saved from mischievous defaulters, the other members, the majority of the small farmers, for whom co-operative credit is the only means to escape from the clutches of the moneylender-traders, must create new sanctions.[26]

Khan's apprehensions were well founded, but new effective sanctions have still not been created. The biggest defaulters are, not surprisingly, the co-operative leaders themselves. According to one study,[27] the members of the Managing Committee of 30 primary societies in the Comilla District had an average amount of *taka* 1,354 in overdue loans, while the corresponding figure for the ordinary member was *taka* 93. In another study it was concluded that a large proportion (52%) of the defaulters were the members of the Managing Committees of the primary societies, while 79% of these defaulting Managing Committee members were Directors and office-bearers of the Managing Committees.[28]

The failure of the experiment became increasingly clear from the point of view of equity as well. Thus, while the co-operatives had been created primarily for the protection of the small and medium farmers against the large owners and the moneylenders, the latter groups soon took over the commanding heights of the movement.

> The whole exercise constitutes a lesson in the futility of such 'co-operation' in a situation of inequality. The programme accepted the unequal distribution of land as an initial condition and hoped to work around the big farmers not by arranging that they 'should be excluded from the new co-operatives', but by hoping that they would 'not be allowed to dominate' (A.H. Khan). The lesson of the Comilla, if there was any need to learn it, was that it is impossible to prevent them from dominating if they are allowed in. In fact, it would be impossible to prevent them from dominating if they are allowed to exist.[29]

The I.R.D.P. and the Replication of Comilla

A Quantitative Overview

The spread of the Comilla model through the Integrated Rural Development Programme (I.R.D.P.) was only temporarily halted by the war of liberation; the extent of the programme's expansion can be seen in Table 10.3.

Table 10.3:
Growth of I.R.D.P., 1971-78

	Cumulative No. of Thanas covered	No. of Primary Societies (K.S.S.)	No. of Individual Members
1971-72	33	n.d.	n.d.
1972-73	87	10,180	261,193
1973-74	152	14,690	387,290
1974-75	161	17,690	480,474
1975-76	162	18,980	525,640
1976-77	200	21,870	649,088
1977-78	250	25,777	708,000

Source: I.R.D.P. *Basic Information on IRDP and RD-1 Project* (1977) and Planning Commission, *Two-Year Plan 1978-80.*

In interpreting the figures, it should, to begin with, be observed that the share of the total agricultural population that has been enrolled as members of the co-operatives remains quite small. After many years of expansion of the Comilla type of co-operative, the number of members is still only around 700,000, a figure which corresponds roughly to the *annual* increase in the rural labour force. The apparently respectable rate of incorporation of new members represents, in fact, only a very small fraction of the number of new rural households each year. To this we should add that the official enrolment figures are grossly inflated — many primary societies exist only on paper, and many registered members have never attended a co-operative meeting or made a deposit. The percentage of inactive societies and members is not known, but is generally assumed to be quite high.

It is too early to make an evaluation of the impact of the still expanding I.R.D.P. in the same way as the Comilla experiment in Kotwali *Thana* could be analysed. The main components of the programmes — the two-tier co-operative structure, the emphasis on credit, subsidized inputs and a rapid dissemination of the H.Y.V. technology — are the same, although the I.R.D.P. version is more diluted and lacks the close links with the Irrigation and Rural Works Programmes that the early Comilla model used to have. It is, for this reason, not quite accurate to talk about 'integrated' rural development in connection with the I.R.D.P., which should rather be seen as a non-integrated attempt to create a co-operative structure capable of distributing subsidized credit and inputs among the co-operative members. Nonetheless the similarities between the Comilla and the I.R.D.P. approaches are greater than the differences, and the basic co-operative structures are virtually identical. The conclusions drawn earlier about the Comilla co-operatives should therefore largely be relevant for the I.R.D.P. as well, a hypothesis which is supported by the few field studies that have been made in areas where the I.R.D.P. has been working for some time.[30]

Before proceeding to the question of the functioning, or malfunctioning, of the I.R.D.P., an important implication of the quantitative difference between the Comilla experiment in Comilla and the I.R.D.P. should be noted. The former operated in one district only, whereas the I.R.D.P. covers over half of all rural *thanas* in the country. Within the District of Comilla, insufficient demand for grain never became a serious problem; the output of rice could, as we have seen, more than double in ten years, and the surplus that arose could easily be sold outside the district, with only marginal effects on the general price level. If, however, lack of effective demand is the most important single long-term obstacle to agricultural growth in the country as a whole — as has been argued elsewhere in this study — then a new dimension is added to the problems of replicating the Comilla experiment all over Bangladesh. In practice, the whole I.R.D.P. approach towards agricultural development is today based on the assumption that all problems originate from the supply side, while a recognition of the key role played by demand makes it imperative to abandon the excessive emphasis on production and concentrate instead on the income distribution and employment creation objectives.

Organizational Problems

The rapid growth of the I.R.D.P. as of 1971 put severe strains on the administrative and supervisory capacity of the organization at all levels. Despite A.H.Khan's warnings from 1971 — 'It must be realized that the pace of co-operative organization must never be forced: that is the road to disaster'[31] — the expansion of the I.R.D.P. as measured by district and *thana* coverage, became a goal in itself. The result was, among other things, that the quality of the institutions that were created tended to be neglected.

There has also been a high degree of inter-departmental competition in the implementation of the different development programmes, and the co-operatives have not always been given priority. In the late 1970s a new problem arose with the Ziahur Rahman government's emphasis on the 'Swanirvar', or self-reliance, movement.[32] Relations between the protagonists of the 'Swanirvar' programme and the I.R.D.P. officials have become quite strained, and a sense of insecurity about the government's official policy has become widespread within the different — and competing — institutions for rural development that have been created.

At the village level, it has often been difficult to achieve the necessary co-operation between competing factions or kinship groups within the same village. Sometimes no I.R.D.P. co-operative can be formed at all, sometimes two competing primary societies have to be established. Within the co-operatives themselves, the members' activities tend to be very low. Weekly meetings are seldom held, and often only the managers attend them. There are many individual exceptions, of course, and quite a few societies work as they are intended, but the general picture that emerges is one of insufficient participation by the members. Also, capital accumulation within the I.R.D.P. co-operatives is not low, but strongly negative.

The co-operatives have, in short, failed to develop into instruments for the mobilization of the farmers' initiative, thrift and innovative spirit. The main reason for this sad state of affairs is not, however, the organizational and other problems referred to in the preceding paragraphs. The fundamental weakness is rather that the copoperatives, as they work today, are institutions for competition rather than for co-operation. They work for the enrichment of the few and powerful instead of for the protection of the poor.

'Closed Clubs of Kulaks'

The fact that land is the only valid security for credit makes the co-operatives useless for the landless labourers and sharecroppers. Even the small farmers have been left out in most of the I.R.D.P. co-operatives, and the entire structure seems to have become dominated by, in the words of the Planning Commission, 'the rural elite . . . in conspiracy with the urban elite'.[33] A few quotations substantiate this rather blunt conclusion:

> In the main body of the report, we have shown that the co-operative societies have turned into closed clubs of kulaks . . . . Membership is dominated by large and medium farmers and the small farmers are grossly under-represented. Leadership in the societies is also dominated by large farmers; medium farmers have some representation, but the small farmers are entirely under-represented in the leadership. These leaders enjoy a greater share of benefits but their participation, as measured by contribution of share capital and savings, is relatively low. The leaders mostly fail to uphold the basic discipline of co-operative action. . . . The co-operative societies are mostly imposed from the top. The spirit of co-operation for economic development is far from engendered. They are kept alive through continued injection of grants and aid. At the level of the village society, the aid comes in the form of highly subsidized inputs. The TCCAs receive outright grants.[34]

> The study demonstrates that, while in Natore and Gaibandha about 30% co-operative farmers fall under the category of big farmers (having more than five acres of cultivable land of their own), almost all the executive committee members are surplus farmers. . . . The benefits of the I.R.D.P. co-operatives, if there be any, have largely gone into the pockets of the big farmers.[35]

It will have become evident by now that the Directors of the Dalalpur

> Thana Central Co-operative Association are by no means an ordinary
> group of farmers. They are, in the context of Bangladesh, large land-
> owners, falling in the top 10% of landholders. However, they are not,
> for the most part, farmers themselves, and have non-agricultural
> occupations and income. As I have shown most of them are in the
> process of acquiring business interests of one kind or another. . . . The
> co-operatives are not simply being taken over by the local rich, but are
> being used as a vehicle for getting started or helping oneself move
> upward; as a means of capital accumulation. Some of the Directors . . .
> come from old business families, but even these are not stable but are
> rather involved in a dynamic process of expansion, e.g. from petty
> trader to small merchant to large fertilizer dealer to large fertilizer
> dealer plus owner and operator of a tractor. But others of the Directors
> are moving up directly from rich peasant families and becoming small
> businessmen (in, for instance, medicine, cloth, or fertilizer) using the
> TCCA to help them consolidate.[36]

The conclusions from these and similar studies all point in the same direction.
The co-operatives, these 'closed clubs of kulaks', as the Planning Commission
labelled them, today work almost exclusively for the benefit of a small
minority of the peasantry and, undoubtedly, in favour of some urban-based
interests as well. The landless or near landless, who are the majority of the
population, are not participating at all, and the total officially registered
membership of all the I.R.D.P. co-operatives is today hardly bigger than the
annual increase in the rural labour force. Instead of converting themselves
into self-reliant, self-sufficient vehicles for the accumulation of local savings
for productive investments, the co-operatives have turned into bottomless
pits each year demanding more and more resources from the state (and from
foreign donors). The integration of many different aspects of rural development, which was the cornerstone of the early Comilla model, has little
meaning for the majority of the I.R.D.P. co-operatives today; the only
successful integration that the I.R.D.P. appears to have achieved is the
accelerated integration between the rural and the urban elites.

Concluding Remarks

The concrete examples used at the beginning of this chapter to illustrate the
'private bias' in Bangladesh's agricultural policies were mainly related to the
use, and misuse, of water. The purpose was to show how technical factors —
in particular the large-scale nature of modern irrigation methods and the
need for co-ordination of water control schemes — and political and
institutional constraints — the fragmented landholding system, the private
ownership of land and water tanks, and the non-availability of credit for the
rural poor — combine to produce a poor rate of utilization of the country's
vast water resources. We also observed how the existing socio-economic

structures militate against collective undertakings in other fields as well, thus hampering the essential expansion and diversification of rural activities outside crop production, and perpetuating a situation characterized by un- and under-utilized capacity at all levels.

Then we turned to the question of organization, comparing the present top-down approach to rural development with a possible mobilization-oriented strategy aimed at releasing the labour and savings potential of the rural people themselves. The conclusion was unambiguous: the former strategy is doomed to failure even from a mere quantitative point of view. The policy based on the distribution of benefits from above cannot possibly be extended to cater for the needs of all farmers, and even if it could, the problem of integrating the hard core of rural poor, the landless or near landless – who, to repeat, constitute some 8 million households, or the majority of the rural population – would remain.

Finally, the review of the Comilla/I.R.D.P. model served to indicate the limitations of all attempts to build up co-operative organizations in the context of an ongoing hierarchical, competitive power structure in society at large. Instead of contributing to overcome the 'private bias' in the present rural development strategy, the I.R.D.P. approach is based on the provision of cheap credit and subsidized agricultural inputs to individual farmers fighting for scarce resources. And the competition cannot possibly be a competition between equals: the idea that the co-operative societies could work in a neutral way, benefiting all categories of farmers, in a non-neutral political and socio-economic environment turned out to be as illusory as Dr. Khan himself had feared. The struggle for control over the primary societies was easily won by the local elites. Today, the I.R.D.P. co-operatives are actually channelling a large part of the meagre resources earmarked for agricultural development to a minority of surplus farmers, contractors and businessmen. The private gains are considerable for the beneficiaries, but co-operation for social benefit has long since lost what relevance it may have had during the early days of the Comilla experiment.

The issue of private versus collective control over the means of production is not exactly new, and in no way have I pretended to give the subject a rigorous treatment, let alone make a blueprint for an alternative strategy. Neither have I relied upon international comparisons to substantiate my arguments; all such comparisons are full of pitfalls, and all one can say with any degree of certainty is that both private and collective ways of organizing agriculture have succeeded in some parts of the world but been less successful in others. There is no universal panacea for agricultural development, and each country has to find its own road, in accordance with its own particular conditions.

In the case of Bangladesh, however, I think there is enough evidence to conclude that an individual-oriented approach towards rural development is doomed to failure, and that a prerequisite for a genuine development favouring the poor is that they themselves get organized. They must be organized for purely defensive purposes: to free themselves from the clutches of landlords and moneylenders, and to defend their interests as wage labourers or sharecroppers. They must be organized in order to benefit from support 'from above' by giving priority to investments that serve the community rather than selected individuals, and by reducing corruption to a minimum through a strict, collective supervision of the use of credits. They must organize themselves in order to be able to stand on their own feet: to mobilize collective savings, to undertake productive investments with their own resources, to take advantage of indivisible technology in a socially efficient way, to create markets for each other's products, etc. And they must, finally, be organized if they are to succeed in their struggle for political power in society as a whole.

Utopian? Perhaps. But it is difficult to envisage a viable alternative.

References

1. For a discussion, see E. Jansen, 'Choice of Irrigation Technology in Bangladesh', *The Journal of Social Studies*, Vol. 1, No. 5, 1979.
2. S. Biggs, C. Edwards and J. Griffith, 'Irrigation in Bangladesh', Discussion Paper No. 22, University of East Anglia, February 1978, p. iv.
3. Agricultural Mission, Fisheries Sector Working Paper No. IV, mimeo (Dacca, 1977), p. 1.
4. A.K. Kaul, 'Bangladesh Agriculture 1987: Are We Preparing For It?', Institute of Nuclear Agriculture, Mymensingh, October 1977, p. 36.
5. A.H. Khan, 'Comilla Revisited', mimeo (Comilla, May–June 1977), p. 11.
6. Ibid., p. 3.
7. A.H. Khan, 'Reflections on the Comilla Rural Development Projects', Overseas Liaison Committee Report, No. 4, March 1974, p. 8.
8. Ibid., p. 16.
9. A.R. Khan, 'The Comilla Model and the I.R.D.P. of Bangladesh: An Experiment in Co-operative Capitalism', draft, mimeo (I.L.O., Geneva, June 1978), p. 7.
10. S.I.D.A./I.L.O., 'Report on Integrated Rural Development Programme', I.R.D.P. (Dacca, August, 1974), p. 80.
11. A.H. Khan, 1974, op. cit., p. 12.
12. Ibid., p. 13.
13. H.W. Blair, 'The Elusiveness of Equity: Institutional Approaches to Rural Development in Bangladesh', Center for International Studies, Cornell University, 1974, p. 21.
14. A.R. Khan, op. cit., p. 14.
15. Blair, op. cit., p. 24.
16. A.R. Khan, op. cit., p. 42.
17. Blair, op. cit., pp. 25 and 27.
18. See, for example, the various studies prepared for the Bangladesh Academy for Rural Development (BARD): A.A. Khan, 'Rural Credit Programme of Agricultural Cooperative Federation', Comilla, 1971; B. Ahmed, 'Leadership in Village Co-operatives', Comilla, April 1972, and 'Who Decides? Role of Managing Committee in A.F.C.', Comilla,

July 1972; M. Solaiman, 'Loan Default by Managing Committee Members', Comilla, 1978.

19. B. Ahmed, July 1972, op. cit., p. 32.
20. Ibid., p. 16.
21. Ibid., p. 32.
22. This paragraph is largely based on A.C. Lindquist, 'Cooperatives, Rural Development and the State: A Bangladesh Case Study', University of Sussex, mimeo, May 1978, where the consequences of this reform are discussed.
23. Ibid., p. 11.
24. Blair, 'Rural Development, Class Structure and Bureaucracy in Bangladesh', *World Development*, No. 1, 1978.
25. A.R. Khan, op. cit., p. 40.
26. A.H. Khan, 'Tour of Twenty Thanas: Impressions of Drainage Roads', Irrigation and Co-operative Programme, BARD, Comilla, 1971, p. 18.
27. A.A. Khan, op. cit., 1971.
28. For similar evidence and conclusions, see for example, Government of Bangladesh, Planning Commission, 'IRDP – An Evaluation', Dacca, 1974, p. 56; Solaiman, op. cit., pp. 31–2; and BARD, 'IRDP in Comilla District – An Evaluation', Comilla, February 1977, pp. 44 and 87.
29. A.R. Khan, op. cit., pp. 42–3.
30. There also exist a number of fairly comprehensive overviews of the I.R.D.P. The evaluations made by the Planning Commission, op. cit., and the S.I.D.A./I.L.O., 'Report on Integrated Rural Development Programme', I.R.D.P., Dacca, August 1974; Hamid and Rahman, 'An Evaluation of Natore and Gaibandha Projects', I.R.D.P./Dept. of Economics, University of Rajshahi, 1977: Lindquist, 'Cooperatives, Rural Development and the State: A Bangladesh Case Study', University of Sussex, May 1978, mimeo; and J.H. Jahangir, 'Differentiation, Polarization and Confrontation in Rural Bangladesh', unpublished thesis, Department of Anthropology, University of Durham, 1976, also contain many useful observations and insights. Minor research reports, newspaper articles, statements by researchers and government officials and I.R.D.P.'s own documentation and analyses – where almost all aspects of the programme's quantitative achievements can be found – also added to the growing body of knowledge about the impact of the I.R.D.P. co-operatives.
31. Quoted in Lindquist, op. cit., p. 10.
32. For a critical analysis, see S.D. Asplund and S. de Vylder, 'Contradictions and Distortions in a Rural Economy: The Case of Bangladesh', S.I.D.A., Stockholm, 1979, Chapter 5.
33. Planning Commission, op. cit., p. 4.
34. Ibid., pp. 4 and 11.
35. M.A. Hamid and M.A. Rahman, op. cit., p. 2.
36. Lindquist, op. cit., p. 90–1.

11. Needless Hunger

Today, the global 'food crisis' has disappeared from the headlines. The spectacular events in the first half of the 1970s, when grain prices tripled in a few years and the 'food weapon' in the hands of the major surplus country, the United States, threatened to become an instrument for international blackmail at least as powerful as OPEC's oil, are a thing of the past. The world has once again, albeit temporarily, adjusted itself to the apparently perfectly normal situation of a peaceful co-existence between food surpluses and hundreds of millions of people going hungry every day.

The situation is paradoxical only if one assumes that the world food system is regulated by a desire to fill empty stomachs. But this is not, of course, the case. Although agriculture has its own characteristics and unpredictable hazards, food production obeys, by and large, the same laws of the market that govern the production of shirts, TV sets, or any other commodity. Food is produced for those who can afford to buy it, and the poor will remain hungry as long as they lack the purchasing power that is necessary in order to translate needs into effective demand.

The barriers to an eradication of mass hunger and undernourishment are neither technical nor Malthusian, but are a product of the unequal distribution of income and power between and within the different countries. The world could easily feed a much larger population than the present one — if it were profitable. In this sense, all hunger is needless. Ecological factors do set an upper limit to our possibilities in most of the industrialized countries to sustain, over a longer period of time, a continuation of the present trends towards a more and more intensive exploitation and chemicalization of the soils. But the most typical feature of the situation, especially in the so-called Third World, is still the gross underutilization of the available resources. Vast areas of fertile land are not being cultivated at all, or are cultivated in a very unintensive way, and in many countries and regions yields per acre are but a fraction of their potential.

Hunger is needless even in a poor and densely populated country like Bangladesh. The tendency in some international aid circles. and in the Western mass media, to relegate Bangladesh to the status of a 'hopeless case', a permanent victim of disasters and misery, has to be refuted; all such attempts are not only cynical, but based on a profound ignorance of the country as well. The reasons why Bangladesh's agricultural sector fails to provide the population with food and productive employment are not a physical shortage of resources, as is sometimes suggested. (In strictly technical terms, the potential is great enough to enable the country to increase its agricultural output several times over.) The real reasons are the various interdependent distortions and constraints which originate from the economic, political and social structure and the concomitant choice of policies.

The main conclusions of this book are that the interaction of these distortions, or biases, results in, first, a low share of total investment going to agriculture and, second, a socially inefficient use of the resources within the agricultural sector. This inefficiency expresses itself in glaring misallocations of investible funds and in an inability to achieve the necessary mobilization of semi-idle or poorly utilized human and natural resources. The economic strategies adopted by successive governments, and implemented by and for those privileged groups whose very existence constitutes the biggest single obstacle to development, have all failed to solve any basic problems. Rather, they have tended to reinforce the last two decades' trends of increasing landlessness, inequality, unemployment and poverty.

It is, however, doubtful whether a different set of policies would have succeeded much better. The class structure that permeates both the state machinery and the village social structure is such that all policies become subverted by a number of biases that begin to operate, thwarting all attempts at long-term improvement for the rural poor. However well conceived particular themes in agriculture may be, they are doomed to failure unless and until the exploited majority manages to change the social structure within which they are living and within which these schemes get implemented.

Bibliography

Abdullah, A., Hossain, M., and Nations, R., 'Issues in Agrarian Development and the IRDP', Appendix 1, in S.I.D.A./I.L.O. Report on Integrated Rural Development Programme, Dacca, June 1974.

Abdullah, A., Hossain, M., and Nations, R., 'Agrarian Structure and the IRDP – Preliminary Considerations', *Bangladesh Development Studies*, No. 2, 1976.

Adnan, S. and Islam, R., 'Social Change and Rural Women: Possibilities of Participation', B.I.D.S., The Village Study Group, Working Paper 7, Dacca, May 1976, mimeo.

Agricultural Mission 1977: *See* FAO/UNDP/GOB 1977.

Ahmed, Badaruddin, 'Leadership in Village Cooperatives', BARD, Comilla, April 1972.

Ahmed, B., 'Who Decides? Role of Managing Committee in A.F.C.', B.A.R.D., Comilla, July 1972.

Ahmed, I., 'Employment in Bangladesh – Problems and Prospects', Dacca, 1973, mimeo.

Ahmed, N.U., 'Cost of Production of Aus Paddy and Jute Cultivation per Acre', U.S. A.I.D., Dacca, August 1976.

Ahmed, N.U., 'Cost of Production of Jute, Wheat and Boro Crops per Acre', U.S.A.I.D., Dacca, August 1977.

Ahmed, R., 'Foodgrain Production in Bangladesh: An Analysis of Growth, its Sources and Related Policies', International Food Policy Research Institute, Washington D.C., 1976.

Alam, Md., 'A Report on the Swanirvar Programme in Athiakhali, Lakshmipur, Noakhali', Locally Sponsored Development Programmes Series, Report No. 19, Rural Studies Project, Department of Economics, Chittagong University, Chittagong, 1976.

Alam, N.S.M., 'A Report on Swanirvar Programmes in Brommothar, Rangunia, Chittagong', Rural Studies Project, Department of Economics, Chittagong University, Report No. 20, October 1976.

Alam, N.S.M., 'Patterns of Chittagong District', Chittagong University, 1979. of Mathazari Thana of Chittagong District', Chittagong University, 1979.

Alam, M., Alamgir, M., and Chowdhury, N., 'Rural and Urban Unemployment and Underemployment in Bangladesh: Concepts, Magnitude, Policies', B.I.D.S., Dacca, 1976, mimeo.

Alamgir, M., 'Some Analysis of Distribution of Income, Consumption, Saving and Poverty in Bangladesh', *Bangladesh Development Studies*, No. 4, 1974.

List of References

Alamgir, M., *Bangladesh: A Case Study of Below Poverty Level Equilibrium Trap*, Dacca, Bangladesh Institute for Development Studies, 1978.

Arens, J., and van Beurden, J., *Poor Peasants and Women in a Village in Bangladesh*, Birmingham, U.K., Third World Publications, 1977.

Arthur, W. Brian, and McNicoll, Geoffrey, 'An Analytical Survey of Population and Development in Bangladesh', *Population and Development Review*, Vol. 4, No. 1, September 1978.

Asian Development Bank (ADB), 'Asian Agricultural Survey 1976, Rural Asia: Challenge and Opportunity', Manila, 1977.

Asplund, D. and de Vylder, S., 'Contradictions and Distortions in a Rural Economy. The Case of Bangladesh', S.I.D.A., Stockholm 1979.

Assaduzzaman, M. and Hossain, M., 'Some Aspects of Agricultural Credit in Two Irrigated Areas in Bangladesh', B.I.D.S. Research Report Series No. 18, Dacca, 1974.

Assaduzzaman, M. and Islam, F., 'Adoption of HYVs in Bangladesh: Some Preliminary Hypotheses and Tests', Research Report Series (new) No. 23, B.I.D.S., Dacca 1976.

Bangladesh Academy for Rural Development (B.A.R.D.), 'Socio-economic Implications of Introducing HYV in Bangladesh', Proceeding of the International Seminar, Comilla, November 1975.

B.A.R.D., 'IRDP in Comilla District — an Evaluation', Comilla, February 1977.

B.A.R.D., 'Annual Report', various issues.

Bangladesh Rice Research Institute (B.R.R.I.), 'Workshop on Experience with HYV Rice Cultivation in Bangladesh', Dacca, 1976.

B.R.R.I., 'Workshop on Ten Years of Modern Rice and Wheat Cultivation in Bangladesh', Dacca 1977.

Bangladesh Rural Advancement Committee (B.R.A.C.), 'Proposal for Bangladesh Rural Credit Trust. An Innovative Approach to Finance the Rural Poor in Productive Pursuits', Dacca 1977.

B.R.A.C., 'Appropriate Technologies Make Pressure: The Case of the Cotton Textile Industry and Post Harvest Rice Processing', Dacca 1979, mimeo.

Bartsch, W.H., 'Employment and Technology Choice in Asian Agriculture', Praeger, New York 1977.

Berry, Albert R. and Cline, William R., 'Agrarian Structure and Productivity in Developing Countries', Johns Hopkins, Baltimore/London 1979.

Bhaduri, A., 'Agricultural Backwardness under Semi-feudalism', *The Economic Journal*, Vol. 83, No. 1, March 1973.

Biggs, S., 'Interaction between Technological and Institutional Development. What is Appropriate Where, When and for Whom?', Dacca 1975, mimeo.

Biggs, S., Edwards, C., and Griffiths, J., 'Irrigation in Bangladesh. On Contradictions and Underutilized Potentials', Discussion Paper No. 22, University of East Anglia, February 1978.

Blair, H.W., 'The Elusiveness of Equity: Institutional Approaches to Rural Development in Bangladesh', Center for International Studies, Cornell University, Ithaca, N.Y., 1974.

Blair, H.W., 'Rural Development, Class Structure and Bureaucracy in Bangladesh', *World Development*, Vol. 1, 1978.

Bose, S.R., 'Trend of Real Income of the Rural Poor', *The Pakistan Development Review*, Autumn 1968.

Bose, S.R., 'Institutional Change and Agricultural Wages in Bangladesh',

Bangladesh Development Studies, No. 4, 1976.

Bose, S.R., 'The Strategy of Agricultural Development in Bangladesh', B.I.D.S., Dacca 1973, mimeo.

Bose, S.R., 'The Comilla Co-operative Approach and the Prospects for Broad-based Green Revolution in Bangladesh', *World Development*, No. 2, 1974.

Brammer, H., 'Costs of Production, Profits and Returns for Paddy and Wheat Cultivation at the New (July 1976) Fertilizer Prices', Soil Survey Department, Dacca, July 1976, mimeo.

Bronfenbrenner, M., 'Second Thoughts on Confiscation', *Economic Development and Cultural Change*, July 1963.

Brown, L., 'Seeds of Change. The Green Revolution and Development in the 1970s', Pall Mall, Overseas Development Council, London, 1970.

Byres, T.J., 'Of Neo-Populist Pipe-Dreams, Dedaelus in the Third World and the Myth of Urban Bias, *Journal of Peasant Studies*, Vol. 6, No. 2, January 1979.

Cain, M.T., 'The Economic Activities of Children in a Village in Bangladesh', *Population and Development Review*, Vol. 3, No. 3, 1977.

Clay, E.J., 'Institutional Change and Agricultural Wages in Bangladesh', *Bangladesh Development Studies*, No. 4, 1976.

Clay, E.J. and Khan, S., 'Agricultural Employment and Under-employment in Bangladesh: The Next Decade', Working Paper, Dacca, June 1977, mimeo.

Clay, E.J., 'Environment, Technology and the Seasonal Patterns of Agricultural Employment in Bangladesh', draft, Dacca 1978, mimeo.

Clay, E.J., 'Employment Effects of the HYV Strategy in Bangladesh: A Rejoinder', Dacca, March 1978, mimeo.

Clay, E.J., 'Food Aid and Food Policy in Bangladesh', *The Bangladesh Journal of Agricultural Economics*, Vol. I, No. 2, December 1978.

Dumont, R., 'Problems and Prospects for Rural Development in Bangladesh', The Ford Foundation, Dacca, November 1973.

Dutta, J.P., 'A Report on Swanirvar Programmes in Shilkup, Monkirchar, Banskhali, Chittagong', Locally Sponsored Development Programmes Series Report No. 23, Rural Studies Project, Chittagong University, October 1976.

Etienne, G., 'Bangladesh: Development in Perspective', Asian Documentation and Research Center, Geneva, 1977.

Faaland, J. and Parkison, J.R., *Bangladesh: A Test Case for Development*, London, Hurst & Co., 1976.

Farmer, B.H., *Green Revolution? Technology and Change in Rice Growing Areas of Tamil Nadu and Sri Lanka*, London, Macmillan, 1977.

Food and Agricultural Organization, (F.A.O.), *F.A.O. Commodity Review,* various issues.

F.A.O./U.N.D.P./Government of Bangladesh, Agricultural Mission, 'Selected Policy Issues and Working Papers I-XIII', Dacca, 1977, mimeo.

Government of Bangladesh (G.o.B.), *Statistical Pocketbook of Bangladesh*, various numbers.

G.o.B., Bureau of Statistics, Ministry of Planning, *Statistical Yearbook of Bangladesh 1979*, Dacca, 1979.

G.o.B., Ministry of Finance, various unpublished reports.

List of References

G.o.B., Ministry of Finance, 'Bangladesh Economic Survey 1978-79', Dacca, 1979.

G.o.B., Planning Commission, 'IRDP – an Evaluation', Dacca, 1974, mimeo.

G.o.B., Planning Commission, *The Two-Year Plan 1978-80*, Dacca, 1978.

Gonoshastaya Kendra (People's Health Centre), 'Progress Report No. 6', Dacca, December 1977.

Griffin, K., 'Foreign Capital, Domestic Savings and Economic Development', *Bulletin of the Oxford University*, Institute of Economics and Statistics, March 1970.

Griffin, K., *The Political Economy of Agrarian Change*, London, Macmillan, 1974.

Griffin, Keith, *International Inequality and National Poverty*, London, Macmillan, 1978.

Griffin, K. and Khan, A.R. (eds.), *Growth and Inequality in Pakistan*, London, Macmillan, 1972.

Griffin, K. and Khan, A.R., 'Poverty in the Third World: Ugly Facts and Fancy Models', *World Development* No. 3, 1978.

Gruening, E., 'United States Foreign Aid in Action – A Case Study', U.S. Printing Office, Washington D.C., 1966.

Hamid, M.A. and Rahman, M.A., 'An Evaluation of Natore and Gaibandha Projects', I.R.D.P./Department of Economics, University of Rajshahi, 1977, mimeo.

Haque, W., Mehta, N., Rahman, A. and Wignaraja, P., 'Towards a Theory of Rural Development', *Development Dialogue*, Vol. 2, 1977.

Hartman, B. and Boyce, J.K., 'Bangladesh: Aid to the Needy?' *International Policy Report*, Vol. IV, No. I, Center for International Policy, Washington D.C., May 1978.

Hossain, Mahabub, 'Farm Size and Productivity in Bangladesh Agriculture. A Case Study of Phulpur Farms', *Bangladesh Economic Review*, No. 1, 1974.

Hossain, Mahabub, 'Farm Size, Tenancy and Land Productivity: An Analysis of Farm Level Data in Bangladesh Agriculture', *Bangladesh Development Studies*, No. 3, 1977.

Hossain, Mahabub, 'Present Agrarian Structure and Agricultural Growth in the Post-partition Period', Paper presented at the Bangladesh Itihashi Samitix, January 1978.

Hossain, Mahabub, 'Nature of Tenancy Markets in Bangladesh Agriculture', *The Journal of Social Studies*, No. 3, 1979.

Hossain, Mahabub, 'Foodgrain Production in Bangladesh. Performance, Potential and Constraints', B.I.D.S., Dacca, March 1980, mimeo.

Hossain, Mahabub, Rahman, Atiur and Akash, M.M., 'Agricultural Taxation in Bangladesh', B.I.D.S., Dacca, 1978, mimeo.

Hossain, Mosharaff, 'Nature of State Power in Bangladesh', *The Journal of Social Studies*, Vol. 1, No. 5, 1979.

Huq, A. (ed.), 'Exploitation of the Rural Poor. A Working Paper on the Rural Power Structure in Bangladesh', B.A.R.D., Comilla, 1976.

Huque, W., Mehta, N., Rahman, A., and Wignaraja, P., 'Towards a Theory of Rural Development', *Development Dialogue*, No. 2, 1977.

International Bank for Reconstruction and Development (I.B.R.D.), 'Land Reform. Sector Policy Paper', Washington D.C., March 1975.

I.B.R.D., 'Bangladesh: Current Trends and Development Issues', Washington D.C., March 1979.

I.B.R.D., 'Bangladesh: Food Policy Issues', December 1979.

I.B.R.D., 'Bangladesh: Current Economic Position and Short-term Outlook', Washington D.C., 21 March 1980.

International Labour Organization (I.L.O.), 'Poverty and Landlessness in Rural Asia', Geneva, 1977.

Isenman, P.J. and Singer, H.W., 'Food Aid: Disincentive Effects and their Policy Implications', *Economic Development and Cultural Change*, June 1977.

Islam, R., 'Approaches to the Problem of Rural Unemployment', Working Paper, Village Study Group, University of Dacca/B.I.D.S., Dacca 1977, mimeo.

Jabbar, M.A., 'Farm Structure and Resource Productivity in Selected Areas in Bangladesh', B.A.R.C., Dacca, December 1977.

Jabbar, M.A., 'Socio-economic Aspects of Lawsuits in Bangladesh', *The Bangladesh Journal of Agricultural Economics*, Vol. I., No. 2, December 1978.

Jacoby, Erich H., 'Effects of the "Green Revolution" in South and South-East Asia', *Modern Asian Studies*, Vol. 6, No. 1, 1972.

Jahan, R., 'Members of Parliament in Bangladesh', Dacca, March 1975, mimeo.

Jahangir, J.K., 'Differentiation, Polarization and Confrontation in Rural Bangladesh', Unpublished thesis, Department of Anthropology, University of Durham, 1976.

Jahangir, J.K., 'Nature of Class Struggle in Bangladesh', *Economic and Political Weekly*, 12 December 1977.

Jannuzi, F. Tomasson, and Peach, James T., 'Bangladesh: A Profile of the Countryside', U.S. A.I.D., Dacca 1979, mimeo.

Januzzi, F. Tomasson and Peach, James T., *Land Occupancy Survey*, 1979.

Jansen, E., 'A Preliminary Report on the Processes of Transfer of Land', B.I.D.S., Dacca 1978, mimeo.

Jansen, E., 'Choice of Irrigation Technology in Bangladesh: Implications for Dependency Relationships between Rich and Poor Farmers', *The Journal of Social Studies*, Vol. 1, No. 5, 1979.

Kamaluddin, S., 'Bangladesh Lures the Investor', *Far Eastern Economic Review*, 23 November 1979.

Kaul, A.K., 'Bangladesh Agriculture 1987. Are We Preparing for it?', Institute of Nuclear Agriculture, Mymensingh, October 1977.

Kendra, G., 'Progress Report No. 6', December 1977, mimeo.

Khan, Akhteer Hamid, 'Three Essays: Land Reform, Rural Works, and The Food Problem in Pakistan', Asian Studies Center, Michigan 1973.

Khan, Akhteer Hamid, 'Reflections on the Comilla Rural Development Projects', Overseas Liaison Committee Report No. 4, March 1974.

Khan, A.H., 'Tour of Twenty Thanas: Impressions of Drainage Roads', Irrigation and Co-operative Programme, B.A.R.D., Comilla, 1971, p. 18.

Khan, Akhteer Hamid, 'Comilla Revisited', Comilla, May-June 1977, mimeo.

Khan, Ali Akteer, 'Rural Credit Programme of Agricultural Cooperative Federation', B.A.R.D., Comilla, 1971

Khan, A.R., 'Capital Intensity and the Efficiency of Factor Use: A Comparative Study of the Observed Capital-Labour Ratios of Pakistan

Industries', *Pakistan Development Review*, Summer 1970.

Khan, A.R., *The Economy of Bangladesh*, London, Macmillan, 1972.

Khan, A.R., 'Poverty and Inequality in Rural Bangladesh', in I.L.O., *Poverty and Landlessness in Rural Asia*, Geneva, 1977.

Khan, A.R., 'The Comilla Model and the I.R.D.P. of Bangladesh. An Experiment in "Co-operative Capitalism" ', draft, I.L.O., Geneva, June 1978, mimeo.

Khan, A.R., 'Employment in Bangladesh during the Second Five-year Plan', ARTEP-I.L.O., Bangkok, 1979.

Khan, Obaidullah A.Z., 'Rural Development in Bangladesh. Problems and Prospects', Dacca, 1973, mimeo.

Lappé, E.M. and Collins, J., 'Food First. Beyond the Myth of Scarcity', Institute for Food and Development Policy, Boston, 1977.

Lifschultz, Lawrence, *Bangladesh: The Unfinished Revolution*, London, Zed Press, 1979.

Lindquist, A.C., 'Cooperatives, Rural Development and the State: A Bangladesh Case Study', University of Sussex, May 1978, mimeo.

Lipton, M., 'Why Poor People Stay Poor. A Study of Urban Bias in World Development', London, Temple Smith, 1977.

Little, I., Scitovsky, T. and Scott, M., *Industry and Trade in Some Developing Countries: A Comparative Study*, London/New York/Toronto, Oxford University Press, 1970.

Majumdar, A.M., 'Reclamation of Derelict Tank Project', B.A.R.D., Comilla, 1978.

Mandal, Md. Abdus Sattar, 'An Economic Analysis of Resource Use with Respect to Farm Size and Tenure in an Area of Bangladesh', unpublished dissertation, Wye College, University of London, August 1979.

Masum, Muhammad, 'Technology and Employment in Bangladesh', in Report of I.L.O. Tripartite Symposium on Choice of Technology and Employment Generation in Asia, Bangkok, 1979.

Maxwell, S.J. and Singer, H.W., 'Food Aid to Developing Countries. A Survey', *World Development*, March 1979.

McHenry, D.F. and Bird, K., 'Food Bungle in Bangladesh', *Foreign Policy*, No. 27, 1977.

Mukhopadyay, A., 'Preparing for Parliamentary Polls', *Economic and Political Weekly*, 26 August 1978.

Munthe-Kaas, H., 'Green and Red Revolutions', *Far Eastern Economic Review*, 19 March 1970.

Muqtada, M., 'The Seed-fertilizer Technology and Surplus Labour in Bangladesh Agriculture', *Bangladesh Development Studies*, No. 4, 1975.

Murshed/Mondal/Mustafi/Sobhan, 'Production of High-yielding and Local Varieties of Aman Paddy in Mymensingh — An Economic Analysis', Department of Agricultural Economics, B.A.U., Mymensingh, 1976, mimeo.

Myrdal, G., *Asian Drama. An Inquiry into the Poverty of Nations*, New York/London, Allen Lane/Penguin, 1968.

N.M.J., 'Murder in Dacca', *Economic and Political Weekly*, 25 March 1978.

Oxfam-America and Institute for Food and Development Policy, 'Aid to Bangladesh: For Better or Worse?', An Interview by Michael Scott, San Francisco, 1979.

Palmer, I., 'The New Rice in Asia: Conclusions from Four Country Studies', U.N.R.I.S.D. Report No. 76:6, Geneva, 1976.

Rahim, S.A., 'Rural Cooperatives and Economic Development of Subsistence Agriculture', B.A.R.D., Comilla, 1972.

Rahim, A.M.A. and Hoque, A.K.M., 'The Terms of Trade of Bangladesh 1972-76. An Analysis and Policy Implications', *Bangladesh Bank Bulletin*, April 1978.

Rahman, Anisur, 'Foreign Capital and Domestic Saving: A Test of Haavelmo's Hypothesis with Cross Country Data', *Review of Economics and Statistics*, February 1968.

Rahman, Anisur, 'The Utilization of Labour in the Strategy for Development in the E.C.A.F.E. Development Region', Paper prepared for the E.C.A.F.E., U.N., undated, mimeo.

Rahman, Atiqur, 'Agrarian Structure and Capital Formation: A Study of Bangladesh Agriculture with Farm Level Data', unpublished dissertation, Clare College, Cambridge, 1979.

Rahman, Atiqur, 'The Debate over Land Reform in Bangladesh: Some Issues Reconsidered', B.I.D.S., Dacca, January 1980, mimeo.

Rahman, Atiqur, 'Usury Capital and Credit Relations in Bangladesh Agriculture. Some Implications for Capital Formation and Capitalist Growth', B.I.D.S., March 1980, mimeo.

Rahman, Atiqur, 'Rural Power Structure: A Study of the Union Parishad Leaders in Bangladesh', *The Journal of Social Studies*, No. 4, 1979.

Rao, C.H.H., 'Urban vs. Rural or Rich vs. Poor?', *Economic and Political Weekly*, 7 October 1978.

Raquibuzzaman, M., 'Share-Cropping and Economic Efficiency in Bangladesh', Research Report No. 2, New Series, Institute of Development Studies, Dacca, 1972, mimeo.

Salimullah, M. and Shamsul, A.B.M., 'A Note on the Conditions of Rural Poor in Bangladesh', *Bangladesh Development Studies*, No. 2, 1976.

Sau, R., 'Growth, Employment and Removal of Poverty', *Economic and Political Weekly*, special number, September 1978.

*Scott, M., 'Aid to Bangladesh: For Better or Worse?', Institute of Food Development Policy/Oxfam-America, San Francisco, 1979.

Shajahan, Md., 'Cost and Return of Amon Cultivation 1976', B.A.R.D., Comilla, July 1977, mimeo.

Siddiqui, A.M.A.M., 'The Public Administration System: An Aid or An Obstacle to Development? An Exposé based on Personal Experience', Dacca, January 1977, mimeo.

* Sobhan, Rehman, 'Politics of Food and Famine in Bangladesh', *Economic and Political Weekly*, 1 December 1979.

Solaiman, M., 'Loan Default by Managing Committee Members', B.A.R.D., Comilla, 1978.

Stevens, R.D., Alavi, H., and Bertocci, P.J. (eds.), *Rural Development in Bangladesh and Pakistan*, Honolulu, University Press of Hawaii, 1976.

Stroberg, P-A., 'Water and Development. Organizational Aspects on a Tube--well Irrigation Project in Bangladesh', S.I.D.A., Stockholm, 1977.

Swedish International Development Authority (S.I.D.A./B.I.D.S.), 'Landless Survey 1978', unpublished.

S.I.D.A./I.L.O., 'Report on Integrated Rural Development Programme',

I.R.D.P., Dacca, August 1974.

Tepper, E.L., 'The Administration of Rural Reform. Structural Constraints and Political Dilemmas', in R.D. Stevens et al., *Rural Development in Bangladesh and Pakistan,* Honolulu, University Press of Hawaii, 1976.

U.S.A.I.D., 'The Poor Majority of Bangladesh', Dacca, undated, mimeo.

Wood, G., 'Class Differentiation and Power in Bandakgram: The Minifundist Case', in A. Huq (ed.), *Exploitation of the Rural Poor,* B.A.R.D., Comilla, 1971.

Yunus, Md., 'Planning in Bangladesh. Format, Technique and Priority and Other Essays', Rural Studies Project, Department of Economics, Chittagong University, June 1976.

Zaman, M.R., 'Share-Cropping and Economic Efficiency in Bangladesh', *The Bangladesh Economic Review,* Vol. 1, No. 2, April 1973.